CAUSAL ANALYSIS

Studying Organizations:
Innovations in Methodology

PROJECT ON INNOVATIONS IN METHODOLOGY
FOR STUDYING ORGANIZATIONS

Project Planning Committee

Thomas J. Bouchard, *University of Minnesota*
Joel T. Campbell, *Educational Testing Service*
David L. DeVries, *Center for Creative Leadership*
J. Richard Hackman (Chair), *Yale University*
Joseph L. Moses, *American Telephone and Telegraph Company*
Barry M. Staw, *University of California, Berkeley*
Victor H. Vroom, *Yale University*
Karl E. Weick, *Cornell University*

Project Sponsorship and Administration

The volumes in this series (listed above) are among the products of a multi-year project on innovations in methodology for organizational research, sponsored by Division 14 (Industrial and Organizational Psychology) of the American Psychological Association.

Support for the project was provided jointly by the Organizational Effectiveness Research Program of the Office of Naval Research (Bert T. King, Scientific Officer), and by the School Management and Organizational Studies Unit of the National Institute of Education (Fritz Mulhauser, Scientific Officer). The central office of the American Psychological Association contributed its services for the management of project finances.

Technical and administrative support for the project was provided by the Center for Creative Leadership (Greensboro, NC) under the direction of David L. DeVries and Ann M. Morrison.

STUDYING
ORGANIZATIONS:
Innovations
in Methodology
1

CAUSAL ANALYSIS

ASSUMPTIONS, MODELS, AND DATA

by
Lawrence R. James, Stanley A. Mulaik,
and **Jeanne M. Brett**

Published in cooperation with Division 14 of the
AMERICAN PSYCHOLOGICAL ASSOCIATION

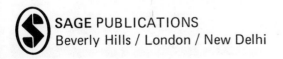 SAGE PUBLICATIONS
Beverly Hills / London / New Delhi

For information address:

SAGE Publications, Inc.
275 South Beverly Drive
Beverly Hills, California 90212

SAGE Publications India Pvt. Ltd.
C-236 Defence Colony
New Delhi 110 024, India

SAGE Publications Ltd
28 Banner Street
London EC1Y 8QE, England

Printed in the United States of America

Library of Congress Cataloging in Publication Data

James, Lawrence R.
  Causal analysis.

  (Studying organizations : innovations in methodology ; v. 1)
  "Published in cooperation with Division 14 of the American Psychological Association."
  Bibliography: p.
  1. Organizational research—Statistical methods.
2. Psychological research—Statistical methods.
3. Causation. I. Mulaik, Stanley A., 1935-
II. Brett, Jeanne M. III. American Psychological Association. Division of Industrial-Organizational Psychology. IV. Title. V. Series: Studying organizations ; v. 1.
HD30.4.J14   1982   001.4'2   82-10723
ISBN 0-8039-1867-4
ISBN 0-8039-1868-2 (pbk.)

THIRD PRINTING, 1983

Contents

Preface

J. Richard Hackman

There has been increasing interest in recent years, both in academia and in society at large, in how—and how well—organizations function. Educational, human service, political, and work organizations all have come under close scrutiny by those who manage them, those who work in them, and those who are served by them.

The questions that have been raised are important ones. How, for example, can organizations become leaner (and, in many cases, smaller) as the birthrate and the rate of economic growth decline? Is there a trade-off between organizational productivity and the quality of life at work? Or can life at work and productivity be simultaneously improved? What changes in organizational practices are required to increase the career mobility of traditionally disadvantaged groups in society? How are we to understand the apparent asynchrony between the goals of educational organizations and the requirements of work organizations? How can public services be provided more responsively and with greater cost effectiveness? What new and nondiscriminatory devices can be developed to test, assess and place people in schools and in industry? The list goes on, and it is long.

Unfortunately, there is reason for concern about our capability to build a systematic base of knowledge that can be used to deal with questions such as these. Available strategies for studying organizations have emerged more or less independently from a variety of disciplines, ranging from anthropology, sociology, and political science to educational, industrial, and organizational psychology. But none of these disciplines appears to be on the verge of generating the kind of knowledge about organizations that will be required to understand them in their full richness and complexity.

Why not? Part of the problem may have to do with the *restrictiveness* of discipline-based research—that is, the tendency of academic disciplines to support specific and focused research paradigms, and to foster intense but narrow study of particular and well-defined research "topics." Another possibility, however, is that the *methodologies* used in research on organizations have been far too limited and conventional.

In general, the methods used in studying organizations have been imported from one or another of the academic disciplines. And while these methods may be fully appropriate for the particular research problems and paradigms that are dominant in the disciplines from which they come, they also may blind those who use them to potentially significant new findings and insights about how organizations operate.

Because the need for higher quality organizational research is pressing, now may be the time to try to break through the constraints of traditional methodologies and seek new approaches to organizational research. This was the thinking of the Executive Committee of Division 14 (Industrial and Organizational Psychology) of the American Psychological Association when, a few years ago, it initiated a project intended to foster innovations in methodology for organizational research. A planning committee was appointed, and support was obtained from the Office of Naval Research and the National Institute of Education. Eighteen scholars were recruited from a variety of disciplines and formed into six working groups to review the state of organizational research methodologies, and to seek innovative approaches to understanding organizations. A three-day conference was held at the Center for Creative Leadership, at which about sixty organizational researchers (representing a variety of disciplinary orientations, and from applied as well as academic settings) reviewed the findings and proposals of the six working groups. The working groups then revised their materials based on the reactions of conference participants, and the six monographs in this series are the result.

The content of the six monographs is wide ranging, from new quantitative techniques for analyzing data to alternative ways of gathering and using qualitative data about organizations. From "judgment calls" in designing research in organizations, to ways of doing research that encourage the *implementation* of the research findings. From innovative ways of formulating research questions about organizations to new strategies for cumulating research findings across studies.

This monograph focuses specifically on confirmatory analysis, a quantitative technique that can help explicate causal relationships among organizational phenomena. The monograph emphasizes the conditions that must be met if causal inferences are to be drawn from nonexperimental data and offers some new tests that readers can use to determine whether or not their data meet those conditions. While the bulk of the monograph deals with the analytic models and techniques of confirmatory analysis, the authors emphasize throughout the importance of strong, well-developed theory as a prerequisite for the appropriate application of this powerful (but easily misused) analytic tool.

The aspiration of the numerous people who contributed their time and talent to the innovations project (they are listed facing the title page) is that readers of this monograph—and of its companions in the series—will discover here some ideas about methods that can be used to benefit both the quality and the usefulness of their own research on organizations.

ACKNOWLEDGMENTS

Support for this project was also provided under Office of Naval Research Contract N00014-80-C-0315, Office of Naval Research Project NR170-904. Opinions expressed are those of the authors and are not to be construed as necessarily reflecting the official view or endorsement of the Department of the Navy.

The authors wish to thank Hugh J. Arnold, Joel T. Campbell, Robert G. Demaree, Robert L. Linn, Jack McArdle, S. B. Sells, B. Krishna Singh, and Gerrit Wolf for their helpful suggestions and advice.

Introduction

☐ The need to pursue questions of causality and causal inference with nonexperimental data—that is, data based on naturally occurring events—has been recognized for some time in disciplines such as biometrics, econometrics, and sociology (see, for example, Blalock, 1971; Duncan, 1975; Goldberger & Duncan, 1973; Heise, 1975; Johnston, 1972; Jöreskog, 1970; Namboodiri, Carter, & Blalock, 1975; Wright, 1934, 1960). More importantly, a family of empirical procedures designed to evaluate the utility of causal hypotheses and to support inferences regarding causality among naturally occurring events is gaining rapid exposure in psychology (see, for example, Bentler, 1980; Bentler & Bonett, 1980; Bentler & Weeks, 1980; Cook & Campbell, 1979; James & Singh, 1978; Jöreskog, 1978; Jöreskog & Sörbom, 1979; Kenny, 1979; Maruyama & McGarvey, 1980; Werts & Linn, 1970). The term "confirmatory analysis" is used here to refer to this family of procedures, which includes confirmatory factor analysis, linear structural relations, path analysis, structural equations, and time series. The term "confirmatory" denotes that these procedures, are designed to evaluate the utility of causal hypotheses by testing the fit between a theoretical model and empirical data. If a theoretical model is shown to have a "good fit" with the data, then the model is regarded as confirmed. Conversely, a theoretical model is disconfirmed if it has a "poor fit" with the data.

Confirmatory analysis is likely to assume an important place in the repertoire of psychological research methods. Bentler (1980, p. 420), for example, described linear structural equation models with latent (i.e., unmeasured) variables as having "the greatest promise for furthering psychological science." Another example is provided by the current editor of *Psychometrika* (Cliff, 1980) who stated, "The development of the rigorous and generalized methods for testing hypotheses concerning underlying structures in covariance matrices is perhaps the most important and influential statistical revolution to have occurred in the social sciences." However, there have also been words of caution about the strong emphasis in the literature on the statistical methods of confirmatory analysis and the comparatively weak emphasis on the assumptions that justify the use of these methods. To illustrate, Cliff (1980) went on to say that while the methods may be "a great boon to social science research, . . . there is some danger that they may instead have been a disaster, a disaster because they seem to encourage us to suspend our normal critical faculties." Billings and Wroten (1978) and James (1980) were less equivocal, noting that failure to pay attention to potential unmeasured causes in path analytic models has resulted in biased estimates of path coefficients and erroneous causal inferences.

There is a serious need to specify the conditions that justify the application of confirmatory analysis and the use of the results of confirmatory analysis to support causal inference. Our objective is to specify and to discuss these conditions. To meet this objective, we will show how these conditions follow from a number of fundamental philosophical assumptions about the nature of causality and about how causes may be known. We will begin our discussion in Chapter 1 with an overview of the philosophical issues surrounding the idea of causation. This section is designed to help the reader who is not familiar with these issues see how philosophical questions about causation must be settled before one proceeds to develop a methodology for dealing with causation in the behavioral and social sciences. In this discussion we will state where we stand philosophically on these issues, recognizing that the topic of causality is still one of the most controversial in the philosophy of science. We will also introduce an interpretation of causality that we feel corresponds to the intuitive use of the concept by scientists (Simon, 1977), and then use this interpretation to establish a rationale for testing the utility of causal hypotheses by confirmatory analysis.

The rationale for testing the utility of causal hypotheses by confirmatory analysis will be developed in greater detail in Chapter 2 by overviewing ten conditions that, if reasonably satisfied, justify confirmatory analysis. The role of confirmatory analysis in causal inference will be addressed in Chapter 3, where we will discuss the advantages and disadvantages of confirmatory analysis in the context of the equivocality of causal inference. Finally, Chapter 4 will be devoted to an overview of latent variable models, which are models designed to evaluate the utility of causal hypotheses among theoretical constructs. As discussed in greater detail later, "latent variables" are abstractions or theoretical constructs that are not amenable to direct measurement (e.g., common factors).

The presentation is relatively nontechnical inasmuch as our goal is to discuss logic and assumptions. Nevertheless, confirmatory analysis cannot be addressed independently of methodology. Those desiring more comprehensive treatments of methods are referred to the references cited throughout this volume. Finally, although this presentation of confirmatory analysis is limited to causal inference with naturally occurring events, we also affirm that the logic and procedures extend to experimental data (see, for example, Kenny, 1979; Miller, 1971).

1

An Interpretation
of Causality

☐ Causality is a complex topic, beset by contro-
versy because of metaphysical and epistemological differences among
philosophers of science. Nevertheless, we believe that an understanding of
causality is helpful for understanding the conditions that justify confirmatory analysis and the use of the results of confirmatory analysis to support
causal inference. It is not our aim to explore exhaustively the theories by
which we come to know things or to delve deeply into the metaphysical
aspects of causation, however important these may be to a full understanding of causality. Rather, we wish to develop an understanding of
causality that is compatible with the methodological treatment of causality in scientific inquiry.

CAUSALITY AND NECESSARY CONNECTION

When we seek to understand an event or an object, what we often want
to know is what caused or determined it. Thus, at first view, causality
seems to involve establishing a necessary connection in the form of an
event A being necessary for the occurrence of an event B. But we shall
argue that causal relations are not necessary relations. Further, our acceptance of a causal relation must be tentative, because there is no logical
guarantee that the relation will be supported by further experience.

The perspective that causal relations are necessary relations is exempli-
fied by the philosophical realist who believes in the independent existence
of a world beyond the senses. Causation, for the philosophical realist,
concerns the manner in which objects are able to effect change in other
objects by means of various forces and powers. The realist wishes to
discover these forces and to show why objects *necessarily* produce the
effects that they do. This is not, however, a sufficient account of causation
for the psychologically minded who wonder how it is that we know about
the world and the causes that objects in the world exert on other objects.
How do external objects cause humans to perceive not just the objects, but

the causal forces they exert on one another? From what information does the human organism construct internal representations of external objects and causal forces?

We know that information about the world comes to the senses in the form of physical energy. Furthermore, information about causes appears to reside in the temporal sequence of stimulus information. For example, people report that they perceive events causing other events as they watch a film. But all the information presented in the film is varying intensities of light and shadow, arranged spatially in images that are presented rapidly in a sequence. People do not report that they perceive events causing other events when the film's image frames are presented in random order. The perception of causation depends on the *order* in which the information is presented and cannot be found in the individual elements of information.

The British empiricists of the eighteenth and nineteenth centuries, reflecting on the problem of causation, reached a similar conclusion. David Hume (1748/1977) argued that the only thing he could find in experience to account for the idea of a causal connection between phenomenal events was an awareness of the repetition of similar instances in which an object of one kind is invariably followed by an object of another kind. Nothing within the objects themselves connects them. Only the repeated pairing of objects gives rise to the idea of a causal relation between objects. "This connexion," Hume wrote, "which we *feel* in the mind, this customary transition of the imagination from one object to its usual attendant, is the sentiment or impression from which we form the idea of power or necessary connexion. Nothing farther is in the case" (Hume, 1748/1977, p. 50).

Hume particularly ruled out any logical necessity, in the form an event A being necessary for the occurrence of an event B, because logical necessity would allow for neither exceptions nor contradictions, such as the occurrence of an event B without the occurrence of an event A. He argued that in considering connections between objects, it is possible that in the future we will experience the connection between objects differently than we have in the past. For a considerable time after Hume, empiricism discounted any role for logical necessity in considerations of matters of fact. The empiricists' rejection of logical necessity led them to avoid deduction from general theories and to stress induction and description.

Modern empiricism, however, restored logic to respectability in science when it came to explanation using hypothetical formal models designed to represent relations between objects of experience. Logic entered in when one deduced the occurrence of specific events from general laws established inductively in prior experience. To illustrate, Hemphill and Oppenheim (1948) offered the following schema for the process of explanation: Let E be an event to be explained, described in observational terms. Let

$C_1, C_2, \ldots, C_k$ be a set of antecedent conditions. Let $L_1, L_2, \ldots, L_p$ be general laws. Then, if from the inductively generated antecedent conditions and the general laws one is able to deduce the event E to be explained, these antecedent conditions *are* the explanation of E. The "logical necessity" that connects the antecedent conditions and general laws is not absolute for these empiricists. Rather, this "logical necessity" is relative to the hypothetical logical system in which one assumes that the antecedent conditions and general laws are valid premises. Furthermore, there can be no absolute necessity for such logically deduced explanations to be always correct, for further experience may show the premises on which they are based to be false.

In general, inductively based theories and explanations—that is, generalizations from the past to the present or future—cannot escape the tentativeness of inductive inferences. As Hume observed, there are no logically necessary connections in experience. Whether the necessary connections of causal relations are established by repeatedly observing invariant successions of an event A followed by an event B, or are deduced logically from inductively established premises, it is not necessary that one will continue to observe such regular successions or to find the empirically induced premises of a deductive argument to be true.

Hume even came to question whether the process of induction, of generalizing from the past to the present or the future, was rationally justifiable. This was particularly disturbing to him because he saw that people used inductive reasoning all the time in their everyday affairs. But he could conceive of no rational argument that could stand up to the logical possibility that events could turn out to be quite different from what was inductively expected. Numerous philosphers after Hume have similarly been unable to find rational arguments to justify the use of induction.

Nevertheless, some philosophers seem willing to live with the unjustifiability of expectations based on past experience. Feigl (1963) regarded the idea that past experience is a guide to what will happen in the present and the future as an essential but unjustifiable premise that one had to make to deal rationally with experience. Cook and Campbell (1979) regarded inductive, cause-inferring behavior as characteristic behavior of our species and suggested that such behavior evolved because it had survival value. Other philosophers have not been so kind in dealing with Hume's skepticism. Wittgenstein regarded Hume's skepticism about induction as "unintelligible," on a par with asking someone to justify breathing or walking (see Dilman, 1973). Capaldi (1969) detected a subtle circularity in Hume's skeptical argument, namely, that Hume must rely on instances in past experience of unfulfilled expectations to support his argument that past experience cannot be relied upon always to fulfill our expectations. But if past experience cannot be relied upon, how can Hume rely upon it to prove that it cannot be relied upon? Thus he presumed the very thing he sought to undermine.

In sum, causal relations are not necessary relations. While a causal relation may be deduced logically from prior theoretical assumptions or based inductively on an observation of a regularity in experience, there is no logical guarantee that the relation will occur similarly in future experience. Thus, our use of causal relations must be tentative. Furthermore, if we do use causal relations as explanations or as guides for action, we do so without any rational justification for why this practice occurs. It is basically a fundamental human practice.

THE FORM OF A CAUSAL RELATION

Some philosophers conceptualize causal relations as following the form of logical implication. These forms are reviewed briefly below. We will then argue that causal relations need not, and perhaps should not, be conceptualized as following the form of logical implication. Rather, we will argue that causal relations follow the form of an asymmetric functional relation in a self-contained system.

In regard to logical implication, causal relations have often been viewed as taking one of the following three interrelated forms (Byerly, 1973):

(1) *sufficient* condition: An event A is causally sufficient for an effect B if B occurs whenever A occurs.
(2) *necessary* condition: An event A is causally necessary for an effect B if B never occurs without A having already occurred.
(3) *necessary and sufficient* condition: An event A is a necessary and sufficient condition for an effect B if B never occurs when A has not occurred and B always occurs when A has occurred.

Treating causation as having one of the forms of logical implication leads to conclusions that are incompatible with the common language conceptions of causation. For example, the statement, "If A, then B" logically implies "If not B, then not A." But, if the causal relation follows the form of logical implication, this would mean "A causes B" implies "not B causes not A," which makes no sense. To use a concrete example, if the causal relation follows the form of logical implication, then the statement, "John's pressing the accelerator pedal causes the car to accelerate" implies "The car's not accelerating causes John not to press the accelerator pedal." Not only does this sound absurd, but also it points out the need for an approach to causality that "corresponds to the intuitive use of that term in scientific discussion" (Simon, 1977, p. 77).

Values on X̲:   1,1,2,2,3,3,4,4,5,5,6,6

Values on Y̲:   1,1,2,2,1,1,3,3,1,1,3,3

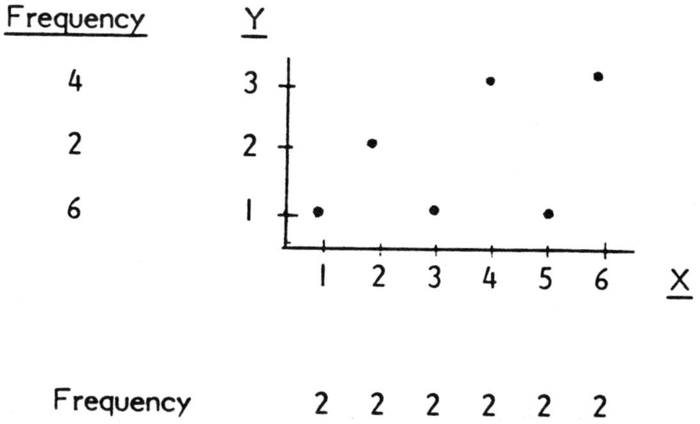

Figure 1.1   The Functional Relation of Variable Y on Variable X in an Asymmetric, Self-Contained System

Simon (1952, 1953, 1977; Simon & Rescher, 1966) argued that, formally speaking, the form of the causal relation does *not* take the form of logical implication. Rather the causal relation takes the form of an *asymmetric functional relation* in a *self-contained* or *closed system*. These points are illustrated in Figure 1.1, which concerns the functional relation between an effect Y and a cause X. As shown at the top of Figure 1.1, there are 12 scores on each variable. The variable X has six possible values (i.e., 1, . . . ,6), and the variable Y has three possible values (i.e., 1, 2, 3). Each separate occurrence of an X or a Y is an *event*. Thus, this example has 24 events. Each *value* of X and Y defines a *class of events*. For example, X = 5 defines a class of events with the common value of 5, and there are two events in the X = 5 class. The *variable* X comprises a *set* of classes of events. The term "set" refers to the six classes of events associated with the six possible values that may be assumed by X. The set of classes of events for Y encompasses the three values that may be assumed by Y.

Simon (1977, p. 108) viewed a causal relation as a function of an effect (Y) on one or more causes (Xs). In this example, we have one cause, and the functional relation takes the form Y = f(X). It is particularly important to note that the causal relation between X and Y is a relation determined over the full range of values on X and Y. It is not merely a relation between the occurrence of two events (e.g., X = 1, Y = 1), or a relation between the occurrence of two classes of events (e.g., X = 6, 6; Y = 3, 3). Let us now address what is meant by self-contained and asymmetric.

The function Y = f(X) is *self-contained* because one and only one value (class of events) of Y is associated with each value (class of events) of X. This implies that the values of Y are determined completely by the values of X; that is, given knowledge that X has occurred and the values of X, we can determine exactly the values of Y. The function is *asymmetric* because it is impossible to reverse the direction of causation (i.e., X = f(Y)) and maintain unique determination. For example, Y = 1 is associated with X = 1, 3, or 5, which means that X cannot be uniquely determined by the knowledge of the values of Y.

In more general terms, Simon considered that causal relations in science usually concern *quantitative* functional relationships, such as the amount of wheat grown is a function of the amount of rain and the amount of fertilizer. In the simple case where an effect (y) is determined by two causes (x_1 and x_2), the functional relation is denoted by $y = f(x_1, x_2)$, where lower-case letters refer to variables in deviation score form. This means that the occurrence of the effect y is dependent on the occurrence of the causes x_1 and x_2 in the manner prescribed by the function f. The function f may take many forms. For simplicity's sake, the treatments in this book are generally predicated on linear functions. Thus, for example, the functional relation $y = f(x_1, x_2)$ expressed in linear form denotes that y is a function of a weighted, additive combination of the values of x_1 and x_2, namely $y = B_{yx_1}x_1 + B_{yx_2}x_2$. When expressed as equations, functional relations are referred to as *functional equations.*

A functional equation implies that the system is self-contained, which is to say that the values of the effect y are determined completely by the function that relates the values of the causes x_1 and x_2 to y. For example, the (linear) functional equation $y = B_{yx_1}x_1 + B_{yx_2}x_2$ represents a self-contained or closed system in which values of y are completely determined by the weighted, additive combination of the values of x_1 and x_2. The asymmetry of causation may at times be illustrated as in our example above, where y is completely determined by the function relating y to x_1 and x_2, but no function can be found that, for example, completely determines the values of x_1 based on a function of y and x_2. However, the asymmetry reflected in a functional equation, in the context of a causal relation, is typically an imposed asymmetry based on the presumed order in which variables occur naturally. To illustrate, the frequency of automobile accidents may be in part a function of the amount of snowfall, but it is unlikely that snowfall is a function of the number of automobile accidents (Darlington, 1968). Thus, the logic of asymmetry of causal relations is that setting $y = f(x)$ does not imply that $x = f(y)$.

Causal analysis is generally predicated on a set of variables, where multiple effects are regarded as functions of multiple causes. Each effect is represented by a functional equation, and, based on the natural causal ordering among the variables, a system of functional equations is devised in which a variable that acts as an effect in one equation is a cause in an equation later in the causal order. For example, a simple system may be composed of two linear equations, such as $y_1 = b_{y_1 x_1} x_1$, and $y_2 = b_{y_2 y_1} y_1$, where the natural causal ordering is x_1, y_1, and then y_2. The y_1 and y_2 equations may be regarded as self-contained *subsystems* within the system of equations. Furthermore, if each of the functional equations embedded in the system of equations is self-contained, then the system is self-contained, which connotes that there are as many equations as effects to be determined. As we shall see later, self-containment of a system of equations suggests that parameters (e.g., $b_{y_1 x_1}$) in functional equations have unique values and may be estimated. We shall also see how these estimates are used to infer the strengths of causal relations.

In summary, what Simon's functional relation conception of causality suggests is that we infer the presence of causal relations when we isolate groups of variables into self-contained systems of functional equations in which the varying values of some variables (causes) appear to determine totally the varying values of other variables (effects). Within these self-contained systems, the causal pathways among variables are determined by the manner in which the values of certain effects in self-contained *sub*systems (functional equations) are themselves determined by the values of causes, which include effects of other self-contained *sub*systems lower in the causal order. The inference of causation is an inductive inference based on presuming that the functional equations/relations describing the causal connections between the values of causal variables and effect variables observed in the past will continue to hold in the future.

IS CAUSALITY REPLACED BY FUNCTIONAL RELATION?

A number of empiricist and positivist writers (e.g., Pearson, 1892/1911; Schlick, 1949; Jeffreys, 1948), have expressed the view, echoed by some psychologists (see Travers, 1981), that causality as a concept has been cast out of science and replaced by the concept of functional relationship or by the even less binding connection of contingency. How does this view contrast with Simon's view of the causal relation as an asymmetric, functional relation?

To begin with, Simon's view does not attempt to settle any metaphysical issues regarding the nature of causality by asserting that causal relations are to be represented formally by functional relations. Simon's view is thus ecumenical in that it seeks to provide a common basis on which scientists of different metaphysical persuasions may agree when dealing with the practical problems of demonstrating causality. These other empiricists, however, have metaphysical commitments when they seek to equate causality with nothing but functional relations, that is to say, mathematical descriptions and summaries of regularities observed in experience. For them the real is only what is known in experience. But because the phenomenalist psychology of empiricism holds that the elements of experience are logically unconnected, this rules out necessary connections in experience. Since, traditionally, causality concerns necessary connections, causality no longer is a viable concept for empiricists. Causality must be replaced by the weaker relation of functional relation, which serves only to describe the regularities of succession of similar kinds of events in experience, these regularities being products of the mind's associative processes.

More important, however, is that those positivists and empiricists rejecting causality in favor of functional relationships have often stressed the interdependence of variables and even the reversibility or symmetry of relationships (see Bunge, 1959). Much of this thinking can be traced to the writings of the physicist Ernst Mach, who had a profound influence on Pearson (1892/1911) and subsequently on the adherents of the Vienna Circle of logical positivists, which included Schlick (1949) cited above. According to Bunge (1959, p. 91) Mach "demanded the replacement of every sort of connection, particularly causal connections, by functional relations expressing a symmetrical interdependence." To illustrate this view, Bradley (1971) reported, Mach would cite how the pressure p of a given mass of gas is uniquely determined by its absolute temperature T and volume V, according to the equation $pV/T = r$ (a constant). But then Mach would caution that none of the quantities p, V, or T should be thought of as a cause of the other, but rather as functions of each other. According to Bradley, Mach was motivated to eliminate the notion of causality (interpreted as a necessary asymmetric connection) and replace it with the less binding and more descriptive symmetric connection of functional interdependence. Functional relations were viewed as describing regular successions of phenomena by summarizing the phenomenal facts.

In contrast, the econometrician and statistician Nicholas Georgescu-Roegen (1971) pointed out how the many examples of functional interdependence cited by Mach and the positivists after him come from Newtonian mechanics. In Newtonian mechanics there is no unique direction in which processes can occur. Events can happen in just the reverse order as we observe them to happen and still be consistent with Newtonian mechanics. But Newtonian physicists, Georgescu-Roegen claimed, were faced with a crisis when they attempted to analyze the phenomenon of heat. The simple law that heat always passes from hotter to colder bodies is an asymmetric relationship not derivable from Newtonian physics (except by invoking an empirically untestable interpretation of probability in what is known as "statistical mechanics"). Yet this simple law, known as the Second Law of Thermodynamics, underlies the asymmetry of countless relationships observed in nature and makes meaningful a conception of causality as an asymmetric relationship.

Simon's functional relation conception of causality is based on asymmetry of relationship. While Simon allowed that asymmetry could be achieved in a definition of the causal relationship by invoking the concept that causal variables would measure events occurring before events measured by effect variables, he chose instead to define causal order independently of time. For him, a system of (linear) causal relations would be represented by a self-contained system of independent and consistent (nonhomogeneous) linear equations. Causal ordering in such a system would be indicated by the order in which one would have to solve for the variables of the system.

We are not yet ready to describe further mathematical details of Simon's self-contained equations and causal order in such a system. As discussed later, the equations selected for such a system would be based on relationships observed in prior experience or on those derived from theory. The important point here is that Simon believed he had distilled what the scientist, of whatever epistemological persuasion, is concerned with when he or she seeks to establish causes, which is to establish asymmetric functional relations among variables in a self-contained, closed system.

The impact of Simon's perspective is seen in econometrics and sociology, where methods of confirmatory analysis using structural equations and path analysis developed partly under Simon's influence. Unfortunately, Simon's views on causality seem to have been overlooked by many philosophers of science as well as by authors of popular textbooks on causality in the social sciences. For example, no reference to Simon appears in Cook and Campbell (1979), Heise (1975), or Kenny (1979), although many treatments in these texts reflect functional relations. In this book we will adopt Simon's view that the causal relation is an asymmetric functional relation among sets of classes of events (i.e., variables) within a self-contained, closed system.

We must make one final observation concerning the metaphysical status of the functional relation conception of causality we will use in this volume. We do not claim to exhaust the idea of causality with such a concept. Actually, we are only interested in formulating conditions under which causal relationships may become known, not in stating what causality *is*. It is the phenomenalist empiricists who wish to make the metaphysical claim that causality as a functional relation merely summarizes regularities of succession in phenomenal experience, which for them is all there is to reality. We will make no such claims, since they are not relevant to our task in this book.

FUNCTIONAL RELATIONS IN PSYCHOLOGY

Theory plays a major role in the formulation of (asymmetric) functional relations in psychological research. The functional relation view of causality suggests that in order to infer causal relations we must isolate groups of variables into self-contained systems in which the varying values of effects appear to be determined totally by functions of values of causes. However, because the number of possible causal relations among psychological variables is infinite, it is necessary to rely on theory to identify the variables to be isolated and included in functional equations in a self-contained system. Not all psychological theories furnish a meaningful basis for accomplishing this chore, and we will devote considerable space in the next section of this monograph to the conditions that must be reasonably satisfied if a theory is to be relied on to develop functional equations in a self-contained system. We preface this discussion with interpretations of functional relations and self-containment in regard to their use in psychology and in other disciplines in which functional relations take the form of probabilistic function equations.

Functional relations were represented above in the form of *deterministic* functional equations. For example, the linear functional equation $y = B_{yx_1}x_1 + B_{yx_2}x_2$ is deterministic because y is completely determined by x_1 and x_2. However, in many areas of psychological research, variation in effects may occur for reasons other than variation in the causes included explicitly in a functional equation. For example, variation may occur in an effect because of variation in causes not included explicitly in an equation. These causes may have minor, independent, and unstable influences on an effect, in which case they are referred to as *random shocks*. The likelihood of the occurrence of random shocks in psychological research suggests that it is usually necessary to think of functional relations and functional equations in probabilistic terms rather than in deterministic terms.

When expressed in probabilistic terms, causal models involving *linear* functional relations take the form $y = f(x_1, x_2, d)$, and a *linear* functional equation has the form $y = B_{yx_1}x_1 + B_{yx_2}x_2 + d$. "Linear" is emphasized because we focus on linear forms of probabilistic functional equations in this discussion. These forms differ from linear deterministic functional equations because probabilistic equations include a *disturbance term,* designated by "d." The disturbance term is a surrogate that represents all causes of y not included explicitly in the (linear) probabilistic functional equation. That is, x_1 and x_2 are the explicitly included causes and d represents all other causes of y. Disturbance terms almost always include random shocks, which, as defined above, are causes of y that are minor, independent, and unstable. Disturbance terms may also include variables that are stable and believed to have nonminor, direct influences on effects. These variables are referred to as "omitted" or "unmeasured" variables or causes. We shall distinguish between unmeasured causes that are *relevant* and unmeasured causes that are not relevant.

A relevant cause is defined as a variable that:

(a) has a nonminor, direct influence on an effect,
(b) is stable,
(c) is related to at least one other cause included explicitly in a functional equation, and
(d) makes a unique contribution to a functional equation, which means that it is not linearly dependent on causes already included in a functional equation (see James, 1980).

An unmeasured cause must satisfy all four conditions above to be an unmeasured *relevant* cause. To illustrate, an unmeasured cause that satisfies conditions a, b, and d, but not condition c, is *not* an unmeasured *relevant* cause because it is not related to causes included explicitly in a functional equation. This type of unmeasured cause is addressed shortly in a discussion of self-containment of probabilistic equations. Also to be considered is a variable that satisfies conditions a, b, and c, but not condition d, which implies that the variable is redundant with respect to explicitly measured causes. This type of variable is discussed in Condition 9.

The distinctions among random shocks, unmeasured relevant causes, and unmeasured causes that are not relevant causes furnish a basis for ascertaining whether or not a probabilistic functional equation is self-contained. We will formally define self-containment for probabilistic functional equations, and then show how this formal criterion can be restated in terms of random shocks, unmeasured relevant causes, and unmeasured causes that are not relevant causes.

Like deterministic equations, probabilistic equations must be self-contained before they can be used to represent functional (causal) relations. However, unlike deterministic functional equations, it is not possible to require that the realized (measured) values of causes determine the values of an effect in probabilistic functional equations, if for no other reason than that the values of effects will include the influences of unstable, and therefore unmeasurable, random shocks. It is possible to define self-containment for probabilistic functional equations in reference to the expected values on an effect, conditional on the values of causes included explicitly in a functional equation (i.e., the [conditional] probability distribution of the effect). Specifically, a probabilistic functional equation is self-contained if the realized values of causes included explicitly in the equation determine the (conditional) probability distribution of the effect variable (Simon, 1977).

For example, the linear probabilistic functional equation:

$$y = B_{yx_1}x_1 + B_{yx_2}x_2 + d \qquad [1.1]$$

is self-contained if the conditional expected values of y, given realized values of x_1 and x_2, are provided by $B_{yx_1}x_1 + B_{yx_2}x_2$. The conditional equation is indicated by:

$$E(y|x_1,x_2) = B_{yx_1}x_1 + B_{yx_2}x_2 \qquad [1.2]$$

where E is the expectation operator.

Equation 1.2 requires that solutions exist for B_{yx_1} and B_{yx_2}, which, combined with the realized values of x_1 and x_2, determine the conditional expected values of y. As shown in the next section of this volume (Condition 5), unbiased solutions exist for B_{yx_1} and B_{yx_2} only if x_1 and x_2 are unrelated to d. This, in turn, connotes that a *probabilistic functional equation will be self-contained if, and only if, the causes represented explicitly in an equation are unrelated to the disturbance term of that equation.* That is, equation 1.2 is dependent on the lack of relationship between d and both x_1 and x_2 in equation 1.1. Thus, a more fundamental definition of self-containment of a probabilistic functional equation is that explicitly measured causes are unrelated to the disturbance term of the equation.

We are now ready to return to the relationship between self-containment and random shocks, unmeasured relevant causes, and unmeasured causes that are not relevant. If the disturbance term is composed of random shocks exclusively, then d in equation 1.1 cannot be related to the explicitly measured causes x_1 and x_2 because, by definition, random shocks are unrelated to all other variables. Similarly, if d includes unmeasured causes that are not correlated with measured causes, in addition to random shocks, then again d is unrelated to x_1 and x_2 because the unmeasured causes are unrelated to explicitly included (i.e., measured) causes. Thus, we may conclude that (a) if the d term in a probabilistic functional equation involves only random shocks and unmeasured causes that are not correlated with measured causes, then (b) the equation is self-contained because explicitly measured causes will be unrelated to do.

However, if d contains at least one *relevant* cause, then d will be related to at least one explicitly measured cause. That is, a relevant cause of y that is not included explicitly in the probabilistic functional equation for y will be included in the disturbance term. By definition, this unmeasured relevant cause is related to at least one explicitly measured cause (see c in definition of relevant cause), from which it follows that either x_1 or x_2, or both, will be related to d in equation 1.1. Consequently, equation 1.2 is not applicable because unbiased solutions do not exist for B_{yx_1} and B_{yx_2}, and the probabilistic equation given by equation 1.1 is not self-contained. On the other hand, if x_1 and x_2 are the only relevant causes of y, then equation 1.1 would be self-contained. This suggests that the most fundamental definition of self-containment for a linear probabilistic functional equation is that *all relevant causes of an effect are included explicitly in the equation.*

Functional equations are assumed to be in linear probabilistic form throughout the remainder of this monograph. We will emphasize, many times, the points that (a) a probabilistic functional equation can be used to represent a causal relation only in the condition that the equation is self-contained, and (b) a probabilistic functional equation will be self-contained only in the condition that all relevant causes of the effect are included explicitly in the equation. We will also demonstrate that, in naturalistic studies, it is necessary to rely on theory to identify relevant causes that should be included in a probabilistic functional equation, and frequently, to build a case that causes not included explicitly in an equation are unrelated (or linearly dependent on) causes represented explicitly in that equation.

SUMMARY

The following ideas were developed in Chapter 1. Causal relations are inductive relations, and take the form of asymmetric functional relations among certain variables, or subsets of variables, in a self-contained structure (Simon, 1977). It is not assumed that causal relations are logically necessary relations or that causal relations take the form of logical implication. It is assumed that theory plays a major role in the formulation of functional relations in psychological research, where functional relations are typically represented by probabilistic, rather than deterministic, equations. The probabilistic equations must be self-contained if they are to represent causal relations.

We have adopted Simon's functional relation perspective of causality in this text. We have also placed major emphasis on the role played by theory in the formulation of functional relations in psychological research. As we shall demonstrate, theory is used to isolate groups of variables into a system of functional equations. It is also used (a) to identify relevant causes that should be included in a functional equation, (b) to build a case that causes not included in a functional equation are not relevant causes, and (c) to specify the causal ordering of equations or subsystems within a system of equations. Finally, we will illustrate the intrinsic interplay between theory and data in the conduct of a confirmatory analysis.

2

Conditions for Confirmatory Analysis and Causal Inference

☐ The objective of this chapter is to describe the conditions that justify the use of confirmatory analysis to evaluate whether the causal hypotheses indicated by functional relations have scientific utility. Ten conditions are introduced and discussed. The first seven conditions pertain to the appropriateness of a theoretical model for confirmatory analysis and causal inference. Reasonable satisfaction of these conditions suggests a well-developed, stable theoretical model in which self-contained (probabilistic) functional equations specify hypothesized causal relations among causes and effects. These conditions are:

(1) formal statement of theory in terms of a structural model,
(2) theoretical rationale for causal hypotheses,
(3) specification of causal order,
(4) specification of causal direction,
(5) self-contained functional equations,
(6) specification of boundaries, and
(7) stability of the structural model.

The final three conditions concern the operational aspects of confirmatory analysis in a population or sample. The conditions are:

(8) operationalization of variables,
(9) empirical confirmation of predictions I: empirical support for functional equations, and
(10) empirical confirmation of predictions II: fit between structural (i.e., theoretical) model and empirical data.

The presentation of Conditions 8 through 10 focuses on variables associated with directly observable events, which are referred to as "manifest variables." As noted earlier, an overview of the latent variable form of analysis is presented separately in Chapter 4. Finally, while reasonable satisfaction of the ten conditions to be described here is required for causal inference, we emphasize their role in confirmatory analysis in this section and their role in causal inference in Chapter 3.

CONDITIONS PERTAINING TO APPROPRIATENESS OF THEORETICAL MODELS

CONDITION 1: FORMAL STATEMENT OF THEORY IN TERMS OF A STRUCTURAL MODEL

Any attempt to explain the occurrence of natural events in terms of functional relations must begin with a well-developed theory. By the term "theory" we mean a set (or sets) of interrelated causal hypotheses that attempt to explain the occurrence of phenomena—physical, biological, social, cultural, or psychological (Singh, 1975). The basic components of a theory, or a theoretical model, are as follows (see Dubin, 1976; Merton, 1968; Singh, 1975):

(1) *Phenomena,* or the variables that act as causes and effects.

(2) *Causal connections* among the variables. A causal connection refers to the hypothesized causal association between one cause and one effect (e.g., $x_1 \rightarrow y_1$). The total pattern or structure of causal connections among ordered variables, where order reflects the natural sequence of occurrences of events represented by variables, is the essence of a theoretical model. It is this structure of causal connections that provides the basis for the development of functional relations and functional equations, which relate each effect to all of its presumed causes. Consequently, the structure of causal connections should specify the variables that are to be related functionally, the causal ordering among the variables, the direction of causation for each connection (unidirectional or reciprocal), and the function that relates each effect variable to all of its relevant causal variables. The last point implies that the structure of causal connections, or the system of functional equations, should be self-contained.

(3) A *theoretical rationale* for each causal hypothesis (causal connection) that describes the processes through which a cause acts on (operates on, produces) an effect.

(4) *Boundaries,* which specify the contexts (e.g., types of subjects and situations) within which the functional relations/equations are expected to hold.

(5) *Stability,* which implies that the hypothesized structure of causal connections will be consistent over specified time intervals. Inasmuch as the structure of causal connections is represented by a system of functional equations, stability suggests that the functional equations will be invariant over specified time intervals.

In its initial development, a theory is based typically on induction, wherein observations of events lead to hypotheses that certain variables are related causally and that certain processes or functions generate the relations. In this regard, previous experience will often suggest to the theory builder the form that functional relations might take. Additional theoretical work is often needed, however, to develop the theory so that it is amenable to confirmatory analysis. This development includes consideration of the form of the theory with respect to (a) its breadth or elaborateness; (b) its depth, which is reflected by the complexity of variables and the molarity of causal hypotheses, and (c) the structure of causal connections, which is typically stated in the form of a structural model. Each of these considerations is discussed below. We will then proceed to discussions of the other aspects of a theory.

Form of a Theory—Elaborateness

A theory may be very simple and involve just one effect and the cause(s) that is (are) presumed to be functionally related to that effect. For example, one might hypothesize that increases in role expectations, communicated by management to subordinates regarding quality and quantity of subordinates' performance, may cause subordinates to perceive that they have too much work to do (i.e., are overloaded—see James & Sells, 1981). This is a "nonelaborate theory," consisting of just one effect (role overload) and two causes (expected quality of role performance and expected quantity of role performance). Nonelaborate theories are acceptable from the perspective of confirmatory analysis if the model is self-contained, which is to say that all relevant causes of role overload are contained in the theoretical model.

A theory may be made more elaborate by adding effects, and as necessary, other relevant causes of those effects. For example, perceptions of role overload may be thought to cause state anxiety, defined as "subjective, consciously perceived feelings of tension, apprehension, [and] nervousness, accompanied by or associated with activation of the autonomic nervous system (ANS)" (Spielberger, 1977, p. 176). The guiding rule is that one should include all relevant causes of each effect in the theoretical model. In this example, if no other causal variables are added to the model, then the theory builder is assuming that role overload is the only relevant cause of state anxiety.

Finally, one can develop highly elaborate theories. To pursue the present illustration, role expectations, role overload, and anxiety might be viewed as a subsystem of a more general system, and one might propose both direct and indirect causes of expected quality and quantity of work (e.g., increases in demand for product), as well as direct and indirect influences of anxiety on other psychological phenomena, such as performance and withdrawal behaviors. The rule remains; each time the theory builder enters an effect into the theoretical model, he or she must also enter all relevant causes of that effect.

In later discussion it will be argued that the more elaborate the theory, the more "faith" one may have in the results of a confirmatory analysis. Nevertheless, confirmatory analysis may be applied to nonelaborate or "moderately" elaborate theories insofar as the theories are self-contained. It must be recognized, however, that nonelaborate and moderately elaborate theories are typically subsystems chosen from more global theoretical subsystems or systems. While acceptable, such selection obviously limits the explanatory value of the chosen theory because the functioning of a specific subsystem depends on the functioning of more general subsystems and systems. For example, expected quality and quantity of role performance may be the only relevant causes of role overload, but this self-contained model will be influenced by the causes of expected quality and quantity of role performance.

Form of a Theory—Molar Causal Connections and Mediating Mechanisms

In addition to elaborateness or breadth of a theory, it is also possible to view a theory in terms of its depth by assessing the "complexity" of variables and "molarity" of causal connections included in functional relations. To contrast extremes, *molar* "refers to causal laws stated in terms of large and often complex objects," whereas *micro*, or *micromediation*, "refers to the specification of causal connections at a level of smaller particles that make up the molar objects on a finer time scale" (Cook & Campbell, 1979, p. 32). To illustrate, a causal hypothesis that perceived role overload will result in state anxiety implies a molar causal connection between two complex variables. A more specific micromediational model, or "micromediational chain," is presented in later discussions of theoretical rationale for causal hypotheses (Condition 2), where it is postulated that perceived role overload produces state anxiety by a model such as: role overload → anticipated failure → anticipated negative consequences of failure (e.g., reprimand) → state anxiety.

As discussed by Cook and Campbell (1979), it is not only acceptable but often necessary to employ theoretical models involving molar causal connections among complex variables. It follows that the micromediating variables that serve to connect complex variables will not be included explicitly as separate variables in the theoretical model, and therefore, in functional relations and equations. It is possible, however, to attempt to identify at least the more important of these mediating variables, and to propose how these variables enter into the causal processes.

That is, one uses mediating variables to attempt to explain how one complex variable produces or acts on another complex variable. Thus, as in the example above, role overload and state anxiety may be the only variables included in a theoretical model. But reference may be made to mediating processes, such as anticipated failure and negative consequences resulting from failure, that lead to associations between role overload and state anxiety. We shall use the term *mediating mechanism* to refer to an intervening or mediating variable that (a) is not included explicitly in a theoretical model, but (b) is used to help to explain the processes by which a complex cause produces a complex effect in a molar causal connection.

Failure of a mediating mechanism to operate as expected for some, but not for all or even most, subjects may be regarded as a relatively random event, and therefore, as one form of random shock. Such failures render molar causal connections, and therefore, functional relations and equations, both fallible and probabilistic (Cook & Campbell, 1979). That is, a cause may not produce an effect because a mediating mechanism on which the causal connection depends is not functioning in the presumed manner for some subjects. Thus, we might say that a cause will produce an effect dependent on the occurrence of the presumed mediating mechanisms for all subjects, which is a probabilistic statement and one of the reasons why functional equations are represented in the form of probabilistic equations. Finally, the probabilistic nature of a causal hypothesis is associated logically with the molarity of the causal connection. Cook and Campbell (1979, p. 33) noted that "it is probably the case that the more molar the causal assertion and the longer and more unspecified the assumed micro-mediational chain, the more fallible the causal law and the more probabilistic its supporting evidence."

To avoid potential confusion, it is helpful to distinguish between the role of mediating mechanisms and relevant causes in functional equations. Consider the following functional equation that relates two complex variables: $y = B_{yx}x + d_y$. If w is a relevant cause of y, then w must be entered into the equation; that is, $y = B_{yx}x + B_{yw}w + d_y$. Note that (a) x is still presumed to have a direct effect on y, (b) the equation is not self-contained without explicit inclusion of w, and (c) w may or may not be a complex variable. However, if w is a mediating mechanism for the function relating y to x, then the model has the form $x \rightarrow w \rightarrow y$. This model indicates two functional equations, namely, $w = B_{wx}x + d_w$ and $y = B_{yw}w + d_y$. This suggests that explicit inclusion of w renders the (x,y) relationship *indirect,* where the effect of x on y must now pass through w. Furthermore, x is no longer a relevant cause of y because, by definition, relevant causes must be *directly* related to effects. On the other hand, if w is unmeasured, then relative to the molarity of the theory, x is a direct cause of y and the molar connection may be regarded as self-contained.

In summary, many theories in psychology are nonelaborate or moderately elaborate, involving molar causal connections linking a few complex variables. Such theories may be quite useful for testing selected, self-contained causal subsystems. However, more elaborate theories involving more holistic subsystems or systems, as well as explication and inclusion of mediating mechanisms in theoretical models, are clearly the long-term objectives. Nevertheless, regardless of the scope of a particular theoretical model, if it is self-contained then it is possible to proceed to the next step in confirmatory analysis, which is the development of a structural model.

Development of Structural Models

It must be possible to propose a theory in quantitative terms if it is to be subjected to confirmatory analysis. The process of confirmatory analysis typically begins by specifying the presumed structure of causal connections among the variables in the form of a graphic model.

Consider the graphic model of the oversimplified theory regarding causes and effects of role overload in Figure 2.1. (All variables are regarded as complex and thus all causal connections are molar.) The model predicts that (a) expected quality (x_1) and expected quantity (x_2) of role performance are causes of perceived role overload (y_1); (b) role overload (y_1) is a cause of state anxiety (y_2); and (c) expected quality (x_1) and quantity (x_2) of role performance do not cause state anxiety (y_2) directly; rather, they affect it indirectly through their effects on the intervening role overload perceptions (y_1). Representations of theory or theoretical models are referred to as causal, or structural, models; the term "structural" is used to denote that the structure of the causal connections has been specified.

Definition of Terms. In regard to the structural model, y_1 and y_2 are referred to as *endogenous* variables; an endogenous variable is a dependent variable (i.e., effect) whose occurrence is to be explained by the structural model. x_1 and x_2 are *exogenous* variables. An exogenous variable is a predetermined variable that acts as a cause but whose occurrence is not to be explained by the model.

The curved (double-headed) arrow between x_1 and x_2 means that although the exogenous variables may be related, their relationship is not to be explained by this particular structural model. The straight (single-headed) arrows in the model represent the hypothesized causal connections. The lack of straight arrows between the two exogenous variables $(x_1$ and $x_2)$ and the endogenous y_2 variable reflects the hypotheses that the exogenous variables do not have direct causal connections with y_2.

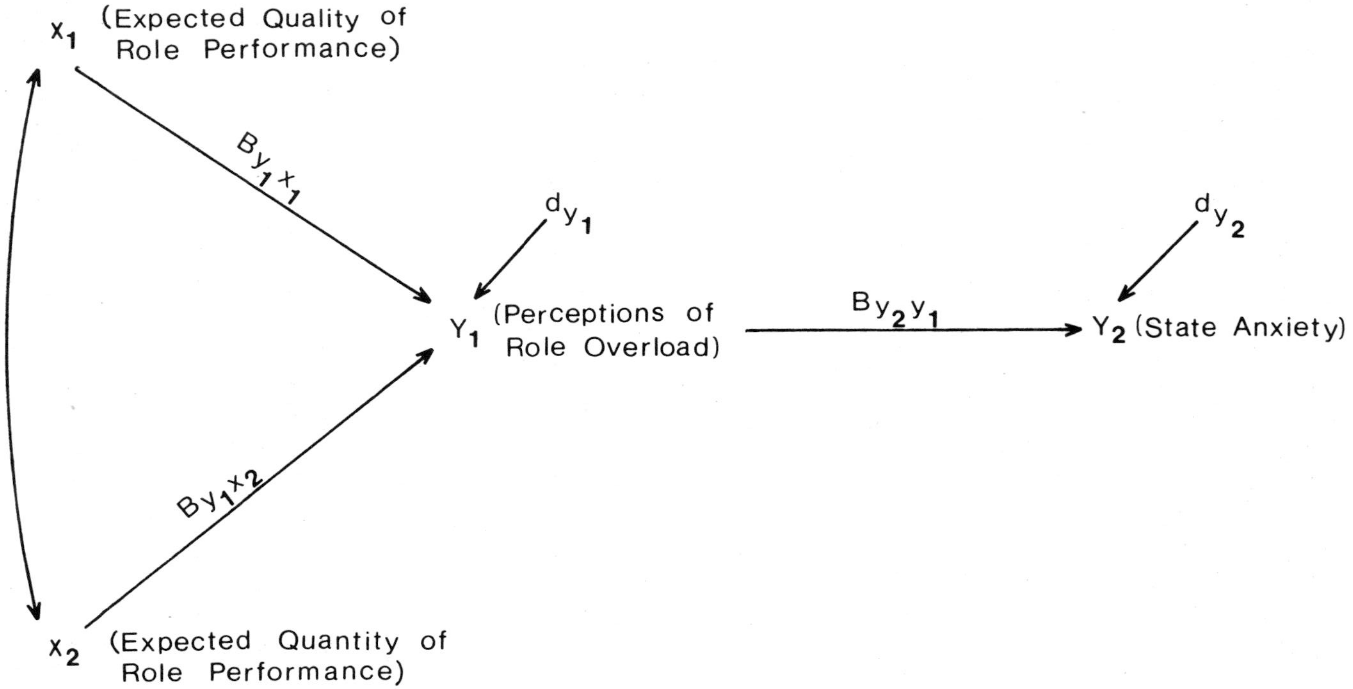

Figure 2.1   Formal Representation of a Structural Model

Associated with each straight arrow is a structural parameter (i.e., $B_{y_1x_1}$, $B_{y_1x_2}$, $B_{y_2y_1}$). The structural parameters assume values that reflect the strengths of the causal relationships. Specifically, each structural parameter reflects the amount of change in an effect (endogenous variable) that results from a unit of change in a cause (exogenous variable or preceding endogenous variable), with all other causes of that effect held constant. For example, $B_{y_1x_1}$ is a shorthand notation for $B_{y_1x_1 \cdot x_2}$, which indicates that x_2, also a cause of y_1, is held constant when the effect of x_1 on y_1 is ascertained. Thus, $B_{y_1x_1}$ is the unique effect of x_1 on y_1. A key objective of confirmatory analysis is to estimate the values of the structural parameters; this process is addressed in Condition 9.

The small "d's" associated with each of the two endogenous variables are the *disturbance terms*. Disturbance terms involve variation in an endogenous variable that is not to be attributed to the causes of that variable included explicitly in a structural model. For example, d_{y_1} accounts for all variation in y_1 that cannot be attributed to x_1 and x_2. The straight arrow from d_{y_1} to y_1 suggests that these other sources of variation are also causes of y_1. In the structural model, the sources of variation in d_{y_1}, as well as in d_{y_2}, include random shocks and/or unmeasured or omitted causes, which may or may not be relevant causes. In an actual confirmatory analysis with realized values on variables, a disturbance term may also include (a) random measurement errors in the effect and the causes, where the primary concern is error in one or more of the causes, and (b) nonrandom measurement errors, such as bias in the scales of measurement and method variance. Random shocks and unmeasured causes are discussed in greater detail in Condition 5; random and nonrandom measurement errors are addressed in Condition 8.

Functional Equations. The formal structural model in Figure 2.1 specifies the form of the functional equations that are to be used to represent the functional relations. There are two endogenous variables in Figure 2.1, and thus two functional relations, namely, $y_1 = f(x_1, x_2, d_1)$ and $y_2 = f(y_1, d_2)$. Assuming linearity and additivity, the functions may be viewed as taking the form of weighted, additive combinations. Specifically, the functional equations are, in deviation form:

$$y_1 = B_{y_1x_1}x_1 + B_{y_1x_2}x_2 + d_{y_1} \qquad [2.1]$$

$$y_2 = B_{y_2y_1}y_1 + d_{y_2} \qquad [2.2]$$

To summarize, the structural model indicates the functional relations that relate effects to causes and specifies the form(s) of the functional equations that are to be used to represent functional relations. However, specifying functional relations and equations does not necessarily mean that the processes by which causes produce effects have been explained. For this we shall often need a theoretical rationale.

CONDITION 2: THEORETICAL RATIONALE FOR CAUSAL HYPOTHESES

Few functional relations are self-explanatory in the sense that the processes by which a cause produces an effect are self-evident. To illustrate, consider the Indian villagers who were taught by a Peace Corpsman to fertilize their wheat crop. The next year, after the Peace Corpsman had left, the villagers erroneously received a double shipment of fertilizer. After their spectacular success with fertilizer the prior year, the villagers decided the more the better, and ruined their crop by applying too much fertilizer. The Peace Corpsman had failed to explain to the villagers the mediating mechanisms between fertilizer and wheat growth. Another problem occurs when what may appear to be a functional relation is instead merely a covariation among variables that are not causally related. A classic example used by philosophers to indicate covariation without causation is the correlation between the occurrence of night and the occurrence of day. This covariation is spurious; covariation between night and day is due to common causes (e.g., the earth's rotation about its axis and the sun). These examples highlight the point that an attempt to specify the processes by which night causes day, or vice versa, would likely preclude an erroneous causal hypothesis that night is a function of day.

An attempt must be made to separate functional relations from simple covariation by proposing a theoretical rationale for the functional relations. Prior experience and observation are helpful in identifying covariation among variables, where the covariation may reflect a functional relation. The theoretical rationale is typically obtained by development of a theory from careful observations, or by deducing from an existing theory a proposal of how causes produce effects, that is, an explanation of why variables covary. It is also typical that the theoretical rationale involves the introduction of mediating mechanisms to help to explain molar causal connections among complex variables.

To illustrate these points, a theoretical rationale is developed for both the causes of role overload and the role overload → state anxiety causal connection in Figure 2.1. Beginning with role overload, prior experience in work environments may suggest that management's decision to increase expectations for quality (x_1) and quantity (x_2) of role performance results in perceptions of overload (y_1) on the part of subordinates. While this observation implies a functional relation between y_1 and x_1 and x_2, it does not necessarily specify how it is that quality/quantity expectations produce role overload. A theory of "stress" might serve this purpose (cf. Katz & Kahn, 1978). For example, it might be postulated that increased expectations for higher quality output in shorter time spans result in perceived overload because these expectations exceed both physical and personnel resources (e.g., demands for quality exceed the tolerances of machinery and the technological training of personnel) as well as time resources (e.g., the quantity of expected output cannot be achieved in the existing workday or workweek). In short, perceived overload occurs when role prescriptions and demands exceed available resources and time.[1]

The explanation above assumes the presence and operation of a number of mediating mechanisms. For example, the presumed causal connection between increased demands for quality and perceived overload is a molar causal connection between two complex variables. This relationship depends on such things as accurate communication of expectations to subordinates from management, cognitive comparisons of resources and demands on the part of subordinates, and assignment of similar meaning to the environment by all or most subordinates (i.e., all or most subordinates perceive similar levels of role overload). The molar causal connection may in fact be true, but can only be stated as a probability because the mediating mechanisms might not function in the presumed manner for all subordinates (e.g., a subordinate who misinterprets the cues from management regarding quality of work).

A theory of stress may also be used to derive a theoretical rationale for the molar causal connection between y_2 (state anxiety) and y_1 (role overload). Subordinates' perceptions that their role performance is adversely affected by inadequate resources should signify to them that they are not likely to succeed. This perceived or anticipated likelihood of failure should arouse conscious affective states of tension and apprehension because failure should result in negative consequences, such as reprimands, failure to be promoted, or dismissals. Thus, the causal connection $y_1 \rightarrow y_2$ is dependent on a theoretical rationale involving several mediating mechanisms, namely y_1 (role overload) → anticipated likelihood of failure → anticipated likelihood of negative consequences → y_2 (state anxiety).

Here again mediating mechanisms render the functional relation probabilistic if any one of the mechanisms does not operate as expected for all subjects. To illustrate, while role overload may be perceived, such perceptions might not lead to feelings of tension and apprehension if subordinates do not anticipate an association between overload and failure. Consequently, the occurrence of role overload might not lead invariably to anxiety for all subordinates and the functional relation is probabilistic.

In conclusion, many functional relations in psychology are nonobvious and involve molar causal connections among complex variables. A theoretical rationale involving mediating mechanisms is therefore required to propose how causes produce effects. An important contribution of a theoretical rationale is that it assists in differentiating functional relations from simple covariation. Another contribution is the identification of at least some of the mediating mechanisms on which functional relations depend. In the situation in which a functional relation receives only weak probabilistic support in a confirmatory analysis, or is disconfirmed by that analysis, the presumed operation of mediating mechanisms is a key source for reevaluation.

CONDITION 3: SPECIFICATION OF CAUSAL ORDER

The causal order is typically thought of as a temporal order or sequence in which causes occur before effects; a causal order must be specified for each causal relation. It is also typical to assume that a time interval, or *causal interval*, intervenes between the occurrence of a cause and the occurrence of an effect. This assumption may prove to be a problem, however, because "in many instances where the scientist speaks of cause (e.g., 'force causes acceleration'), no time sequence is involved" (Simon, 1977, p. 82). Simon (1977) "avoided" the time sequence and causal interval issue by arguing that the causal order among a set of variables is given by the order in which variables occur naturally in an asymmetric, self-contained system of functional relations, and, therefore, the order in which one would solve for the values of the variables in a system of ordered functional equations.

Figure 2.1 and functional equations 2.1 and 2.2 illustrate a presumed causal order; the ordering of equations 2.1 and 2.2 denotes that x_1 and x_2 occur before y_1, and that y_1 occurs before y_2. Causal intervals are not specified for the causal connections. This does not imply that causal intervals are unimportant (in our opinion), and we will discuss causal intervals both below (briefly) and in a number of the remaining conditions. Nevertheless, the point here is that the causal ordering among variables, with the exception of purely exogenous variables (i.e., x_1 and x_2), is given by the presumed ordering of functional relations and, therefore, by the ordering among the functional equations. This rationale is especially pertinent to cross-sectional designs in which no time intervals are involved empirically (i.e., all data are collected at the same time). On the other hand, this reasoning means that one is relying on theory to establish a causal ordering among variables inasmuch as the functional equations are themselves given by theory. This may also prove to be troublesome, as discussed below.

The important question with respect to causal order is whether the presumed causal ordering is correct. Consider, for example, that causal order is easily established for many naturally occurring events, such as the use of heroin precedes withdrawal symptoms. On the other hand, causal ordering among other variables is not generally obvious and is subject to misspecification. To illustrate, Zajonc (1980) challenged the widely accepted model that perceptions (P) of situations (S) precede affective reactions (A) to situations (i.e., S → P → A). Focusing on the cognitive processing of "hot cognitions" (e.g., perceptions of danger), Zajonc proposed and supported a model of the form S → A → P, which suggests that differentiated cognitive interpretations (P) are a result of an attempt to explain the affect (A), which occurred almost simultaneously with the presentation of S. If generalized to the structural model in Figure 2.1, one might argue that anxiety (y_2) occurs prior to perceptions of role overload (y_1).

This illustration serves to point out that (a) causal ordering among variables, especially subjective constructs such as perceptions and affect, is often not obvious, (b) one must rely frequently on theory to propose a causal order, and (c) the theory may be wrong. Now, it is true that a causal order must be specified before a confirmatory analysis is conducted, and that one should not explore different causal orders with the same set of data in order to optimize goodness of fit between a model and data (Duncan, 1970, 1975). But it is also true that one may test for alternative causal orders with the same set of data (see Billings & Wroten, 1978). This is possible only if structural models specifying different orders are proposed prior to the analysis of data. In other words, if different theories suggest different causal orders, and if the theories furnish structural models with conflicting (and empirically testable) predictions, then it is possible to determine which of the models, if any, has the best fit with the data (see Griffin, 1977).

As a final point, it is often thought that the establishment of a causal order is facilitated by the use of a time-series form of design, where measurement of presumed causes precedes measurement of presumed effects by a discrete, identifiable time period (see Ostrom, 1978). However, measuring presumed causes before presumed effects in no way implies that the true causal order is consistent with order of measurement (see Rozelle & Campbell, 1969). Moreover, the times of measurement (measurement intervals) must correspond closely to the true causal intervals in a time-series design (see Kenny, 1979), which raises an obvious problem for psychology inasmuch as causal intervals are often unknown. Time-series designs are discussed in the next condition and in later conditions. The key points here are that causal ordering and time of measurement in a time-series analysis should be dictated by prior knowledge of causal intervals and a structural model; time of measurement should not dictate causal order, causal intervals, or the structural model.

CONDITION 4: SPECIFICATION OF CAUSAL DIRECTION

Up to now we have focused on unidirectional, or recursive relations of the form x → y. This emphasis was intentional and designed to maintain consistency with Simon's (1977) view of causality as an asymmetric functional relation. However, studies of causality in science also allow for *nonrecursive* relations, which take the form $y_i \rightleftarrows y_j$. This form implies reciprocal causation between y_i and y_j, where the variables mutually affect one another. The criterion for Condition 4 is that all direct causal connections within a structural model must be specified as either recursive or nonrecursive.

Nonrecursive Models

A nonrecursive model involving reciprocal causation is presented and discussed below. The discussion includes an interpretation of causality which, following an amendment to Simon's views, allows for reciprocal causation. A distinction is then made between nonrecursive and *cyclical recursive* models.

A nonrecursive structural model based on a study by Kritzer (1977) and used by James and Singh (1978) to illustrate reciprocal causation is presented in Figure 2.2. As with recursive models, the x_j designate exogenous events, the y_i designate endogenous events, the Bs reflect structural parameters, and the d_{y_i} designate disturbance terms. Functional equations for nonrecursive models are developed in the same manner as those for recursive models; an equation is constructed for each effect, and it includes all causes having a direct causal connection with that effect. The functional equations for Figure 2.2 are (assuming linearity and deviation scores):

$$y_1 = B_{y_1 y_2} y_2 + B_{y_1 x_1} x_1 + B_{y_1 x_2} x_2 + d_{y_1} \qquad [2.3]$$

$$y_2 = B_{y_2 y_1} y_1 + B_{y_2 x_3} x_3 + B_{y_2 x_4} x_4 + d_{y_2} \qquad [2.4]$$

By convention, endogenous variables involved in a reciprocal relation are included in a functional equation before the exogenous variables (e.g., y_2 is placed before x_1 and x_2 in equation 2.3).

The structural model and functional equations are based on the following causal hypotheses:

(1) The amount of violence employed by police at a political protest event (y_1—the extent to which police use increasingly more dangerous controls) is a function of (a) the degree to which police are prepared for or anticipate violence, as indicated by the presence of riot equipment (x_1), and (b) verbal provocation by protesters, operationalized by the extent to which obscenities are collectively shouted by demonstrators (x_2). x_1 and x_2 are exogenous causes of y_1, and precede y_1 in the causal order.

(2) The amount of violence evidenced by protesters collectively (y_2—operationalized on a scale ranging from protestors' use of antipolice

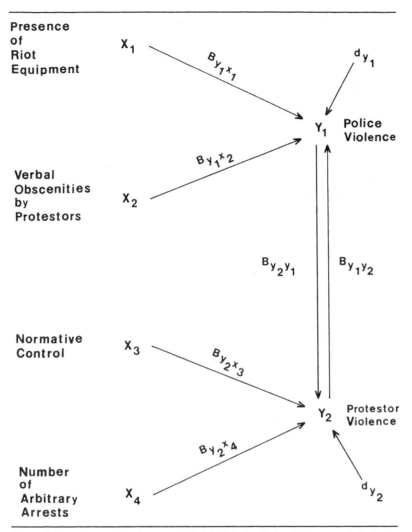

Figure 2.2 Nonrecursive Structural Model Relating Police Violence and Protestor Violence

SOUCE: From "An Introduction to the Logic, Assumptions, and Basic Analytic Procedures of Two-Stage Least Squares," by L. R. James and B. K. Singh, *Psychological Bulletin*, 1978, 85, 1104-1122. Copyright 1978 by the American Psychological Association. Reprinted by permission of the authors and publisher.

slogans to protestors' use of weapons) is a function of (a) the conscious attempt by protesters to effect normative controls on violence (x_3), and (b) the number of (perceived) arbitrary arrests of protesters made by police (x_4). x_3 and x_4 are exogenous causes of y_2 and precede y_2 in the causal order (x_3 is related negatively to y_2).

(3) Police violence (y_1) and protester violence (y_2) are reciprocal causes of each other. A causal order is not especially relevant here; either police or protesters may initiate violence. The point is that an initiation or escalation of violence on the part of police (protesters) is followed by an initiation or escalation of violence by the other party. Furthermore, an escalation by one party influences escalation by the other, resulting in a dynamic system of mutual causation. It is presumed, however, that the mutual escalation of violence will level off, or reach an "equilibrium-type condition" (see Namboordiri, Carter, & Blalock, 1975), which in part is determined by the values on the exogenous variables (equilibrium-type conditions are discussed in Condition 7). For example, the mutual effects between police and protester violence are less likely to reach the stage of joint use of weapons if protesters exercise normative control and police do not have riot equipment available. Finally, and of major importance, it is assumed that the reciprocal effects between police and protester violence are essentially instantaneous, or at least so rapid that reliable causal intervals cannot be determined for either the $y_1 \rightarrow y_2$ or $y_2 \rightarrow y_1$ causal effects.

The discussion above illustrates only one of many reciprocal causation models for the social sciences. With respect to psychology, reciprocal causation is intrinsic to many theoretical models. For instance, reciprocal causation is indicated in social learning and cognitive social learning models (see Bandura, 1978; Mahoney, 1977; Mischel, 1977), interactional psychology (see Bowers, 1973; Ekehammer, 1974; Endler & Magnusson, 1976; Pervin, 1968), and social system and organizational theory (see Dansereau, Graen, & Haga, 1975; James & Jones, 1976; Roberts, Hulin, & Rousseau, 1978). Furthermore, confirmatory analysis provides analytic techniques to test nonrecursive models involving reciprocal causation. Two of the most popular of these techniques were reviewed recently in the psychological literature. These methods are two-stage least squares (James, 1981; James & Singh, 1978) and maximum likelihood estimation (Maruyama & McGarvey, 1980). A review of these procedures is beyond the scope of this volume, although it is noteworthy that Kritzer (1977) used the two-stage least squares technique to test (and support) the hypothesized reciprocal causation between police and protester violence.

To summarize, each causal connection in a structural model must be specified as either recursive or nonrecursive. It is also necessary to stipulate that not all relations in a structural model may be nonrecursive. This stipulation evolves from the "identification" question, which is concerned with whether sufficient information is available to obtain unique mathematical solutions for the structural parameters in functional equations (see Fisher, 1966; Theil, 1971). Identification is discussed in Conditions 9 and 10. At this time we note only that functional equations representing nonrecursive relations are identified if there exists at least one "instrument" for each endogenous variable involved in a reciprocal relationship. In general terms, an instrument is an exogenous variable that affects only one of the endogenous variables involved in a reciprocal relationship. For example, each of the exogenous variables in Figure 2.2 is an instrument because each of these variables is a cause of either y_1 or y_2, but not of both y_1 and y_2.

We now turn to the apparent paradox of defining causality as an asymmetric functional relation and then entertaining the concept of reciprocal causation. To review briefly, the stipulation of asymmetric functional relations was designed (a) to avoid confusion of causation with logical implication, and (b) to differentiate functional relations from ordinary mathematical functions, where, for example, $e = mc^2$ implies $c^2 = e/m$. The fidelity of the stipulation is preserved by stating that $y_2 = f(y_1, d_{y_2})$ does not imply that $y_1 = f(y_2, d_{y_1})$. This does not rule out, however, the offering of a causal hypothesis that $y_1 = f(y_2, d_{y_1})$. That is, hypothesizing a functional relation does not automatically imply a reciprocal form of relation, but a reciprocal relation may be proposed as part of a structural model. For example, the hypothesis that child behavior = f(mother behavior) does not imply mother behavior = f(child behavior). However, we may propose two functional relations, namely child behavior = f(mother behavior) and mother behavior = f(child behavior). (Based on the preceding discussion, instruments would have to be added to each of the functions before analyses could be performed.)

In sum, reciprocal causation is amenable to confirmatory analysis and is consistent with a functional definition of causality. It is necessary, however, to amend Simon's (1977) definition of causality to allow for reciprocal causation. This amendment is: "Causality is a functional relation among certain variables, or subsets of variables, in a self-contained structure, where functional relation does not imply reciprocal relation but reciprocal relations may be postulated."

Cyclical Recursive Models

The concluding objective of this section is to distinguish between reciprocal causation and "cyclical causation." Reciprocal causation refers to relations of the form $y_i \rightleftarrows y_j$, where the causal intervals for the $y_i \rightarrow y_j$ and $y_j \rightarrow y_i$ causal connections are rapid and essentially indiscernable. If, however, a causal interval can be established for the $y_i \rightarrow y_j$ and $y_j \rightarrow y_i$ causal connections, then one has a structural model such as shown in Figure 2.3. The essence of this model is that the occurrence of y_1 at time t (i.e., y_{1t}) causes the occurrence of y_2 at time t+1 (i.e., y_{2t+1}), where the time interval between t and t+1 is discernible. The occurrence of y_2 at time t+1 then, through a feedback loop shown at the top of Figure 2.3,

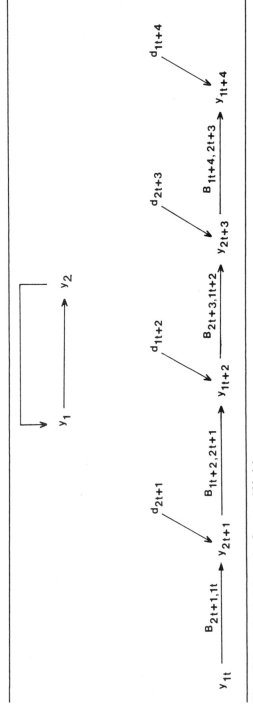

Figure 2.3   A Cyclical Recursive Structural Model

causes the occurrence of y_1 at time t+2 (i.e., y_{1t+2}), where again the time interval between t+1 and t+2 is discernible. This cycle repeats itself and we have cyclical causation.

The structural model in Figure 2.3 is a form of time-series design. Of special importance is the fact that it is a recursive model inasmuch as all causal relations are asymmetric. That is, each causal relation is recursive because a time interval may be specified between the occurrence of a cause and the occurrence of an effect (see Strotz & Wold, 1971). We shall refer to this design as a "cyclical recursive model."

The functional equations for Figure 2.3 are shown below. y_1 and y_2 are specified in the subscripts of structural parameters and disturbance terms by a "1" or a "2" preceding the time indicator. y_1 at time t assumes the role of an exogenous variable (i.e., its occurrence is not to be explained by this model).

$$y_{2t+1} = B_{2t+1,1t}y_{1t} + d_{2t+1} \qquad [2.5]$$

$$y_{1t+2} = B_{1t+2,2t+1}y_{2t+1} + d_{1t+2} \qquad [2.6]$$

$$y_{2t+3} = B_{2t+3,1t+2}y_{1t+2} + d_{2t+3} \qquad [2.7]$$

$$y_{1t+4} = B_{1t+4,2t+3}y_{2t+3} + d_{1t+4} \qquad [2.8]$$

Linear relations and deviation scores are assumed. Furthermore, it must be assumed not only that the causal intervals are known, but also that the times of measurement of variables representing y_1 and y_2 (i.e., measurement intervals) correspond closely to the causal intervals. Finally, as discussed in greater detail in Condition 7, the model and functional equations must be "stationary." Stationarity refers to the stability of a structural model, and would be indicated here if the structural parameters with common causes and effects are equal (i.e., $B_{1t+2,2t+1} = B_{1t+4,2t+3}$, and $B_{2t+1,1t} = B_{2t+3,1t+2}$).

In conclusion, while there is much to be said in favor of reciprocal causation (nonrecursive relations) and cyclical causation (cyclical recursive relations) in psychological research, we shall continue to employ simple recursive models for illustrative purposes.

CONDITION 5: SELF-CONTAINED FUNCTIONAL EQUATIONS

Simon (1977) discussed self-containment in the context of an ordered system of functional equations representing a recursive structural model. However, an overview of the basic logic and requirements of self-containment is made easier by focusing on a single functional equation. We will discuss self-containment in this context.

As discussed previously, a (probabilistic) functional equation is representative of a causal relation only if the functional equation is self-contained, and an equation is self-contained only if all relevant causes of the endogenous variable are included in the functional equation. To illustrate, consider the part of the model in Figure 2.1 that deals with causes of role overload. This part is reproduced in Figure 2.4a. The linear functional equation for role overload is, in deviation form:

$$y_1 = B_{y_1 x_1} x_1 + B_{y_1 x_2} x_2 + (d_{y_1} = RS) \qquad [2.9]$$

Equation 2.9 is the same as equation 2.1 with the exception that d_{y_1} has been specified as being made up exclusively of random shocks (RS). This specification implies that x_1 and x_2 are the only relevant causes of y_1, which suggests that no other variable exists that simultaneously (a) has a direct, nonminor influence on y_1, (b) is stable, (c) is related to x_1 and/or x_2, and (d) is not linearly dependent on x_1 and x_2. That is, no other relevant cause exists for y_1. Consequently, x_1 and x_2 will not be related to d_{y_1} because, by definition, the expected value of the covariance between a variable and random shock is zero (e.g., $E(x_1 d_{y_1}) = E(x_1 RS) = \sigma_{x_1 RS} = 0$). Given that d_{y_1} is unrelated to x_1 and x_2, it follows that the conditional expected values of y_1 are determined by a conditional function, or $E(y_1 | x_1, x_2) = B_{y_1 x_1} x_1 + B_{y_1 x_2} x_2$.[2] In other words, the equation is self-contained and the functional equation, and functional relation $y_1 = f(x_1, x_2, d_{y_1})$, may be used to represent a causal relation (assuming that other conditions have been met).

Now, suppose a relevant cause of role overload is not included explicitly in the functional equation. A possible example of such a relevant cause is the degree to which the work environment is perceived to be "impersonal." An impersonal environment suggests that management focuses on productivity and profit, with little attention given to employees' needs and capabilities. By contrast, a "personal" environment connotes consideration of employees' needs and capabilities in addition to concerns for productivity and profit. Employees are predicted to be overloaded in impersonal environments, in comparison to personal environments, because management in such environments strives for economic and performance goals even after the personal capacities of employees have been exceeded. Thus, "impersonality" might be hypothesized to be a major cause of role overload.

Another important characteristic of a relevant cause is that it covaries with a causal variable(s) included explicitly in a functional equation. Impersonality is likely to covary with both expected quality and quantity of role performance because managers who focus only on productivity and profit are more likely to demand higher levels of quality and quantity of

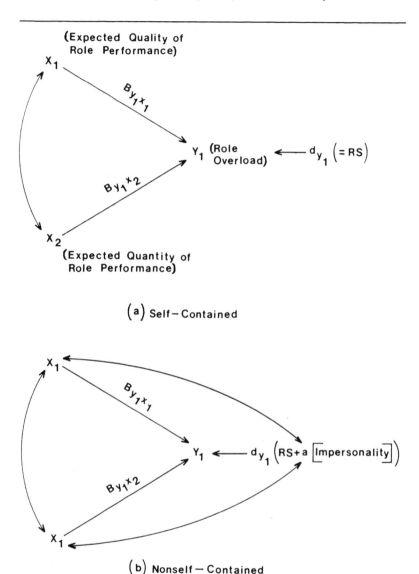

Figure 2.4   Illustrations of Self-Contained and Non-Self-Contained Structural Models

performance than managers more attuned to the effects of their demands on employees. On the other hand, impersonality is not expected to be redundant with, or linearly dependent on, quality and quantity of role performance. In other words, impersonality might be viewed as having a unique effect on role overload.

A model including impersonality is displayed in Figure 2.4b. The unmeasured *a* (impersonality) is represented in the disturbance term for y_1, along with the RS component. It is assumed that *a* fits all the criteria for a relevant cause of y_1, including relationships with x_1 and x_2 (indicated by the curved, double-headed arrows between *a* and both x_1 and x_2), but not linear dependence on x_1 and x_2. The curved, double-headed arrows also indicate that the relationships between *a* and the x's are not to be explained by this model.

The functional equation for Figure 2.4b is

$$y_1 = B_{y_1 x_1} x_1 + B_{y_1 x_2} x_2 + (d_{y_1} = RS + a) \qquad [2.10]$$

The curved (double-headed) arrows relating *a* to x_1 and x_2 in Figure 2.4b show that both x_1 and x_2 should covary with d_{y_1}. The expected value of the covariance between x_1 and d_{y_1} is:

$$
\begin{aligned}
E(x_1 d_{y_1}) &= E[x_1(RS + a)] \\
&= E(x_1 RS) + E(x_1 a) \\
&= \sigma_{x_1 a}, \qquad [2.11]
\end{aligned}
$$

where $\sigma_{x_1 a}$ is a (population) covariance. A similar derivation demonstrates covariation between x_2 and d_{y_1}.

Assuming linearity and additivity, covariation between d_{y_1} and x_1 and x_2 brought about by inclusion of *a* in d_{y_1} implies that the functional equation (equation 2.10), and the model from which it was derived, are not self-contained. To be specific, the model in Figure 2.4b is not self-contained because the conditional expected values of y_1 are no longer determined by the conditional function $B_{y_1 x_1} x_1 + B_{y_1 x_2} x_2$. To achieve self-containment, not only should this function include a term for *a* (i.e., $B_{y_1 a} a$), but also the structural parameters for x_1 and x_2 should include controls for *a* (e.g., $B_{y_1 x_1} \cdot x_2 a$). Thus, with *a* unmeasured, equation 2.10 is misspecified because it omits a relevant cause. In fact, equation 2.10 is not a functional equation because it is not self-contained. Consequently, neither the equation nor the functional relation represents a causal relation.

In summary, the condition of self-containment is satisfied only if the causes included explicitly in a functional equation are unrelated to the disturbance term of that equation. Pragmatically, failure to satisfy this condition results in biased estimates of structural parameters, which is demonstrated in Condition 9. Of importance here is the fact that many published confirmatory studies in psychology have paid no attention whatever to the need for self-contained equations and systems (Billings & Wroten, 1978; James, 1980; Cliff, 1980). Review of these studies reveals obvious and serious violations of the self-containment condition. Consequently, it is our opinion that the confirmatory literature in psychology is inundated with biased estimates of structural parameters, or, if you wish, with equations that have only remote bearing on causal relations. This is rather difficult to understand inasmuch as almost all introductory texts on confirmatory analysis highlight the need to include relevant causes in functional equations, although the terminology and format used to present this condition vary. For example, the condition is discussed in terms of covariation between causes and disturbance terms (Duncan, 1975; Johnston, 1972), covariation among disturbance terms (Namboodiri et al., 1975), and nonspuriousness (Kenny, 1979).

This problem deserves immediate attention. Unfortunately, such attention is unlikely to result in total resolution of the problem because all relevant causes of endogenous variables are not likely to be known (Duncan, 1975; Heise, 1975; Kenny, 1975). As noted by James (1980, p. 415), "The operative question is not whether one has an unmeasured variables problem but rather the degree to which the unavoidable unmeasured variables problem biases estimates of path coefficients [a form of structural parameter] and provides a basis for alternative explanations of results." This statement was grounded on the logic that (a) scientific investigation must proceed based on what is known at the present time, recognizing that present knowledge is incomplete; (b) one must judge whether enough information has accumulated to justify both the development of a structural model and the conduct of a confirmatory analysis; and (c) all known relevant causes should be included in a model and in its functional equations. In other words, given that one believes that it is reasonable to proceed with confirmatory analysis, then the pragmatic question is whether known, relevant causes are included in the functional equations. In this regard, it is fair to ask whether prior failures to include relevant causes in structural models and functional equations could have been avoided by not only an awareness of the self-containment condition, but also by more thoughtfully developed structural models. We recommend that investigators submit their models to their own and others' careful scrutiny, attempting to identify unmeasured relevant causes, before data are collected. In the discussion of Condition 9 we present a set of decision steps that assist in evaluating the likelihood that unmeasured relevant causes will bias estimates of structural parameters. At that time we will also discuss briefly the use of a time-series design that makes possible the minimization of bias in estimates of structural parameters created by unmeasured relevant causes.

CONDITION 6: SPECIFICATION OF BOUNDARIES

Boundaries specify the contexts (e.g., types of subjects and environments) within which functional relations are expected to generalize. Given linearity in both parameters and variables, this condition is satisfied if the functional equation relating an effect to its causes is not contingent on other variables (Kenny, 1979). In other words, the functional relation should be additive. The condition is violated if the functional relation is contingent on, or moderated by, the values on a third or more variables. This is because a significant moderator effect implies interaction, from which it follows that direct causal connections of the form $x \rightarrow y$ cannot be interpreted unambiguously.

Tests for interaction/moderation should be conducted as part of a confirmatory analysis when prior research and/or theory suggest the presence of a moderator. If the potential moderator is a categorical variable, then the values of the structural parameters may be estimated separately for each value of the moderator, such as one analysis for males and another analysis for females. Tests for moderation are then often based on an assessment of whether the estimates of the structural parameters vary as a function of the "subgroups" established by different values of the moderator (see Schoenberg, 1972; Jöreskog & Sörbom, 1979; Specht & Warren, 1976). The term "subgroup" refers to subpopulations (subsamples) in which all relationships are linear and additive (see Zedeck, 1971). If the moderator (or moderators) is a continuous variable (e.g., age), then more complex analytic procedures are required. In general, these procedures assume a form similar to moderated regression (see Cohen & Cohen, 1975), although more sophisticated methods are required for causal interpretation. An excellent and readable discussion of these methods was presented recently by Stolzenberg (1979). Methods for estimating structural parameters given nonlinearity in the variables are also presented by Stolzenberg.

In summary, our primary concern here is to point out that the existence of a moderator, or moderators, requires careful specification of the boundaries of a structural model. Taking the simple case in which a moderator is a categorical variable, a different structural model and accompanying functional equations are required for each value of the moderator (i.e., each subgroup). In other words, each value of the moderator forms the boundary for each structural model. Clearly, moderators inflate the complexity of confirmatory analysis, and attempts should be made to specify the original boundaries of a structural model in a manner that reduces the likelihood of moderation. Conversely, failure to identify a significant moderator will result in inaccurate estimates of structural parameters and erroneous causal inferences regarding the magnitudes of causal effects.

CONDITION 7: STABILITY OF THE STRUCTURAL MODEL

A structural model is expected to be stable. Stability is indicated if the values of structural parameters in functional equations are invariant, or stationary, over specified time intervals (see Pindyck & Rubinfeld, 1976). The importance of stability becomes clear if its obverse is considered. If the variables in a structural model are in a state of flux, then the relationships among the variables are likely to change rather rapidly. Consequently, data collected at two points in time, within a relatively short time interval, would provide two different sets of equations for the same set of variables; that is, the estimated structural parameters would assume different values at each point in time. This is an impossible situation because the structural model could not be generalized beyond a few days or weeks. On the other hand, if the parameter estimates remain the same over time periods that are reasonable and meaningful for the variables of interest, then a basis is provided for generalizing the results of a confirmatory analysis beyond very restricted time intervals. Note, however, that the stability condition does not suggest that a particular structural model will be invariant with respect to long periods of time. The point is that a structural model should possess enough stability for generalization across a reasonable and meaningful time interval (see Simon, 1977).

Equilibrium-Type Condition

A subtle but critical implication of the stability condition is that the values on the variables in a functional equation should have reached a temporary state of approximate constancy before an attempt is made to measure them and to use the data to estimate structural parameters. This temporary state of constancy is referred to as the *equilibrium-type condition* (Namboodiri et al., 1975). The equilibrium-type condition is almost unheard of in the psychological literature, a literature that relies heavily on cross-sectional designs in confirmatory analysis. Stated directly, it is precisely the *assumption* that the equilibrium-type condition has been satisfied that justifies using cross-sectional designs to estimate structural parameters. Specifically, cross-sectional designs attempt to model (capture) causal processes that have already occurred via functional equations that employ fixed constants (i.e., structural parameters; Pindyck & Rubinfeld, 1976). Estimation of the fixed constants is justified only in the condition that the effects of the exogenous variables on the endogenous variables have worked their way through the causal system. This means that subjects' scores on the endogenous and exogenous variables are temporarily fixed, or "equilibrated" (Heise, 1975), or at least that any effect that does occur during the equilibrium period is so rapid that a temporary equilibrium is rapidly reestablished (Simon, 1977). Given an equilibrium-type condition, in combination with (a) sampling that has been of sufficient breadth to guarantee large differences among subjects on each of the variables, and (b) functional equations that are appropriate for all subjects in the population from which a random sample was drawn, one may model prior causal processes by relying on cross-sectional comparisons across subjects to infer processes that have been at work for a particular subject over time (Heise, 1975; Miller, 1971; Namboodiri et al., 1975).

Consider, for example, the structural model for role overload and state anxiety (Figure 2.1—which, for illustrative purposes, is considered self-contained). The preceding discussion suggests that, for a cross-sectional design, one would want to sample work environments and individuals so as to guarantee large variations in expected quality and quantity of role performance, perceptions of role overload, and state anxiety. Data should be collected only after the effects of role expectations on role overload, and the effects of role overload on state anxiety, have had a chance to stabilize (equilibrate) in each work environment and for each subject, that is, only after values on the variables have reached a temporary state of constancy. Assuming the functional relations are applicable for all subjects and work environments (see Condition 6), analytic procedures discussed in Conditions 9 and 10 could then be used to capture the prior causal processes that generated the particular configuration or pattern of values on the variables obtained in the cross-sectional analysis.

An equilibrium-type condition is also assumed for each wave (time) of measurement in a time-series analysis. However, the temporary equilibrium at a particular time is lost as soon as changes occur in one or more causal variables. The changes in causal variables produce changes in effects, and a new temporary equilibrium is established when the values on all variables reach a new temporary state of constancy. This is referred to as a "shift in equilibrium levels" (see Namboodiri et al., 1975). Given changes in a causal variable, the time period required to reestablish a temporary equilibrium in an effect is referred to as the "equilibration time" (Heise, 1975), which is the causal interval. (It is assumed that the values of causes remain constant within the causal interval.) If (a) the functional relations are stationary (i.e., the structural parameters are invariant with respect to shifts in equilibrium levels) and (b) times of measurement correspond closely to causal intervals, then (c) it is possible to attempt to fit functional equations to the shifts in equilibrium levels. Only then can we use these functional equations to infer the causal processes that produced the shifts (see Namboodiri et al., 1975).

To summarize, the stability condition is satisfied if the values on variables have reached a temporary state of constancy for each time of measurement (equilibrium-type condition) and if the functional equations are the same over specified time intervals (stationarity). These points apply to recursive models, including cyclical recursive models. They apply also to nonrecursive models, although the process by which the endogenous variables involved in dynamic, reciprocal relationships reach an approximate state of equilibrium requires advanced mathematics. A relatively nontechnical overview of this process is presented in Heise (1975) and Namboodiri et al. (1975)

Equilibrium-Type Conditions and Causal Order

It was suggested in Condition 3 that the causal ordering among variables is often less than obvious and subject to misspecification. Consider, as an example, the popular "social systems" concept (see Katz & Kahn, 1978), which in many areas of psychology gives rise to serious concerns about causal ordering because all variables in the social system are regarded as causally related to each other, directly or indirectly. We illustrate this by the simple, nonelaborate model shown in Figure 2.5a. This model predicts that increases in organizational control processes (e.g., implementation of weekly time and effort statements) cause increases in employee dissatisfaction. These in turn lead to increases in dysfunctional behaviors (e.g., absenteeism, clock watching, work slowdowns). Dysfunctional behaviors may then serve as a stimulus for even greater organizational controls, which lead to greater dissatisfaction, and so on, so that an iterative, recurring cycle of control → dissatisfaction → dysfunctional behaviors → control is established. Note that the point at which the cycle begins is arbitrary; the cycle might also have started with employee dissatisfaction or dysfunctional behaviors.

This model does not present a major problem for a time-series design. In this type of design, the feedback processes could be captured by a cyclical recursive model, beginning at an arbitrary point and, for example, obtaining two measures of each variable, where time of measurement corresponds to causal intervals (equilibration times). On the other hand, this model creates a major problem for cross-sectional designs because once the cycle is operative, the causal relationships are in a system of infinite regress and specification of causal order is arbitrary.

Translated into the terminology of structural models, this reasoning implies that all variables are endogenous in a cross-sectional application of Figure 2.5a. Confirmatory analysis cannot proceed in such an ambiguous situation. It is necessary to identify predetermined, exogenous variables that are not caused by endogenous variables, and to use these predetermined variables to establish causal precedence. In pursuit of this objective, Miller (1971) reasoned that even though all variables in a structural model

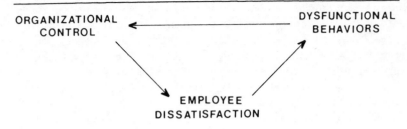

Figure 2.5a   Social System: Nonbounded Time Interval

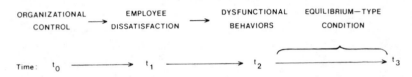

Figure 2.5b   Causal Order Assuming Rapid Equilibration Times and an Equilibrium-Type Condition

Figure 2.5   Causal Order and the Equilibrium-Type Condition

may be related, particularly over long periods of time, it is possible that the effects of some variables on others will be so small or infrequent as to be negligible in a particular interval in time. Consequently, within a specific time interval that is relatively short but generalizable, it is possible to establish a causal order for cross-sectional designs by specifying that (a) causes must have at least a moderate influence on effects within the time interval, and (b) a variable whose causal influence is slow and thus does not occur within the bounds of the time interval should be treated only as an effect.

For example, in the illustration in Figure 2.5a one might postulate that the effects of organizational control on dissatisfaction, and of dissatisfaction on dysfunctional behaviors, occur much more rapidly than the effects of dysfunctional behaviors on organizational control. This is reasonable given that affective and behavioral outcomes are individually determined and may occur quickly, whereas changes in organizational control may require multiple inputs from different line managers and staff (e.g., legal opinions), deliberations regarding alternatives, and time to implement formal decisions. Consequently, a time interval could be identified in which control influences dissatisfaction and then dissatisfaction influences behaviors, but behaviors do not significantly influence control. Thus, dysfunctional behaviors could be treated only as an effect. That is, we expect the influence of dysfunctional behaviors on organizational control to take a period of time greater than that bounded by the time interval. It must be emphasized, however, that the model could not be generalized beyond the specified temporal bound.

In effect, the preceding argument rests on establishing a causal order using differences in equilibration times and assumptions regarding strengths of causal influences in a short but generalizable equilibrium-type condition. To illustrate, consider Figure 2.5b, which displays the presumed causal ordering in the time interval extending from t_0 to t_2, and an equilibrium-type condition extending from time t_2 to time t_3. Organizational control is assumed to have stabilized (equilibrated) at time t_0, and to remain constant until time t_3. The interval between t_0 and t_1 is the equilibration time required for employee dissatisfaction to stabilize, that is, the causal interval for the organizational control → employee dissatisfaction causal effect. Once employee dissatisfaction has stabilized, it, like control, is expected to remain constant through at least time t_3. The time interval between t_1 and t_2 is the equilibration time for the employee dissatisfaction → dysfunctional behaviors causal influence. Finally, the period encompassed by t_2 to t_3 is the equilibrium-type condition, where the values on all three variables, including dysfunctional behaviors, are expected to remain relatively constant. This is the time period within which data should be collected for a cross-sectional analysis.

The equilibrium-type condition will end at the time that values on the variable representing organizational control begin to change as a result of the causal influences of dysfunctional behaviors. However, the equilibration time for the dysfunctional behaviors → organizational control causal relation is expected to be substantially longer than the time period extending from t_0 to t_3. This implies that (a) the equilibration times represented by t_0 to t_1 and t_1 to t_2 are much more rapid (i.e., shorter) than the equilibration time for the dysfunctional behaviors → organizational control causal influence, and (b) given the slow dysfunctional behaviors → organizational control causal effect, values on the variables may be regarded as equilibrated during the equilibrium-type condition (t_2 to t_3).

To summarize, in this subsection we have shown how the equilibrium-type condition is useful when theorizing about causal ordering in cross-sectional designs. Salient implications of using differences in equilibration times and assumed lengths of equilibrium-type conditions to predict causal orderings are (a) "time" is an important consideration in cross-sectional designs, (b) researchers must be specific about assumptions regarding time, especially the generalizability of a presumed causal ordering in regard to time, and (c) different assumptions regarding time may lead to different causal orderings. On the other hand, assumptions regarding time are less demanding in cross-sectional designs than in time-series designs. For example, one may "get by" with only assumptions regarding "relative differences" in equilibration times in cross-sectional designs, whereas time-series analysis requires specific knowledge (or predictions) of actual causal intervals.

SUMMARY

This completes the discussion of the seven conditions pertaining to the appropriateness of theoretical/structural models for confirmatory analysis. The seven conditions are summarized in Figure 2.6. It must be stressed that lack of reasonable satisfaction of one or more of these conditions results in questionable use of confirmatory analysis. We shall continue to emphasize this point in the remaining presentations in this text, where false conclusions regarding empirical confirmation or disconfirmation are shown to result from violation of aspects of Conditions 1 through 7, as well as of Condition 8 (operationalization of constructs).

We now turn to a review of the conditions pertaining to the operational aspects of confirmatory analysis. Because these operational aspects are the subject of a rapidly growing literature in psychology, not to mention large literatures in areas such as econometrics and sociology, the presentation emphasizes the logic of confirmatory analytic procedures. References are suggested for more extensive treatments of methods.

CONDITIONS PERTAINING TO OPERATIONAL ASPECTS OF CONFIRMATORY ANALYSIS

CONDITION 8: THE OPERATIONALIZATION OF VARIABLES

We have used the term "variable" to refer to sets of classes of events formed because the classes of events have some attribute in common. For example, we may form a class of events from all those things weighing X_i pounds. If we have several such classes, each associated with a different weight, then we may join these classes together to provide a set of classes of events, all of which have the common attribute weight. This set will provide the basis for the variable "weight." Now, operationalization of a variable means specifying the operations by which we would seek to assign a specific event (thing) occurring in the world to one of the classes of events of a variable, where the events in each class share a common value on a scale in which all classes of events have a common attribute.

An important aspect of operationalization is *measurement,* which concerns the *assignment of numbers to classes of events* so that relationships among the numbers correspond to empirical relationships among the classes of events. Measurement is not, however, merely the assignment of numbers to classes of events of a variable. The relations among the assigned numbers must correspond to an already established empirical relationship among the classes of events. A common but grave mistake is to assume that by assigning numbers in an arbitrary, or at best not well understood, way one has achieved measurement. The mistake is especially compounded if one believes there will be magical mathematical techniques, such as exploratory factor analysis or multidimensional scaling, that will salvage clear empirical meaning from the numbers.

When numbers have been assigned to the classes of events of a variable, we then have a *quantitative variable.* Moreover, when the numbers assigned to classes of events represent meaningful empirical relationships among the classes, then we may give empirical meaning to quantitative relationships among the variables. In particular, we will be interested in establishing functional relationships between variables by employing quantitative variables to represent variables in functional equations. To do this, we must presume in our applications that the scientist has quantitative variables with at least an *interval level of measurement.* Thus, for the purposes of discussion, we will assume that all forms of variables are, or may be, represented as quantitative variables with interval scales.[3] Consequently, the term "quantitative" is not specified explicitly.

The preceding discussion of operationalization of variables and measurement focused on *manifest* variables, which were defined earlier as variables associated with directly observable events. The empirical content of a manifest variable is reflected directly by assigning observable events to values on the measurement scale of the variable. We also introduced earlier the term *"latent"* variable, which was defined as an abstract or theoretical construct associated with presumed, but not directly observable, events. Latent variables cannot be measured directly; rather, they derive their empirical content through linkages with the directly measurable manifest variables. A latent variable is usually portrayed as a common factor that acts as a cause of one or more manifest variables and whose empirical content can only be assessed indirectly by examining empirical relations among manifest variables. A latent variable is operationalized in the sense that attempts are made to articulate not only linkages between hypothetical constructs and manifest variables, but also linkages among hypothetical constructs. Both of these attempts to articulate a latent variable are dependent on empirical relations among manifest variables.

When each theoretical construct (latent variable) is represented by a single corresponding manifest variable in a structural model, the model is referred to as an observed or manifest variable design. In this case, each manifest variable is used as a direct surrogate of a theoretical construct, and relationships among the manifest variables are used as direct surrogates of relationships among the constructs. When manifest variables are used in this manner, it is critical that the variables be accurate representations of

Condition 1: Formal statement of theory in terms of a structural model.

Development of a structural model that specifies variables, causal connections among variables, and functional relations and equations that relate each effect to all of its relevant causes.

Condition 2: Theoretical rationale for causal hypotheses.

Use of theory to propose how causes produce effects by introduction of mediating mechanisms to help to explain nonobvious covariation among variables and molar causal connections among complex variables.

Condition 3: Specification of causal order.

Hypothesized order in which variables occur naturally in a system of ordered functional equations, given an equilibrium-type condition for cross-sectional designs and specified causal intervals, stationarity, and an equilibrium-type condition for time series designs.

Condition 4: Specification of causal direction.

Hypothesized direction of causation for each causal connection in a structural model. The direction may be asymmetric, denoting a recursive causal relation, or reciprocal, denoting a nonrecursive causal relation.

Condition 5: Self-contained functional equations.

   The functional equation for each effect (endogenous
   variable) in a structural model contains all the relevant
   causes of that effect, which is indicated by lack of
   covariation between the explicitly measured causes in
   an equation and the disturbance term of that equation.

Condition 6: Specification of boundaries.

   Given linearity in parameters and variables, the
   functional equations are additive within the populations
   (e.g., subjects and environments) to which inferences are
   to be made.

Condition 7: Stability of structural model.

   The values of structural parameters are invariant
   (stationary) over specified time intervals, and the values
   on variables representing events are in an equilibrium-
   type condition.

Figure 2.6   Conditions Pertaining to Appropriateness of Theoretical Models for Confirmatory Analysis

the constructs. Accurate representations are indicated when (a) the manifest variables are, technically, perfectly reliable, although high reliability is generally considered sufficient for reasonable satisfaction of this condition (cf. Duncan, 1975); and (b) the manifest variables, and relationships among the manifest variables, are not subject to, or at least are minimally influenced by, nonrandom measurement errors introduced by extraneous, unmeasured influences or improper measurement procedures. Included in the broad category of nonrandom measurement errors are: (a) aggregation and disaggregation bias (see Borgatta & Jackson, 1980; Firebaugh, 1978; Hannan, 1971); (b) ceiling and floor effects in measurement scales (see Carroll, 1961); (c) classification errors, such as reducing a psychometrically reliable and valid continuous scale to a dichotomy (see Namboodiri et al., 1975); (d) method variance, which suggests that covariation among manifest variables representing different constructs is spuriously inflated due to a common measurement procedure (see Campbell & Fisk, 1959; Cronbach & Meehl, 1955); and (e) serially correlated errors of measurement resulting from the use of the same measurement scale(s) in two or more waves of data collection (see Werts, Linn, & Jöreskog, 1971).

Psychologists are generally aware of the basic tenets of scale development and reliability and with most of the concerns associated with nonrandom measurement errors. They are also aware of the fact that it is extremely difficult, and at times impossible, to develop measurement instruments that encompass only small amounts of measurement error and are free of nonrandom measurement errors. Nevertheless, while some slippage is allowed in meeting assumptions regarding random and nonrandom measurement errors in confirmatory analysis with manifest variables, the degree of slippage allowed is comparatively smaller than psychologists have enjoyed in exploratory (e.g., correlational) analysis.

The reason for insisting on more rigorous psychometric and statistical criteria is that the investigator is playing for higher stakes in confirmatory analysis. Because the aim of confirmatory analysis is causal inference and explanation, confirmatory analysis must be based on a firmer psychometric and statistical base than is often found in exploratory studies. Thus, for example, "reasonable satisfaction" of the reliability assumption in a confirmatory analysis on manifest variables still requires high reliabilities. While available research does not allow for an unequivocal specification of "high," it is also the case that rationale such as "a reliability of .70 was sufficient for exploratory purposes" is unacceptable because a reliability of .70 may result in serious attenuation of parameter solutions or estimates. Furthermore, attenuation in parameter solutions and estimates is only one of many possibilities when a functional equation involves multiple causal variables, each of which involves random measurement error (e.g., the bias may be upward and signs may be reversed—see Blalock, Wells, & Carter, 1970; Kenny, 1979). In this regard, Kenny (1979) suggested that in the multivariate case the bias due to measurement error may be negligible if (a) reliabilities are high, (b) the (true) causal effects are small, and/or (c) the causal variables have low intercorrelations. We suggest that researchers focus their attention on option a.

The implication of the need for rigorous standards regarding operationalization of manifest variables is that the use of confirmatory procedures may be restricted for manifest variable designs in psychology. We illustrate this point in the introduction to Chapter 4 (latent variables) by demonstrating the bias in estimates of structural parameters resulting from random measurement errors in observed variables. In Chapter 4 we also demonstrate how one can proceed with confirmatory analysis given some random measurement error in manifest variables and certain types of nonrandom measurement errors (e.g., presence of method variance, serially correlated measurement errors) if one uses a *latent variable* form of analysis. However, for the present we will introduce and overview the logic of confirmation and disconfirmation using manifest variable designs.

CONDITION 9: EMPIRICAL CONFIRMATION OF PREDICTIONS I: EMPIRICAL SUPPORT FOR FUNCTIONAL EQUATIONS

If Conditions 1 through 7 are considered reasonably satisfied, and if manifest variables are reasonably accurate representations of the constructs they are designed to measure, then it is possible to proceed with confirmatory analysis using manifest variables. The objective of such an analysis is to confirm or disconfirm a structural model. This is the process that is generally thought of as confirmatory analysis, where *confirmation* implies that a structural model, and the functional relations and equations representing the model, are useful for making causal inferences to explain how variables occur and why they covary (excluding purely exogenous variables). *Disconfirmation* implies that the structural model (functional relations and equations) are not useful in this regard. Given linear functional equations, the logical foundation of confirmation and disconfirmation is often viewed in terms of the following three principles.

(1) The functional relations and equations relating effects to causes in a linear structural model may be used to derive a set of *predictions* regarding the observed correlations (or variances/covariances) among the manifest variables.

(2) A structural model is *confirmed* if the predictions regarding correlations (variances/covariances) among manifest variables are consistent with the observed (i.e., empirically derived) correlations (variances/covariances) among manifest variables. A structural model is *disconfirmed* if predictions and observed correlations (variances/covariances) are inconsistent.

(3) Confirmation of predictions implies corroborative support for the structural model represented by the functional relations and equations. Disconfirmation of predictions implies that one or more components of the structural model (functional relations and equations) is false, in which case it is concluded that the structural model as proposed originally is invalid.

The present condition and Condition 10 focus on Principles 1 and 2. It is shown that predictions regarding correlations (variances/covariances) among manifest variables, and confirmation/disconfirmation of these predictions, can be addressed empirically by testing predictions regarding the magnitudes of estimates of structural parameters. In the present condition, we consider tests of whether or not structural parameters that are predicted by the structural model to be nonzero are different from zero. In Condition 10 we discuss tests of whether or not structural parameters that are predicted by the structural model to be equal to zero are zero, or approximately zero. When combined, these two sets of tests furnish the information needed to ascertain whether a model has been confirmed or disconfirmed.

Principle 3 is considered in Chapter 3 of this volume, where we address the roles of empirical confirmation and disconfirmation in causal inference.

The discussion of Condition 9 is organized as follows: (a) tests of predictions regarding structural parameters associated with causes, which includes an overview of identification, ordinary least squares (OLS) estimation, and tests of significance for a recursive model; (b) the use of standardized versus unstandardized manifest variables, where advantages and disadvantages of the path analytic approach to confirmatory analysis are reviewed; and (c) a specification error of major interest to psychologists, namely, unmeasured relevant causes in equations that are presumed to be self-contained functional equations.

Tests of Predictions Regarding Structural Parameters Associated with Causes

Stated simply, inclusion of a variable as a cause in a functional equation indicates that the structural parameter associated with that variable is hypothesized to be different from zero. It follows that if (a) we employ a statistical estimating equation to represent the functional equation, then (b) the estimates of the structural parameters provided by the statistical equation are predicted to be different from zero. Given reasonable satisfaction of Conditions 1 through 8, the predictions regarding estimated structural parameters can be tested in random samples from well-defined (i.e., boundaries specified) populations by estimating statistically the values of structural parameters and conducting tests of significance on the estimates. If the estimate of a structural parameter is significanly different from zero, then the prediction is regarded as confirmed, which implies that the functional equation is consistent with empirical data (i.e., the statistical estimating equation). If one or more estimates is not significantly different from zero, then the prediction(s) is (are) disconfirmed, implying that the functional equation is not consistent with the data.

The preceding points are illustrated using the structural model shown in Figure 2.7. Of initial importance is that all (manifest) variables in Figure 2.7 are represented by an x. This notation is adopted to simplify subscripting parameters and statistics in equations. The subscripts for the x's denote causal order, the B_{ij} $(i > j)$ are structural parameters, and the d_i are disturbance terms. The structural model is "fully recursive," which means that (a) the model includes only one exogenous variable (x_1), (b) the direction of all causal connections is asymmetric, and (c) each variable higher in the causal order is a function of all variables lower in the causal order, plus a disturbance term (e.g., $x_4 = f(x_1,x_2,x_3,d_4)$). For illustrative purposes, we presume that empirical data are to be collected on a cross-sectional basis on a random sample of subjects from a well-defined population.

The linear functional equations, in deviation form, are shown in Figure 2.7 (equations 2.7a through 2.7c). In confirmatory analysis, a functional equation is often referred to as a *structural equation.* This suggests that the structure of causal connections among variables is represented by the equations. We will, however, continue to use the term "functional equation." The objective now is to estimate the values of the structural parameters in equations 2.7a through 2.7c.

Identification. The first step in this process is to ascertain whether *each* of the functional equations is identified. As discussed earlier, this concerns the question of whether sufficient information is available to obtain unique mathematical solutions of the structural parameters. For recursive, manifest variable models, a functional equation will be identified (i.e., sufficient information is available) if (a) the causes included explicitly in the functional equation are uncorrelated with the disturbance term of that equation, and (b) all such causes have a unique, direct effect on the endogenous variable and are not linearly dependent on other causes included explicitly in the equation.[4] We will focus here on the assumption that causes are uncorrelated with disturbances.

For the purpose of describing identification, we will regard the manifest variables in equations 2.7a through 2.7c as hypothetical random variables defined on a hypothetical population. Now, in the functional equation for x_2 (equation 2.7a), it is (theoretically) possible to solve for (note, not estimate) the structural parameter B_{21} directly by (a) multiplying through equation 2.7a by x_1, (b) taking expectations on the resulting equation,

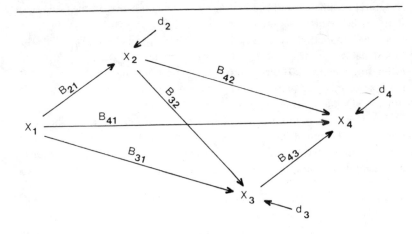

Functional Equations

$$x_2 = B_{21}x_1 + d_2 \qquad\qquad\qquad [2.7a]$$
$$x_3 = B_{31}x_1 + B_{32}x_2 + d_3 \qquad\qquad [2.7b]$$
$$x_4 = B_{41}x_1 + B_{42}x_2 + B_{43}x_3 + d_4 \qquad [2.7c]$$

Figure 2.7   Structural Model and Functional Equations for a Fully Recursive Design

and, if justified, (c) solving for B_{21} algebraically (see Duncan, 1975). The first two steps are as follows:

Functional equation for x_2:

$$x_2 = B_{21}x_1 + d_2 \qquad\qquad\qquad [2.12]$$

Multiplying through the equation by x_1:

$$x_2x_1 = B_{21}x_1x_1 + d_2x_1$$

Taking expectations:

$$E(x_2x_1) = B_{21}E(x_1x_1) + E(d_2x_1)$$
$$\sigma_{21} = B_{21}\sigma_1^2 + \sigma_{d_21} \qquad\qquad [2.13]$$

where σ_{21} and σ_{d_21} are covariances and σ_1^2 is a variance. Equation 2.13 is often referred to as a "normal equation."

The values assumed by the random variables x_1 and x_2, and therefore σ_{21} and σ_1^2, may be regarded as "known" because the random variables can be operationalized as manifest variables. It is not possible to regard d_2

as known, one obvious reason being that the random shock component of disturbances, which may be the only component, is by definition unmeasurable. Thus, d_2, and therefore $\sigma_{d_{21}}$, are considered "unknowns." B_{21} is also unknown; we must solve for its value based on the known values of σ_{21} and $\sigma_1{}^2$ in equation 2.13. This is not possible at the present time because equation 2.13 has two unknowns (i.e., B_{21} and $\sigma_{d_{21}}$—or, one equation and two unknowns). This is an illustration of *underidentification*, which means that sufficient information is not available to obtain a unique mathematical solution for B_{21}. However, if we can assume that x_1 is unrelated to d_2, then $\sigma_{d_{21}} = 0$ and the equation is *identified*. That is, we now have one unknown and one equation, and B_{21} is easily solved for: $B_{21} = \sigma_{21}/\sigma_1{}^2$. As shown in Condition 5, $\sigma_{d_{21}} = 0$ if d_2 is composed of random shocks exclusively (or by random shocks and unmeasured causes that are unrelated to measured causes).

This logic may be generalized directly to the functional equations for x_3 and x_4 (equations 2.7b and 2.7c). Equation 2.7b is identified if $\sigma_{d_{31}} = \sigma_{d_{32}} = 0$, and equation 2.7c is identified if $\sigma_{d_{41}} = \sigma_{d_{42}} = \sigma_{d_{43}} = 0$. Furthermore, algebraic derivation will show that lack of covariation between the causes in each functional equation and the disturbance of that equation implies that the disturbance terms in the system of equations are themselves unrelated (Duncan, 1975).

Lack of relationship among the disturbances of different equations implies that the system of equations is identified. This is an important consideration if all structural parameters from all equations are to be estimated simultaneously. On the other hand, if the structural parameters for each functional equation are to be estimated separately, then it is possible to estimate parameters for the identified equations but not for the underidentified equations. Finally, note that no assumption is required for covariations of the form $\sigma_{d_{ji}}$, where $i > j$. For example, x_4 may be related to d_2 (i.e., $\sigma_{d_{24}}$ not equal to zero) without affecting identification.

Solutions and Estimates of Structural Parameters. Requirements for identification vary as a function of the type of structural model (see Fisher, 1966). We will return to the critical assumption that causes included explicitly in a functional equation are unrelated to the disturbance of that equation (and by implication all disturbances later in the causal order). For the present, we regard this assumption as satisfied. Thus, functional equations 2.7a through 2.7c are considered identified. As shown above, this implies that the solution for B_{21} is $\sigma_{21}/\sigma_1{}^2$. Solutions for the structural parameters in equations 2.7b and 2.7c may be determined in a manner similar to that used to solve for B_{21}. For example, it is possible to solve for B_{31} and B_{32} in equation 2.7b by (a) multiplying through equation 2.7b by x_1 and then x_2, thus providing two equations, and (b) taking expectations on each of these equations. The resulting normal equations are:

$$\sigma_{31} = B_{31}\sigma_1{}^2 + B_{32}\sigma_{21} + \sigma_{d_{31}} \qquad [2.14]$$

$$\sigma_{32} = B_{31}\sigma_{21} + B_{32}\sigma_2{}^2 + \sigma_{d_{32}} \qquad [2.15]$$

$\sigma_{d_{31}}$ (equation 2.14) and $\sigma_{d_{32}}$ (equation 2.15) are assumed to be zero. Therefore, we have two unknowns (B_{31} and B_{32}) and two equations, and it is possible to solve for B_{31} and B_{32} using determinants. The resulting solutions are:

$$B_{31} = (\sigma_{31}\sigma_2{}^2 - \sigma_{21}\sigma_{32})/(\sigma_1{}^2\sigma_2{}^2 - \sigma_{21}{}^2) \qquad [2.16]$$

$$B_{32} = (\sigma_{32}\sigma_1{}^2 - \sigma_{21}\sigma_{31})/(\sigma_1{}^2\sigma_2{}^2 - \sigma_{21}{}^2) \qquad [2.17]$$

Inspection of equations 2.16 and 2.17 demonstrates that the solutions for B_{31} and B_{32} are the same as those that would have been obtained if we had simply used Ordinary Least Squares (OLS) estimation to solve for B_{31} and B_{32}. That is, B_{31} and B_{32} have the form of *unstandardized regression weights*. The same is true for B_{21} in equation 2.7a; $\sigma_{21}/\sigma_1{}^2$ is the solution for an unstandardized regression weight in a bivariate relation. Finally, if $\sigma_{d_{41}} = \sigma_{d_{42}} = \sigma_{d_{43}} = 0$, then B_{41}, B_{42}, and B_{43} in equation 2.7c have the form of unstandardized regression weights and may be solved by using OLS.

To summarize, given a recursive, cross-sectional design, if the causes in a functional equation are unrelated to the disturbance of that equation, then OLS may be used to solve for the values of the structural parameters (note that OLS is applied separately to each equation). This conclusion was predicated on hypothetical random variables in a hypothetical population, but extends to operationalized designs, although one must be mindful of the fact that disturbances can not be measured directly. To illustrate, the causes and effects in functional equations 2.7a through 2.7c may be replaced with manifest variables defined on a population (with boundaries specified) if the manifest variables satisfy the assumptions discussed in Condition 8. It is also possible to employ manifest variables in the algebra used to derive the variance and covariances shown in equations 2.13 through 2.17, including covariances between causes and disturbances and solutions of the structural parameters. However, the covariances involving disturbances involve relations between manifest variables and hypothetical variables that cannot be measured directly. It follows, then, that these covariances cannot be solved for, nor estimated, in operationalized designs. In other words, assumptions regarding covariances between causes and disturbances are a theoretical concern. As shown shortly, an erroneous assumption that a covariance between a manifest variable and a disturbance is zero has serious consequences for estimates of structural parameters.

Let us continue the illustration with the assumptions that the functional equations are operationalized in a well-defined population of subjects, with manifest variables that satisfy reasonably Condition 8 and are unrelated to disturbances. An OLS regression equation may now be employed to represent a functional equation, where the values of the unstandardized regression weights represent the values of the structural parameters. Under these assumptions, the OLS error (residual) term represents accurately the disturbance term. However, this does not suggest that one may relate the manifest variables with the OLS error, designated e_i, to test the assumption that the manifest variables in a functional equation are unrelated to the disturbance of that equation. By definition, an e_i will be unrelated to all manifest variables included in an OLS equation. This point may appear trivial, but some researchers have in fact calculated covariances (correlations) between manifest variables and e_i's to test the assumption that causes are unrelated to disturbances. Still others have defined a disturbance as a form of statistical residual (e.g., an OLS error term), which is misleading. To reiterate, a disturbance cannot be measured directly, and the covariation (correlation) between a disturbance and manifest variables in a particular equation cannot be solved for, or estimated, directly. A statistical residual, such as an e_i in OLS, represents (estimates) a disturbance only in the condition that the manifest variables in an equation are theoretically unrelated to the disturbance of that equation.

We hope we have made the point that while a functional equation involving manifest variables and an OLS equation involving manifest variables may assume identical forms, it is only in the functional equation that covariation between manifest variables and a disturbance has meaning, and it is only when all such covariations are theoretically zero that an OLS equation truly represents a functional equation. Let us now proceed to the question of estimation given that the OLS population equation is an accurate representation of the functional equation. This is a simple step because it is identical to the requirements for estimating population unstandardized regression weights based on the unstandardized regression weights derived in a sample. In general, the unstandardized regression weights derived in a sample will be unbiased estimates of population unstandardized weights, and therefore, of the structural parameters, if the sample was obtained randomly from a well-defined population in which errors (and by implication disturbances) have a mean of zero and a constant variance (i.e., homoscedasticity). (We are, of course, also assuming linearity, interval scales, and essentially perfect reliability).

Let us presume that the assumptions above have been reasonably satisfied. An illustration of the empirical estimation of structural parameters by means of a structural equation analysis on a recursive model is then straightforward. Consider, as an example, the hypothetical sample data shown in Figure 2.8. Figure 2.8a is a replication of the structural model in Figure 2.7, only here we have placed variances of the variables in parentheses below the variables and covariances in parentheses above the arrows connecting the variables. The sample OLS regression equations (equations 2.8a through 2.8c) in Figure 2.8b were used to estimate the values of the structural parameters in the structural equations in Figure 2.7. That is, the unstandardized regression weights in equations 2.8a through 2.8c (i.e., the $\hat{B}_{ij}$) were used as estimates of the B_{ij} in equations 2.7a through 2.7b. A separate OLS analysis was conducted for each of the OLS regression equations. The results of the analyses are shown in Figure 2.8c. Given reasonable satisfaction of Conditions 1 through 8 and the assumptions for OLS analysis, the $\hat{B}_{ij}$ are unbiased estimates of the B_{ij}.

Given unbiased estimates, we are now in a position to confirm or disconfirm the predictions that estimates of structural parameters associated with causes in functional equations should be significantly different from zero. This is accomplished by employing the conventional significance test for unstandardized regression weights. (This test requires the additional assumption that the population OLS error term [and the disturbance] is distributed normally.) If all estimated structural parameters for a particular functional equation are significant, then all predictions are confirmed in regard to our first test of confirmation. If all predictions in all equations are confirmed, then the structural model is regarded as being consistent with the data, again in regard to the first test of confirmation. For example, given a large sample, the $\hat{B}_{ij}$ in Figure 2.8c would be significant, which suggests that the structural model in Figure 2.7 is confirmed in regard to the first test of confirmation. However, if one or more estimated structural parameters is not significant, then not only are the predictions associated with those estimates disconfirmed, but the structural model is regarded as inconsistent with the data.

In sum, simple multiple regression may be used to test predictions that estimated structural parameters (unstandardized regression weights) associated with causes are significant. If the estimated parameters are significant in each and every statistical (OLS) equation, then, based on the first test of confirmation/disconfirmation, a structural model is confirmed. Confirmation implies that the structural model is consistent with the data. If one or more estimated structural parameters is not significant, then the model is disconfirmed, implying that the model is not consistent with the data. Now, given the consensus that confirmatory analysis should be conducted on large samples, it follows that the significance tests for estimated structural parameters are powerful. Consequently, unstandardized regression weights of rather trivial magnitudes are likely to be significant. This suggests that the present test is not likely to disconfirm many

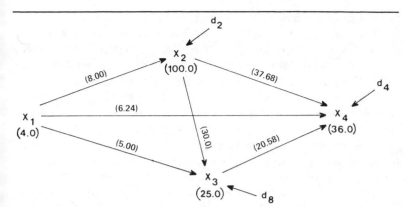

2.8a Variances and Covariances Among Variables

$$x_2 = \hat{B}_{21}x_1 + e_2 \qquad [2.8a]$$
$$x_3 = \hat{B}_{31}x_1 + \hat{B}_{32}x_2 + e_3 \qquad [2.8b]$$
$$x_4 = \hat{B}_{41}x_1 + \hat{B}_{42}x_2 + \hat{B}_{43}x_3 + e_4 \qquad [2.8c]$$

2.8b OLS Regression Equations

x_2 equation: $\hat{B}_{21} = 2.00$

x_3 equation: $\hat{B}_{31} = .75, \hat{B}_{32} = .25$

x_4 equation: $\hat{B}_{41} = .60, \hat{B}_{42} = .18, \hat{B}_{43} = .48$

2.8c Estimates of Unstandardized Regression Weights

Figure 2.8   An Empirical Example of Structural Equation Analysis for a Recursive Model

predictions, or, it is weighted in favor of confirming predictions. As we shall see in Condition 10, precisely the opposite problem occurs in our second test of confirmation/disconfirmation.

Theory Trimming. It is, of course, possible for unstandardized regression weights to be nonsignificant, even with large samples. How serious is this source of disconfirmation? The answer to this question depends on the model and the salience of the causal hypothesis underlying the structural parameter. For example, in Figures 2.7 and 2.8, it may be critical to the theory underlying the model that the estimate of B_{43}, namely $\hat{B}_{43}$, be significant. Consequently, a nonsignificant $\hat{B}_{43}$, or a significant $\hat{B}_{43}$ of trivial magnitude, may be a serious blow. On the other hand, a nonsignificant, or significant but low, $\hat{B}_{41}$ may not be a serious theoretical blow. Thus, the particular source of disconfirmation of predictions (i.e., the causal hypotheses involved) may vary from rather minor to drastic. If confirmation of a prediction is of particular importance to a model, and the prediction is disconfirmed, then one may decide that there is little reason to proceed with additional analyses. We recommend that one proceed in order to test fully all of the predictions of the model.

If the source of disconfirmation is not of major importance, then the investigator may consider "theory trimming." Theory trimming consists of deleting causal connections from a structural model (Heise, 1969), which is to say, deleting a cause and its associated structural parameter from a functional equation. It is extremely important to note that theory trimming is a form of exploratory, and not confirmatory, analysis. That is, the investigator is now making decisions based on data, and is no longer confirming/disconfirming a priori theory. The crucial implication of this point is that the structural parameters for which trimming might be indicated in this first test of confirmation/disconfirmation should never be used to test confirmation/disconfirmation in the second test (Condition 10). The reasoning is simple; the second test of confirmation/disconfirmation assesses whether estimated structural parameters that are predicted to be zero are in fact not significantly different than zero. If, after looking at the data, one knows that an estimated parameter is essentially zero, then a test that this same parameter is predicted to be zero is nonsense.

In conclusion, theory trimming of minor sources of disconfirmation is acceptable as long as one remembers that, following trimming, one is no longer dealing with an a priori, theoretical model. This leaves two avenues for further analysis, specifically (1) test the trimmed model in a new sample, or (2) do not trim prior to conducting the second test of confirmation/disconfirmation discussed in Condition 10. One may theory trim after all analyses are conducted and interpreted, and the researcher is proposing a revised theoretical model for future research.

Standardized versus Unstandardized Manifest Variables

Up to now we have treated manifest variables in deviation form, one result being that the OLS estimates of structural parameters are unstandardized regression weights. It is also possible to treat the manifest variables in standardized form, in which case the values on the variables are standard scores (i.e., $z = (X - \mu)/\sigma$), and the variables have a mean of zero and a standard deviation of 1.0. When the variables are in standardized form, the structural parameters are referred to as standardized structural parameters, or *path coefficients*. The estimates of path coefficients provided by OLS are "standardized regression weights," or beta weights. Moreover, it is customary to refer to the structural model as a *path model,* the functional equations as *path equations,* and the confirmatory analysis as a *path analysis*. A full recursive path model and its corresponding set of path equations are shown in Figure 2.9, where z_i's are used to designate standard scores, and p_{ij} $(i > j)$ designate path coefficients. It is customary to employ the symbol "u_i" to designate disturbance terms in path models and path equations.

There are advantages and disadvantages associated with both path coefficients and (unstandardized) structural parameters (cf. Tukey, 1964; Wright, 1960). The advantages of path coefficients are as follows:

(1) Algebraic and statistical manipulations are simplified.
(2) Path coefficients are based on readily interpretable correlation coefficients.
(3) Path coefficients themselves are readily interpretable inasmuch as all variables are based on the same metric.
(4) Path analysis provides simplified expressions for decomposing correlations into functions of path coefficients.[5]

Structural parameters typically have none of the advantages above because the variables are based on different metrics (see Figure 2.8) and variance/covariance matrices replace correlation matrices. However, structural parameters have the advantage that they can be compared directly across different populations (for the same variables) or for the same population over time. We have chosen to illustrate the former case because we wish to demonstrate how the subgrouping moderator approach can be applied in confirmatory analysis. By doing so, our intention is to discourage carrying over into confirmatory analysis the practice among some investigators of conducting subgrouping moderator analysis on standardized regression weights (beta weights, correlation coefficients in the bivariate case).

Consider a linear bivariate model in which both variables (x_1 and x_2) have been measured in each of two specified populations (e.g., males and females). The path equation in each population is $z_2 = p_{21}z_1 + u_2$; the corresponding structural equation in each population is $X_2 = A_2 + B_{21}X_1 + d_1$. The structural equation is presented in raw score form, where A_2 is the intercept. The structural parameter B_{21} may be thought of as the slope of a regression line, where the slope reflects the amount of change in X_2, in units of X_2, brought about by a unit of change in X_1. This suggests that the structural parameter reflects the *concrete* contribution that X_1 makes directly to X_2 in X_2 units. If the same metrics are employed across the two populations, then the contribution that X_1 makes to X_2 can be compared across the populations in an absolute sense; that is, in terms of units of X_2.

The path coefficient p_{21} may also be thought of as the slope of a regression line. However, the path coefficient is an *abstract* measure of the

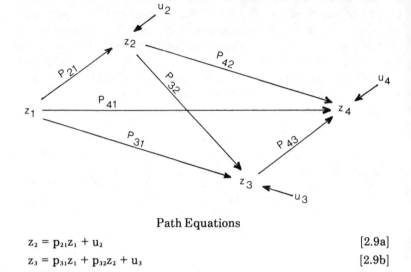

Path Equations

$$z_2 = p_{21}z_1 + u_2 \qquad\qquad [2.9a]$$

$$z_3 = p_{31}z_1 + p_{32}z_2 + u_3 \qquad\qquad [2.9b]$$

$$z_4 = p_{41}z_1 + p_{42}z_2 + p_{43}z_3 + u_4 \qquad\qquad [2.9c]$$

Figure 2.9   A Fully Recursive Path Model and Corresponding Path Equations

slope because it is based on an abstract scale that varies as a function of a ratio of standard deviation units within a particular population. That is, $p_{21} = B_{21} (\sigma_{x_1}/\sigma_{x_2})$, which means that path coefficients are unstandardized regression weights adjusted by a ratio of the standard deviations in each population. Thus, a comparison of path coefficients is in actuality a comparison of abstract scales, each adjusted for population idiosyncrasies in standard deviations. This suggests that while the concrete contribution (causal effect) indicated by B_{21} may remain invariant across populations, the path coefficients may vary simply because the standard deviations of X_1 and/or X_2 vary across populations. Thus, the general rule is that path coefficients should not be employed in the comparison of causal effects for different populations, or in the comparison of causal effects in the same population over time (see Blalock, 1967, 1968, 1969; Spaeth, 1975; Tukey, 1964; Wiley & Wiley, 1971).

On the other hand, path analysis has the advantages discussed earlier. When research is focused on a specific population using cross-sectional data collected during an equilibrium-type condition, the advantages may outweigh the disadvantages (Wright, 1960). For our purposes, the opportunity to simplify statistical derivations is important, and thus a path-analysis paradigm is employed frequently in the remaining discussion.

Specification Error Due to an Unmeasured Relevant Cause

Specification error is a general term that refers to errors (misspecifications) in the form of a structural model and its accompanying functional equations, or in the operationalization of variables. In this discussion we will demonstrate a specification error of particular concern to psychologists, namely, unmeasured relevant causes. We will also return to the question of relations between causes and disturbances, the resulting underidentification, and the consequences of proceeding with OLS estimation given violation of conditions for confirmatory analysis.

In the presentation of Condition 5, we demonstrated that an unmeasured relevant cause would result in a theoretical covariation between causes included explicitly in a functional equation and the disturbance term of that equation (see Figure 2.4 and equation 2.11). We also demonstrated that covariation between a measured cause and a disturbance implies that the functional equation is not self-contained. Finally, we noted that psychologists have paid scant attention to the need for self-contained functional equations, although increased attention is not likely to solve this problem completely because all relevant causes of an effect are unlikely to be known. Nevertheless, it is possible to reduce substantially the influence of unmeasured relevant causes, or what we will refer to as the "unmeasured variables problem," by (a) recognizing that the problem exists, (b) judging whether sufficient information has accumulated to justify a confirmatory analysis, and (c) including all known, relevant causes in the appropriate functional equations. Given a and assuming an affirmative answer to b, the operational question is c, namely, have known, relevant causes been omitted from one or more functional equations. As we shall see, this question consists of postulating the degree to which an unmeasured variables problem is believed to lead to bias in estimates of structural parameters.

Within psychology, a primary cause of an unmeasured variables problem appears to be the failure to recognize that "focused" theoretical models are not amenable to confirmatory analysis. To illustrate, it is frequently the case that psychological models are designed around sets of focused causal variables, where by "focused" we mean causes that are of interest to an investigator(s). Leader behaviors are one example. In contrast, the endogenous variables are typically less focused, and include such things as attrition, overall satisfaction, and performance. One of the certain ways to create a serious unmeasured variables problem is to analyze focused causal variables, such as leader behaviors, in relation to a global endogenous variable, such as overall job satisfaction. The latter includes a plethora of additional causal influences, such as pay, working conditions, opportunities for advancement, job stability, and so forth.

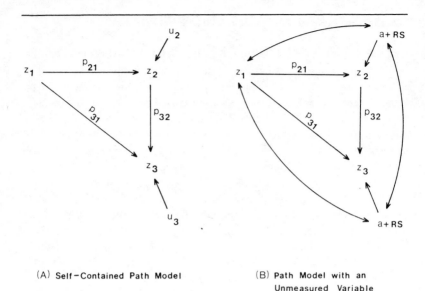

(A) **Self-Contained Path Model**

(B) **Path Model with an Unmeasured Variable**

Figure 2.10 Illustrations of a Self-Contained Path Model and a Path Model with an Unmeasured Variable

By way of simple illustration, Figure 2.10a displays a self-contained path model in which the manifest exogenous variable z_1 is a cause of the two endogenous variables, z_2 and z_3. z_2 is also a cause of z_3. The u_i (u_2 and u_3) are disturbance terms, and are assumed to be composed exclusively of random shocks (RS). (It is assumed that, with the exception of an unmeasured variables problem in Figure 2.10b, all conditions for confirmatory analysis have been satisfied.). Population path equations, expectations, and normal equations for the model in Figure 2.10a are shown in the upper portion of Figure 2.11. Note that the functional equations are identified; the normal equation for z_2 (equation 2.11a) has one equation and one unknown (i.e., $p_{21} = r_{21}$), and the normal equations for z_3 (equations 2.11b and 2.11c) have two unknowns in two equations. The correlations are assumed to be known, and are indicated by "r_{ij}." (These are population correlations; the conventional ρ is not used because it is easy to confuse ρ [population correlation] with p [path coefficient].)

Figure 2.10b illustrates a condition in which the u_i are not composed of RS components exclusively. Rather, an unmeasured causal variable, *a*, is present in both u_i terms. The variable *a* is regarded as a relevant cause of both z_2 and z_3, which includes relationships with z_1 (indicated by the curved, double-headed arrows from *a* to z_1). Moreover, because *a* appears in both disturbance terms (i.e., the curved arrow between *a* for z_2 and *a* for z_3), the disturbances are also correlated. (The *a*'s need not be the same for this to occur; different but correlated a's for z_2 and z_3 also lead to correlated disturbances.)

Path equations, expectations, and normal equations for Figure 2.10b are shown in the lower portion of Figure 2.11. As shown in the normal equation for z_2 (equation 2.11d) and the normal equations for z_3 (equations 2.11e and 2.11f), the equations are underidentified because the unmeasured a covaries with both z_1 and z_2 (i.e., equation 2.11d has two unknowns, and equations 2.11e and 2.11f contain four unknowns—the relations between a and the z's are represented as covariances because if d_i = RS + a_i, and if d_i is in standardized form, then a_i cannot be in standardized form). Consequently, OLS cannot be used to solve for the path coefficients in the population or to estimate the coefficients in a sample.

Now, consider the case that the path model displayed in Figure 2.10b is operable, but that an investigator assumes that u_2 and u_3 are composed of RS components exclusively. It is possible to use OLS to solve for the path coefficients; however, the path coefficients will be biased. To illustrate the bias, a false model (a is not included in the path equation) is compared with a true model (a is included in the path equation) in order to determine the consequences of employing the false model to solve for the path coefficient(s) (Duncan, 1975; James, 1980). A comparison of the false and true models for the z_2 equation is presented in Figure 2.12. The "true" path coefficients are designated by primes (e.g., p'_{21} and p'_{2a}).

As shown in equation 2.12a, p_{21} in the false model differs from p'_{21} in the true model by a factor of $p'_{2a}r_{a1}$. This implies that p_{21} will be biased if *both* p'_{2a} and r_{a1} are different than zero. In other words, if the unmeasured a is (a) a cause of z_2 and (b) correlated with z_1, then p_{21} will be biased. If we disregard suppressors, then the bias will result in a p_{21} that is too large; this is a direct result of failure to control for the effects of a in solving for p_{21} in the false model. The ramification of this bias is that causal influence that rightfully belongs to a is instead attributed to z_1.

Let us now address the question of the *degree* to which p_{21} may be biased. If either p'_{2a} or r_{a1} is zero, or approximately zero, then little or no bias will exist in p_{21}. This suggests that bias will not occur if an unmeasured variable is in fact a cause of the endogenous variable but is unrelated to the measured causes of that same variable. (Note that the unmeasured cause is not a relevant cause if it is unrelated to measured causes.) Consequently, one need not assume that *all* major causes of an endogenous variable have been measured. Rather, an unmeasured cause must also be related to a measured cause before bias will ensue.

We must also entertain the fact that there are degrees of causation; the magnitude of p'_{2a} might be anywhere on a continuum from low, to moderate, to high. Similarly, the magnitude of r_{a1} may vary from zero, or

Equations for Figure 2.10a (Self-Contained Path Model)

Path Equations
$$z_2 = p_{21}z_1 + (d_2 = RS)$$
$$z_3 = p_{31}z_1 + p_{32}z_2 + (d_3 = RS)$$

Expectations
$$E(z_2z_1) = p_{21}E(z_1z_1) + E(RSz_1)$$
$$E(z_3z_1) = p_{31}E(z_1z_1) + p_{32}E(z_2z_1) + E(RSz_1)$$
$$E(z_3z_2) = p_{31}E(z_1z_2) + p_{32}E(z_2z_2) + E(RSz_2)$$
Note: $E(RSz_1) = E(RSz_2) = 0$

Normal Equations
$$r_{21} = p_{21} \tag{2.11a}$$
$$r_{32} = p_{31} + p_{32}r_{21} \tag{2.11b}$$
$$r_{32} = p_{31}r_{21} + p_{32} \tag{2.11c}$$

Equations for Figure 2.10b (Path Model with an Unmeasured Variable)

Path Equations
$$z_2 = p_{21}z_1 + (RS + a)$$
$$z_3 = p_{31}z_1 + p_{32}z_2 + (RS + a)$$

Expectations
$$E(z_2z_1) = p_{21}E(z_1z_1) + E(RS + a)z_1$$
$$E(z_3z_1) = p_{31}E(z_1z_1) + p_{32}E(z_2z_1) + E(RS + a)z_1$$
$$E(z_3z_2) = p_{31}E(z_1z_2) + p_{32}E(z_2z_2) + E(RS + a)z_2$$

Normal Equations
$$r_{21} = p_{21} + \sigma_{a1}: \quad E(RS + a)z_1 = \sigma_{a1} \tag{2.11d}$$
$$r_{31} = p_{31} + p_{32}r_{21} + \sigma_{a1} \tag{2.11e}$$
$$r_{32} = p_{31}r_{21} + p_{32} + \sigma_{a2} \tag{2.11f}$$

Figure 2.11   Path Equations, Expectations, and Normal Equations for Figures 2.10a and 2.10b

approximately so, to low, moderate, or high. Thus, the product term $p'_{2a}r_{a1}$ can assume many values, only some of which result in serious bias of p_{21}. From a pragmatic standpoint, we shall assume that the permutations most likely to lead to serious bias are high-high, moderate-high, high-moderate, and moderate-moderate. Moreover, an unmeasured variable will not result in bias if this variable is highly correlated with a measured cause. This point is easily demonstrated in the "true" equation for z_2, which is presented below with appropriate controls indicated for the path coefficients.

$$z_2 = p'_{21 \cdot a}z_1 + p'_{2a \cdot 1}a + u_2$$

The path coefficient for a is theoretically equal to, or approximately equal to, zero if a and z_1 are correlated highly (e.g., .95). Consequently, there is no reason to include a in the z_2 equation because it is essentially redundant with, or linearly dependent on, z_1. Note also that inclusion of a in the z_2 equation would result in a multicollinearity problem if OLS were used to solve for the path coefficients. Thus, with a unmeasured essentially no bias will ensue for the p_{21} path coefficient (i.e., $p'_{2a\cdot1}r_{a1} = 0$ because $p'_{2a\cdot1} = 0$). Here again, a would not be an unmeasured relevant cause if it is linearly dependent on the causes already included in an equation.

In sum, an unmeasured variable must be a relevant cause before it will lead to bias in the solutions (estimates) of path coefficients for measured causes. In particular, it must have at least a moderate effect on the endogenous variable after controls have been effected for measured causes, and it must have at least a moderate correlation with one or more measured causes without being linearly dependent on the measured causes. The implication of these points is that if an unmeasured causal variable is not a relevant cause, then one does not have a serious unmeasured variables problem.

If, however, the unmeasured variable is a relevant cause, then as shown in Figure 2.12, bias will ensue in the solution (estimate) of a path coefficient(s). This point is illustrated empirically in Figure 2.13. Figure 2.13a is a self-contained or true model with relevant causes z_1 and a (in standardized form) in the path equation for z_2. Hypothetical population correlations associated with the relation between the two exogenous variables (i.e., $r_{a1} = .50$) and the causal connections are presented in parentheses. Solutions for the path coefficients in the true model, designated by a prime, were obtained by OLS; the path coefficients (beta weights) were: $p'_{21} = .50$ and $p'_{2a} = .40$. A false model with a unmeasured is shown in Figure 2.13b. The OLS solution for p_{21} is .70, or simply r_{21}. The bias in p_{21} resulting from the failure to include a in the path equation for z_2 is shown in Figure 2.13c. The bias is equal to $p_{21} - p'_{21} = .70 - .50 = .20$. This is equivalent to $p'_{2a}r_{a1} = (.40)(.50) = .20$.

The discussion above transfers directly to more complex equations involving multiple causes, although, given an unmeasured relevant cause, the direction of bias may be either positive or negative. Nevertheless, the unmeasured cause must be a relevant cause before serious bias will ensue in the solutions (estimates) of path coefficients. We will forego a statistical demonstration of this point. Rather, we shall proceed to summarize the salient points from the preceding discussion in the form of "decision steps." The decision steps, presented by James (1980), are designed to assist investigators in making a judgment of whether an unmeasured

False Model	True Model
Assumes $u_2 = RS$ when in fact	Assumes a is measured, and
$u_2 = RS + a$	thus u_2 *is equal* to RS

Path Equations

$$z_2 = p_{21}z_1 + u_2 \qquad\qquad z_2 = p'_{21}z_1 + p'_{2a}a + u_2$$

Expectations

$$E(z_2z_1) = p_{21}E(z_1z_1) + E(u_2z_1) \qquad E(z_2z_1) = p'_{21}E(z_1z_1) + p'_{2a}E(az_1) + E(u_2z_1)$$

$$E(z_2a) = p'_{21}E(z_1a) + p'_{2a}E(aa) + E(u_2a)$$

Normal Equations

$$r_{21} = p_{21} \qquad\qquad\qquad r_{21} = p'_{21} + p'_{2a}r_{a1}$$

Note: False assumption that $\qquad\qquad r_{2a} = p'_{21}r_{a1} + p'_{2a}$

$$E(u_2z_1) = E(RS + a)z = \sigma_{a1} = 0$$

Bias in Using r_{21} as Solution for p'_{21}

$$r_{21} = p_{21} \text{ (false model)}$$
$$= p'_{21} + p'_{2a}r_{a1} \text{ (true model)},$$

thus, p_{21} (false model) differs from p'_{21} (true model)

by a factor of:

$$p'_{2a}r_{a1} \qquad\qquad\qquad [2.12a]$$

Figure 2.12   Biased Solution of a Path Coefficient

variables problem is of sufficient seriousness to preclude the use of path analysis (or of other forms of confirmatory analysis). The decision steps are prefaced on the logic that while it is unrealistic to expect obviation of the unmeasured variables problem in research, it is possible to attempt to minimize bias in path coefficients (structural parameters) to the point that the bias is within "tolerable limits" for research purposes. It is also prefaced on the logic that investigators will exercise "good judgment" in deciding initially that enough information has accumulated to justify confirmatory analysis, which is a pragmatic but defensible reason for focusing on known causes. (We address this issue further in Chapter 3.)

The decision steps are presented in Figure 2.14. The steps are written from the standpoint of designing a cross-sectional, manifest variable analysis involving recursive causal connections, although the rationale generally transfers to other types of designs. Furthermore, the steps apply to one endogenous variable, and should be applied to each endogenous variable in a structural model.

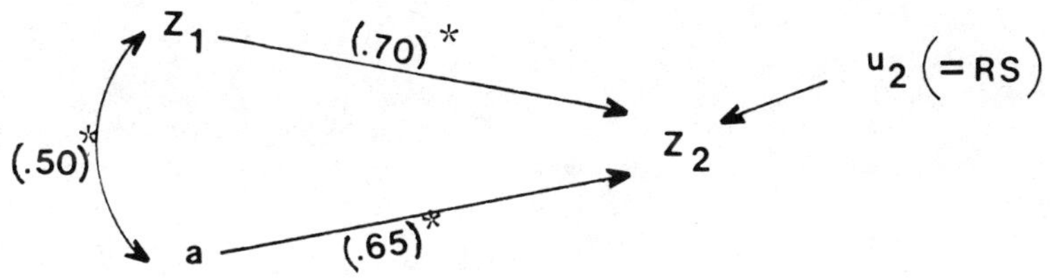

Path Equation: $z_2 = p'_{21}z_1 + p'_{2a}a + u'_2 (= RS)$

Solutions for Path Coefficients: $p'_{21} = .50$, $p'_{2a} = .40$

Figure 2.13a Solutions for Path Coefficients in a Self-Contained Path Equation
(true model)

*Indicates correlations.

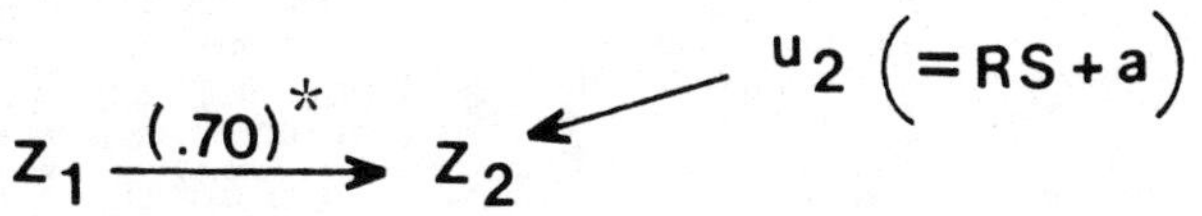

Path Equation: $z_2 = p_{21}z_1 + u_2 (= RS + a)$

Solution for Path Coefficient: $p_{21} = r_{21} = .70$

Figure 2.13b Solution for Path Coefficients in a Non-Self-Contained Path Equation
(false model)

$$p_{21} = p'_{21} + p'_{2a}r_{a1}$$
$$.70 = .50 + (.40)(.50)$$
$$= .50 + .20$$

Bias in $p_{21} = p'_{2a}r_{a1} = .20$

Figure 2.13c Bias in Estimate of P_{21} (false model)

Figure 2.13 Empirical Illustration of Bias Resulting from an Unmeasured Relevant
Cause and a Non-Self-Contained Path Model

The decision steps, while subjective, are the most help that we can give
researchers who are using cross-sectional designs with manifest (or latent)
variables. However, with longitudinal designs, it is possible to minimize
statistically the bias in estimates of structural parameters resulting from
unmeasured relevant causes. Of particular importance is time-series analysis combined with generalized differencing and generalized least squares
(see James & Singh, 1978; Johnston, 1972; Ostrom, 1978; Pindyck &
Rubinfeld, 1976). The logic of these methods is that if a disturbance term

Step I. Attempt to identify known major and moderate causes of the endogenous variable.

A. If data have not been collected, then attempt to measure the major/moderate causes unless there appears to be a good reason not to include one or more of these variables, as determined in Step II.

B. If data have already been collected, then attempt to identify known major/moderate unmeasured causes. If one or more such causes is believed to exist, proceed to Step II. If no major/moderate unmeasured causes are believed to exist, then exit from the decision steps at this point [i.e., a serious unmeasured variables problem appears to be unlikely for this endogenous variable, at least from the perspective of the decision-maker(s)].

Step II. Postulate whether each (major/moderate) unmeasured cause is correlated with one or more of the measured causes, using prior empirical evidence whenever possible to support the postulates. In designing a path analysis study, this step and those to follow are meant to be viewed in terms of causes that are not as yet in the causal model, as compared to causes already included in the model.

A. If the correlations between an unmeasured cause and all of the measured causes are presumed to be low (e.g., 0 to ± .20, although this is arbitrary), then exit here for that unmeasured cause. Note, however, that if a different unmeasured cause is included later in the causal model, then the decisions regarding prior unmeasured causes should be reevaluated (this applies to all of the following steps). Furthermore, an exit at this point suggests that the explanatory power of the causal model in regard to the endogenous variable of interest will be reduced. On the other hand, if the judgment is correct that all correlations between the unmeasured cause and the measured causes are low, then the solutions of the path coefficients for the measured causes are not likely to be seriously biased.

B. If an unmeasured cause is believed to have a moderate to high correlation with one or more of the measured causes, then consider whether the unmeasured cause is essentially linearly dependent on some combination of the measured causes. If prior research and/or judgment allow one to have confidence in an affirmative response to one of these considerations, then exit at this point. Note again, however, that while the exit suggests lack of serious bias, this will occur only if the judgments are correct.

Step III. By reaching Step III, it has been decided that (a) at least one unmeasured major/moderate cause exists for the endogenous variable of interest, (b) the unmeasured cause is correlated at least moderately with one or more of the measured causes, and (c) the unmeasured cause is not linearly dependent on some combination of the measured causes. This suggests that a serious unmeasured variables problem exists and that an attempt to solve for the path coefficients for this endogenous variable based on the measured causes is likely to result in at least one seriously biased solution. Consequently, it is recommended that path analytic procedures not be employed for this endogenous variable until the unmeasured cause(s) is in fact measured. A less desirable possibility might be to delete measured causes that are presumed to be correlated with unmeasured causes.

Figure 2.14 Decision Steps for Assessing the Seriousness of the Unmeasured Variables Problem

SOURCE: From "The Unmeasured Variables Problem in Path Analysis," by Lawrence R. James, *Journal of Applied Psychology*, 1980, 65, 415, 415, 421, Copyright 1980 by the American Psychological Association. Reprinted by permission of the author and publishers.

is estimated for the same endogenous variable(s) at each of several times of measurement, it is possible to estimate relationships among the disturbance terms. If the disturbance terms are composed of random shocks exclusively, then these relationships will be zero, or approximately so. If, however, unmeasured causes are contained in the estimated disturbance terms, then it follows that the unmeasured causes will correlate with themselves over time because they are, by definition, stable. These correlations are referred to as autocorrelations, or serial correlations, among the disturbance terms. Statistical procedures can be used to remove the serial correlation from the estimated disturbance terms, and, in the process, obviate relationships between measured causes and disturbances. The result is that consistent estimates of structural parameters may be obtained even though one may have an unmeasured variables problem.

Summary

Considerable territory has been covered in presenting Condition 9, and there is more to come in the discussion of latent variables. Nevertheless, with a minimum of statistical development we have attempted to make three points. First, predictions regarding estimates of structural parameters (standardized or unstandardized) must be confirmed if a structural model is to be consistent with empirical data. This is the first test of confirmation/disconfirmation. Second, erroneous conclusions may be drawn regarding confirmation/disconfirmation of predictions if the estimates of structural parameters are biased. Third, the degree of bias in estimates of structural parameters is a function of specification errors brought about by the failure to satisfy reasonably one or more of the preceding eight conditions. An illustration was provided for unmeasured relevant causes (a violation of the self-containment condition). An illustration of the effects of random measurement error in manifest variables is presented in Chapter 4. Illustrations of the effects of violations of other conditions, such as specification errors in causal order, causal direction, causal interval, and operationalization of variables, are furnished in the confirmatory literature (see Billings & Wroten, 1978; Bohrnstedt & Carter, 1971; Cook & Campbell, 1976; Darlington & Rom, 1972; Deegan, 1974; Goldberger & Duncan, 1973; Griffin, 1977; Heise, 1969; Werts & Linn, 1971; Young, 1977; Cliff, 1980).

CONDITION 10: EMPIRICAL CONFIRMATION OF PREDICTIONS II: FIT BETWEEN STRUCTURAL MODEL AND EMPIRICAL DATA

The estimation of structural parameters in Condition 9 is based (conditional) on the assumption that the structural model, as proposed originally, is valid. It is, however, quite possible for all of the estimated parameters to be significantly different from zero when the structural model is invalid. To illustrate, consider the two path models and their accompanying path equations in Figure 2.15. Model 2.15a predicts that similarity of interests (z_1) leads to felt attraction (z_2), which in turn leads to a higher probability to form a friendship (z_3). This is a simple chain model in which a direct $z_1 \rightarrow z_3$ effect is not hypothesized. Rather, the effect of z_1 on z_3 is indirect, which is to say that the effect of similarity of interests on friendship is mediated by the intervening process of experienced attraction. Model 2.15b predicts that z_1 affects both z_2 and z_3 directly, where both z_1 and z_2 are relevant causes of z_3 (z_1 also affects z_3 indirectly through z_2). If model 2.15a were tested in Condition 9, when in fact model 2.15b is the true model, then the estimate of the path coefficient for z_2 in equation 2.15b (i.e., p_{32}) would be biased. This would occur even though estimates of p_{31} in equation 2.15a and p_{32} in equation 2.15b were significant. The rationale here is that failure to include a measured relevant cause in a functional equation (i.e., z_1 in equation 2.15b) has the same implications as failure to include an unmeasured relevant cause (i.e., lack of self-containment and biased parameter estimates). However, unlike unmeasured relevant causes, it is possible to test empirically for direct causal effects for measured causes. This is a form of goodness-of-fit test, and brings us to the second test of confirmation/ disconfirmation.

The key condition required for the second test of confirmation/ disconfirmation is that no direct causal connection is hypothesized between at least one causal variable and an endogenous variable in the original structural model. This is analogous to hypothesizing that the value of the structural parameter relating these two variables is zero. For example, in Figure 2.15a, there is no direct arrow between z_1 and z_3; this means that p_{31} is hypothesized to be equal to zero. Thus, the path equation for z_3 in Figure 2.15a (equation 2.15b) may be thought of as $z_3 = (p_{31} = 0)z_1 + p_{32}z_2 + u_3 = p_{32}z_2 + u_3$. It cannot be emphasized strongly enough that setting structural parameters equal to zero must be *based on theoretical grounds (i.e., accompanied by a theoretical rationale) and proposed as part of the original structural model.*

To continue the illustration, the hypothesis that $p_{31} = 0$ in Figure 2.15a and equation 2.15b leads directly to the prediction that the OLS estimate of p_{31} should not differ significantly from zero. This hypothesis can be tested by estimating p_{31} in equation 2.15d, which is a test of the goodness of fit of model 2.15a. If the estimate of p_{31} is significant, then model 2.15a is disconfirmed and model 2.15b is a viable (but untestable, as explained below) possibility. This form of test is referred to as the *omitted parameter* test of goodness of fit, and is described later in this section. A test that accomplishes essentially the same purpose, but in a

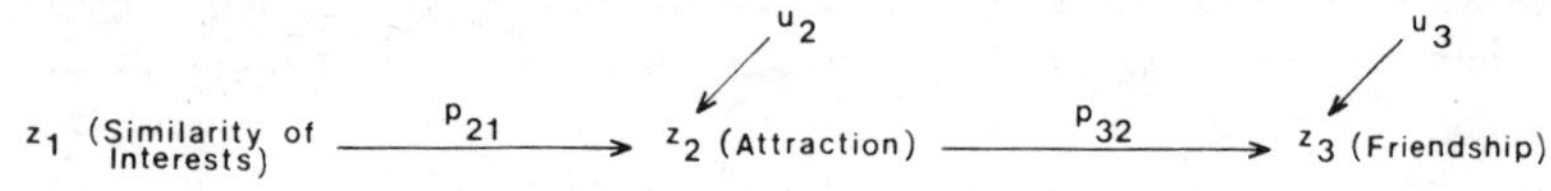

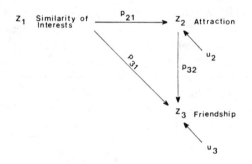

Path Equations

$$z_2 = p_{21}z_1 + u_2 \qquad [2.15a]$$
$$z_3 = p_{32}z_2 + u_3 \qquad [2.15b]$$

Figure 2.15a z_1 Is an Indirect Cause of z_3

Path Equations

$$z_2 = p_{21}z_1 + u_2 \qquad [2.15c]$$
$$z_3 = p_{31}z_1 + p_{32}z_2 + u_3 \qquad [2.15d]$$

Figure 2.15b z_1 Is a Direct Cause of z_3

Figure 2.15   Contrasting Path Models with z_1 Treated as an Indirect Cause and as a Direct Cause

more subtle manner, is to demonstrate that the correlation between z_1 and z_3 is equal to the product of the paths that link, indirectly, z_1 to z_3, or $r_{31} = p_{21}p_{32}$, in Figure 2.15a. This is referred to as the *reproduced correlation* test. The reproduced correlation test, or reproduced variance/ covariance test if variables are not standardized, is prominent in theoretical discussions of confirmatory analysis, and is described prior to the omitted parameter test. It is noteworthy that the reproduced correlation (variance/ covariance) test is not often used in manifest variable designs because significance tests are not available if OLS is used to estimate structural parameters (Kenny, 1979). On the other hand, it is, at the present time, the method of choice in latent variable analysis, where significance tests do exist.

The objectives of this section are (a) to describe the reproduced correlation test and the omitted parameter test, (b) to demonstrate the relations between the tests, and (c) to combine the two tests of confirmation/disconfirmation (i.e., Condition 9 and Condition 10). Path models based on a cross-sectional design are used to illustrate the process. Initial derivations are based on population data, although the processes are the same for the sample data. We assume that Conditions 1 through 8 and the assumptions required for OLS have been reasonably satisfied.

Reproduced Correlation Test

We begin with the path model shown in Figure 2.16 (which is the same as Figure 2.9). The key to the reproduced correlation test is to decompose correlations among variables in a structural model into functions of path coefficients and, if necessary, unanalyzed correlations among exogenous variables (the latter case is not treated in our examples). Aside from the correlation of a variable with itself, there are six population correlations associated with Figure 2.16, namely, r_{21}, r_{31}, r_{32}, r_{41}, r_{42}, and r_{43} (the order of subscripts reflects causal priorities, although this is arbitrary). The decomposition may be accomplished by the long method using expectations (see Duncan, 1975) or by the short method using the following equation (Namboodiri et al., 1975):

$$r_{ij} = \sum_k p_{ik} r_{kj} \qquad [2.18]$$

i represents the endogenous variable (i > k,j), j refers to the causal variable, and k begins with i-1 and ranges down to 1 (i.e., z_1). The short method is employed below, where correlations of the form r_{jj} (k = j) are deleted because they are equal to 1.0.

Direct application of equation 2.18 provides:

$$r_{21} = p_{21} \qquad [2.19]$$

....

$$r_{31} = p_{32} r_{21} + p_{31} \qquad [2.20]$$

$$r_{32} = p_{32} + p_{31} r_{12} \qquad [2.21]$$

....

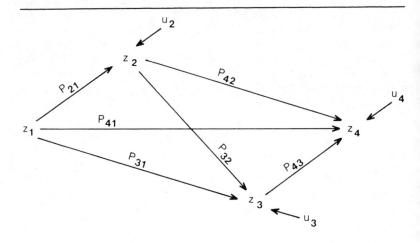

Path Equations

$$z_2 = p_{21}z_1 + u_2 \qquad\qquad [2.16a]$$

$$z_3 = p_{31}z_1 + p_{32}z_2 + u_3 \qquad\qquad [2.16b]$$

$$z_4 = p_{41}z_1 + p_{42}z_2 + p_{43}z_3 + u_4 \qquad\qquad [2.16c]$$

Figure 2.16 A Just-Identified Path Model

$$r_{41} = p_{43}r_{31} + p_{42}r_{21} + p_{41} \qquad\qquad [2.22]$$

$$r_{42} = p_{43}r_{32} + p_{42} + p_{41}r_{12} \qquad\qquad [2.23]$$

$$r_{43} = p_{43} + p_{42}r_{23} + p_{41}r_{13} \qquad\qquad [2.24]$$

Equations 2.19 through 2.24 do not represent a full decomposition; they are the normal equations used to solve for the path coefficients in equations 2.16a through 2.16c in Figure 2.16. Dotted lines separate the normal equations associated with each path equation. As discussed in regard to identification in Condition 9, it is possible to compute the six correlations directly from the data and thus the correlations are "known values." There are also six unknown path coefficients. When the number of known values (normal equations) for each path equation is equal to the number of unknown values, each path equation is referred to as *just identified* or *exactly identified*. If all equations are just identified, then the path model is said to be just identified (exactly identified). This means that one has a sufficient number of knowns (six correlations) to estimate the number of unknowns (six path coefficients) in the path model. In just identified models, *all* of the known information is employed to calculate the unknown path coefficients.

Assuming that OLS has justifiably been used to solve for the path coefficients (i.e., the p_{ij} and population OLS beta weights are equivalent), we can now fully decompose the correlations by replacing the correlations on the right side of equations 2.19 through 2.24 with their decompositions from earlier equations. For example, r_{21} in equation 2.20 and r_{12} in equation 2.21 are equal to p_{21} (equation 2.19). Applying this process to the remaining equations results in the following set of decomposed correlations.

$$r_{21} = p_{21} \qquad\qquad [2.25]$$

$$r_{31} = p_{32}p_{21} + p_{31} \qquad\qquad [2.26]$$

$$r_{32} = p_{32} + p_{31}p_{21} \qquad\qquad [2.27]$$

$$r_{41} = p_{43}p_{32}p_{21} + p_{43}p_{31} + p_{42}p_{21} + p_{41} \qquad\qquad [2.28]$$

$$r_{42} = p_{43}p_{32} + p_{43}p_{31}p_{21} + p_{42} + p_{41}p_{21} \qquad\qquad [2.29]$$

$$r_{43} = p_{43} + p_{42}p_{32} + p_{42}p_{31}p_{21} + p_{41}p_{32}p_{21} + p_{41}p_{31} \qquad\qquad [2.30]$$

The objective of these "decomposition equations" is to see if one can reproduce the correlations with functions of path coefficients. This is clearly circular for these equations. That is, if all the known information (correlations) is used to solve for the unknown information (path coefficients) in the normal equations (equations 2.19 through 2.24), then it should be possible to reverse the process and reproduce the correlations exactly by functions of the path coefficients. This is precisely the case; equations 2.25 through 2.30 will reproduce exactly the original six correlations used to solve for the path coefficients in equations 2.19 through 2.24. Thus, in just-identified models, goodness-of-fit tests are inappropriate inasmuch as solutions of path coefficients and reproduction of correlations are circular or mirror reflections of the same statistical process.

It is possible to break out of this circular process by omitting one or more causal connections from the path model and path equations. This is accomplished by assuming a priori that at least one path coefficient is equal to zero; that is, a z_j does not cause a z_i ($i > j$) directly. For example, in Figure 2.16, suppose it is assumed that z_3 does not cause z_4 directly. Mathematically this is equivalent to assuming that $p_{43} = 0$. The new path equation for z_4 is now

$$z_4 = p_{41}z_1 + p_{42}z_2 + u_4 \qquad\qquad [2.31]$$

The effects of this assumption may be demonstrated with the normal equations (see Duncan, 1975), although it is straightforward to deal directly with the decomposition equations. To see the results of the assumption that $p_{43} = 0$, we will omit all terms in equations 2.25 through 2.30 that involve p_{43}. The terms to be omitted have a line crossed through them.

$$r_{21} = p_{21} \tag{2.32}$$

$$r_{31} = p_{32}p_{21} + p_{31} \tag{2.33}$$

$$r_{32} = p_{32} + p_{31}p_{21} \tag{2.34}$$

$$r_{41}{}^* = \cancel{p_{43}p_{32}p_{21}} + \cancel{p_{43}p_{31}} + p_{42}p_{21} + p_{41} \tag{2.35}$$

$$r_{42}{}^* = \cancel{p_{43}p_{32}} + \cancel{p_{43}p_{31}p_{21}} + p_{42} + p_{41}p_{21} \tag{2.36}$$

$$r_{43}{}^* = \cancel{p_{43}} + p_{42}p_{32} + p_{42}p_{31}p_{21} + p_{41}p_{32}p_{21} + p_{41}p_{31} \tag{2.37}$$

Of initial importance is the fact that there are still six known correlations. However, only five unknowns now exist (i.e., p_{43} is considered known and equated to zero). When more knowns than unknowns exist in the normal and decomposition equations, the model is said to be *overidentified*. (Technically, the z_4 path equation is overidentified because z_3 was deleted from equation 2.31). Overidentification has a number of technical implications; however, our concern here is with the substantive outcome. This outcome is that (a) any correlation in the set of six correlations represented by equations 2.32 through 2.37 that has a term crossed out (i.e., equations 2.35, 2.36, and 2.37) is (b) not constrained to be exactly reproduced by the path coefficients. In more specific terms, $r_{41}{}^*$, $r_{42}{}^*$, *and* $r_{43}{}^*$ are subject to an *overidentifying restriction* (i.e., $p_{43} = 0$), and the reproduced (sometimes referred to as *implied*) correlations resulting from equations 2.35 through 2.37 may differ from their observed counterparts (r_{41}, r_{42}, r_{43}). Asterisks are used to designate correlations subject to overidentifying restrictions.

The hypothesis that $p_{43} = 0$ leads to the predictions that $r_{41}{}^*$, $r_{42}{}^*$, and $r_{43}{}^*$ will be equal to their observed counterparts, namely, r_{41}, r_{42}, r_{43}. Consequently, if the reproduced correlations are equal to their observed counterparts, then the predictions are confirmed. This implies that p_{43} is equal to zero. Suppose, however, that the a priori hypothesis that $p_{43} = 0$ is wrong, and $p_{43} > 0$. In this situation, $r_{41}{}^* \neq r_{41}, r_{42}{}^* \neq r_{42}$, and $r_{43}{}^* \neq r_{43}$. For example, if all correlations and path coefficients are positive, then $r_{41}{}^*$ will underestimate r_{41} by a value equal to $p_{43}p_{32}p_{21} + p_{43}p_{31}$; the terms deleted from equation 2.35. Thus, the goodness-of-fit test leads to disconfirmation of the predictions evolving from a model with $p_{43} = 0$. The implication of disconfirmation is that z_3 has a direct effect on z_4.

We will now demonstrate the above rationale with an empirical illustration, using the prediction that $p_{41} = 0$ in place of $p_{43} = 0$. Figure 2.17 presents a path model (Figure 2.17a) and path equations (Figure 2.17b) that are similar to the model and equations in Figure 2.16, except for the

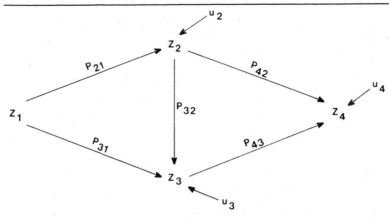

Figure 2.17a Path Model with P_{41} Predicted to Be Equal to Zero

$$z_2 = p_{21}z_1 + u_2 \qquad [2.17a]$$
$$z_3 = p_{31}z_1 + p_{32}z_2 + u_3 \qquad [2.17b]$$
$$z_4 = (p_{41} = 0)z_1 + p_{42}z_2 + p_{43}z_3 + u_4 = p_{42}z_2 + p_{43}z_3 + u_4 \qquad [2.17c]$$

Figure 2.17b Path Equations

$$r_{21} = p_{21}$$
$$r_{31} = p_{32}p_{21} + p_{31}$$
$$r_{32} = p_{32} + p_{31}p_{21}$$
$$r_{41}{}^* = p_{43}p_{32}p_{21} + p_{43}p_{31} + p_{42}p_{21} + \cancel{p_{41}}$$
$$r_{42}{}^* = p_{43}p_{32} + p_{43}p_{31}p_{21} + p_{42} + \cancel{p_{41}p_{21}}$$
$$r_{43}{}^* = p_{43} + p_{42}p_{32} + p_{42}p_{31}p_{21} + \cancel{p_{41}p_{32}p_{21}} + \cancel{p_{41}p_{31}}$$

Figure 2.17c Decomposition Equations
*Denotes correlations subject to overidentifying restriction.

| | Correlation Matrix A | | | | | Correlation Matrix B | | | |
	z_1	z_2	z_3	z_4		z_1	z_2	z_3	z_4
z_1	1.0				z_1	1.0			
z_2	.60	1.0			z_2	.50	1.0		
z_3	.64	.64	1.0		z_3	.50	.55	1.0	
z_4	.44	.56	.59	1.0	z_4	.65	.78	.82	1.0

Figure 2.17d Correlation Matrices

Figure 2.17 Reproduced Correlation Test for a Path Model with p_{41} Predicted to Be Equal to Zero and Two Correlation Matrices

Matrix A

$p_{21} = .60$

$p_{31} = .40, p_{32} = .40$

$p_{42} = .30, p_{43} = .40$

Matrix B

$p_{21} = .50$

$p_{31} = .30, p_{32} = .40$

$p_{42} = .40, p_{43} = .50$

Figure 2.17e Solution of Path Coefficients for Correlation Matrices A and B

Matrix A

Observed	Reproduced
r_{41}^*: .44	$.44 = (.40)(.40)(.60) + (.40)(.40) + (.30)(.60)$
r_{42}^*: .56	$.56 = (.40)(.40) + (.40)(.40)(.60) + .30$
r_{43}^*: .59	$.59 = .40 + (.30)(.40) + (.30)(.40)(.60)$

Matrix B

Observed	Reproduced
.65	$.45 = (.50)(.40)(.50) + (.50)(.30) + (.40)(.50)$
.78	$.68 = (.50)(.40) + (.50)(.30)(.50) + .40$
.82	$.72 = .50 + (.40)(.40) + (.40)(.30)(.50)$

Figure 17f   Observed and Reproduced Correlations for Correlation Matrices A and B

Figure 2.17 (Continued)

fact that p_{41} is predicted to be equal to zero in Figure 2.17a. Consequently the $p_{41}z_1$ term is deleted from the z_4 path equation (equation 2.17c). The decomposition equations are shown in Figure 2.17c. All terms involving p_{41} have a line crossed through them (i.e., are omitted), which results in r_{41}^*, r_{42}^*, r_{43}^* being subject to an overidentifying restriction. Two different hypothetical population correlation matrices for the model in Figure 2.17a are shown in Figure 2.17d. Given that all conditions and assumptions for confirmatory analysis and OLS have been reasonably satisfied, the population OLS solutions of the path coefficients for each of these correlation matrices are reported in Figure 2.17e. (Only the correlations differ; the path model is the same for both correlation matrices). The observed correlations subject to an overidentifying restriction and the reproduced correlations, based on the decomposition equations in Figure 2.17c, are presented in Figure 2.17f. For matrix A, the observed and reproduced correlations are identical, which suggests that (a) $p_{41} = 0$; (b) the path model in Figure 2.17a has a good fit with the data—that is, the correlations in matrix A; and (c) the path model is confirmed in regard to the second test of confirmation/disconfirmation. For matrix B, however, discrepancies exist between the observed and reproduced correlations. These results connote that (a) p_{41} is not equal to zero and the terms crossed out of the decomposition equations for $r_{41}{}^*$, $r_{42}{}^*$, $r_{43}{}^*$ should have been retained; (b) the path model in Figure 2.17a does not have a good fit with the data represented by matrix B; and (c) the path model is disconfirmed.

To summarize, the a priori prediction that $p_{41} = 0$ in Figure 2.17a resulted in an overidentification condition in which three correlations were subject to an overidentifying restriction. In other words, three reproduced correlations were not constrained to be equal to their observed counterparts, although they were predicted to be equal to their observed counterparts. The correlations subject to the overidentifying restriction may be ascertained by deriving the decomposition equations using equation 2.18 for a just-identified model (i.e., all paths included), and then crossing out those terms in the decomposition equations that involve a path coefficient assumed to be equal to zero. Reproduced correlations may then be calculated and compared to observed correlations. Divergence of reproduced from observed correlations disconfirms predictions regarding the reproduced correlations and implies that a priori hypotheses are incorrect. Reproduced correlations equal to observed correlations denote confirmation of predictions and imply that the a priori hypotheses may be valid.

Note that only correlations subject to overidentifying restrictions should enter into goodness-of-fit tests. It would make no sense whatever to use r_{21}, r_{31}, or r_{32} in Figure 2.17 as a basis for testing goodness of fit inasmuch as these correlations will be reproduced exactly. Moreover, the assumption that $p_{ij} = 0$ must be made a priori. To reiterate a point, consider a scenario in which a just-identified model is used to calculate the values of all path coefficients, and p_{41} is found equal to zero. p_{41} is then deleted from the model, and the model is regarded as overidentified. A goodness-of-fit test of predictions evolving from $p_{41} = 0$ could not miss because one would know that the calculated $p_{41} = 0$. Thus, the reproduced correlations would equal the observed correlations. This is obviously not a legitimate goodness-of-fit test, and the time has arrived for authors and reviewers to recognize that the researcher must test the goodness of fit of the model he or she begins with and not the model obtained by theory trimming (i.e., after seeing the data).

The preceding discussion was based on population values. With sample values, goodness-of-fit tests are designed to ascertain whether reproduced correlations subject to overidentifying restrictions are different than their observed counterparts. (A method of estimation other than OLS, e.g., maximum likelihood, must be used to estimate structural parameters if a significance test is desired to compare the reproduced and observed correlations.) However, the comparison between reproduced and observed correlations is often not recommended for actual practice with manifest variable designs because (a) it is complex statistically, (b) it is difficult to interpret when more than one path is omitted from a model, and most importantly, (c) the omitted parameter test is a more direct method that is easier both to compute and to interpret (see Duncan, 1975; Namboodiri et al., 1975). We illustrate the difficulty of interpretation issue below, and then demonstrate how it is possible to address the same issue more directly with the omitted parameter test.

Consider the model in Figure 2.18, which predicts that both p_{32} and p_{41} are equal to zero. The path equations are as follows:

$$z_2 = p_{21}z_1 + u_2 \qquad\qquad [2.38]$$

$$z_3 = p_{31}z_1 + u_3 \qquad\qquad [2.39]$$

$$z_4 = p_{42}z_2 + p_{43}z_3 + u_4 \qquad\qquad [2.40]$$

If the model were just identified, the decomposition equations would be the same as equations 2.25 through 2.30. These equations are shown below, where all terms involving p_{32} and p_{41} have been crossed out. With these terms omitted, there are six known correlations and four unknown path coefficients. Thus, the model is overidentified. Once the four path coefficients are solved for in the population (estimated in a sample), all correlations except r_{12} are shown to be subject to an overidentifying restriction.

$$r_{21} = p_{21} \qquad\qquad [2.41]$$

$$r_{31}{}^* = \cancel{p_{32}p_{21}} + p_{31} \qquad\qquad [2.42]$$

$$r_{32}{}^* = \cancel{p_{32}} + p_{31}p_{21} \qquad\qquad [2.43]$$

$$r_{41}{}^* = \cancel{p_{43}p_{32}p_{21}} + p_{43}p_{31} + p_{42}p_{21} + \cancel{p_{41}} \qquad\qquad [2.44]$$

$$r_{42}{}^* = \cancel{p_{43}p_{32}} + p_{43}p_{31}p_{21} + p_{42} + \cancel{p_{41}p_{21}} \qquad\qquad [2.45]$$

$$r_{43}{}^* = p_{43} + \cancel{p_{42}p_{32}} + p_{42}p_{31}p_{21} + \cancel{p_{41}p_{32}p_{21}} + \cancel{p_{41}p_{31}} \qquad\qquad [2.46]$$

Suppose all $r_{ij}{}^*$ are equivalent to their observed counterparts. This denotes that predictions regarding reproduced correlations are confirmed, and implies that $p_{32} = p_{41} = 0$. Now, suppose $r_{31}{}^* = r_{31}$ and $r_{32}{}^* = r_{32}$, but $r_{41}{}^*$, $r_{42}{}^*$, and $r_{43}{}^*$ are not equal to their observed counterparts. This pattern suggests that (a) p_{32} is equal to zero, and (b) p_{41} is different from zero. That is, the $r_{ij}{}^*$ involving only p_{32} led to accurate reproduced correlations, while the $r_{ij}{}^*$ involving p_{41} (and p_{32}) did not. Predictions regarding correlations containing z_4 are disconfirmed because p_{41} is presumably not equal to 0.

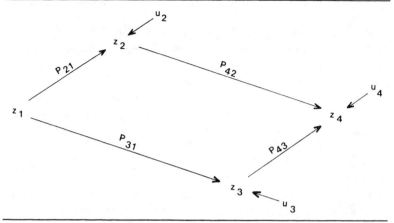

Figure 2.18 An Overidentified Recursive Path Model with p_{32} and p_{41} Predicted to Be Equal to Zero

Finally, suppose that all of the r_{ij}^* diverge from the observed r_{ij}. $r_{31}^* \neq r_{31}$ and $r_{32}^* \neq r_{32}$ imply that $p_{32} \neq 0$. However, the $r_{4j}^* \neq r_{4j}$ ($j = 1,2,3$) may be a result of either (a) $p_{32} \neq 0$ (which appears to be the case) or (b) p_{32} and $p_{41} \neq 0$. That is, we can not infer whether p_{41} is equal or not equal to zero with this test. This is hardly a trivial concern if one wishes to ascertain sources of disconfirmation. As a result, the reproduced correlation test applied to a single model is of questionable use in actual practice with moderately to highly overidentified manifest variable designs. Duncan (1975) and Bentler (1980) review other problems of a statistical nature. A refinement of this test has been suggested for latent variable analysis, and will be discussed in that section.

The Omitted Parameter Test

The logic of the reproduced correlation test is that if the values of p_{ij} assumed equal to zero are in fact zero, then reproduced correlations subject to overidentifying restrictions should be equal to their observed counterparts. It would seem that one could save considerable fuss by simply estimating, in a sample, the values of the p_{ij} assumed equal to zero to see if, in fact, they do not differ significantly from zero. That is, if a path coefficient is hypothesized to equal zero, then one would predict that its estimated value should not differ significantly from zero. If the estimated path coefficient is not significantly different from zero, then the prediction is confirmed. If it is significantly different from zero, then the prediction is disconfirmed. This is the omitted parameter test, and it is logically equivalent to the reproduced correlation test. More importantly, it provides a method to locate sources of disconfirmation in recursive models.

To begin the illustration, let us return to Figure 2.17, in which it was shown that the (population) path model did not have a good fit with matrix B. This implied that the omitted parameter p_{41} was not equal to zero. It is possible to solve for the value of p_{41} by including p_{41} in the path equation for z_4 (equation 2.17c) and conducting a new OLS analysis on the equation: $z_4 = p_{41}z_1 + p_{42}z_2 + p_{43}z_3 + u_3$. The population value of p_{41} given by an OLS analysis using the correlations in matrix B is .20, which differs considerably from zero. Thus, the omitted parameter test and the reproduced correlation test result in the same conclusion for this simple model. Note also that if (a) the terms deleted from the decomposition equations in Figure 2.17c are instead retained, and if (b) the value of .20 is used for p_{41}, then (c) the observed and reproduced correlations for r_{41}, r_{42}, and r_{43} are identical.

Things are often not this simple. Let us continue with a discussion of the omitted parameter test, where sample data are now assumed because we wish to address significance tests. Consider the path coefficients in the original path equations for Figure 2.18 (equations 2.38 through 2.40). We will presume that the values of these coefficients are estimated using OLS. The goodness-of-fit test is then conducted by inserting the variables with path coefficients predicted to equal zero into the appropriate equations and conducting new OLS analyses. In the present case, OLS would be conducted to estimate the path coefficients in the following equations (the z_2 equation does not have an omitted parameter):

$$z_3 = \hat{p}_{31}z_1 + \hat{p}_{32}{}^*z_2 + \hat{u}_3 \qquad\qquad [2.47]$$

$$z_4 = \hat{p}_{41}{}^*z_1 + \hat{p}_{42}z_2 + \hat{p}_{43}z_3 + \hat{u}_4 \qquad\qquad [2.48]$$

where asterisks indicate the path coefficients that should be equal to zero, and circumflexes denote that we are dealing with sample estimates of path coefficients (and disturbances).

If $\hat{p}_{32}{}^*$ and $\hat{p}_{41}{}^*$ are not significantly different from zero, then the predictions are confirmed. Confirmation implies that the parameters or path coefficients p_{32} and p_{41} are zero and that this part of the original path model is valid. That is, the omitted paths should have been omitted. If $\hat{p}_{32}{}^*$ and/or $\hat{p}_{41}{}^*$ are significant, then at least one prediction is disconfirmed. Disconfirmation implies that the original path model is invalid, which is to say that at least one omitted path should not have been omitted (i.e., p_{32} and/or p_{41} are not equal to zero). It is particularly important to note that this process allows one to ascertain the source of disconfirmation.

In samples, $\hat{p}_{32}*$ and $\hat{p}_{41}*$ are tested for significance using standard tests for regression weights. There are, however, some problems with the use of these significance tests. First, confirmatory analysis is usually conducted on large samples. Thus, the test of significance is rather powerful, and paths with rather trivial magnitudes (e.g., $\hat{p}_{ij}* = .05$) may be statistically significant and lead to disconfirmation. There are no clear rules of thumb here; one may wish to go beyond the data and argue that a significant but very low path coefficient, less than $|\pm.05|$ for example, does not do serious damage to a model. This is a matter of judgment, however, and the author must have a strong theoretical defense in support of such a decision.

A second problem is multicollinearity, which occurs when two or more variables in the same equation are correlated highly with one another (see Johnston, 1972, and Gordon, 1968, for discussions of indicators of multicollinearity). A key product of multicollinearity is that "it becomes very difficult, if not impossible, to disentangle the relative influences of the various X [causal] variables" (Johnston, 1972, p. 160). In effect, one can place little faith in sample estimates of structural parameters and significance tests (see Gordon, 1968). The probability of a multicollinearity condition is of serious concern in omitted parameter tests (James & Jones, 1980). Consider, for example, equation 2.48, in which $\hat{p}_{41}*$ is to be tested for significance. Variable z_1 is included in an equation with two variables for which it is a cause, namely, z_2 and z_3. If z_1 is a strong cause of z_2 and z_3, then z_1 will be correlated highly with z_2 and z_3. It is possible, therefore, that the equation used for the omitted parameter test (equation 2.48), which considers, z_1, z_2, and z_3 as causes, could be subject to a multicollinearity condition. Given multicollinearity, one has several options, including (a) hierarchical regression (see Cohen & Cohen, 1975) or (b) a disturbance term regression test described in James and Jones (1980). Inasmuch as these tests concern primarily statistical issues, they are not discussed here.

A final issue is protection of the significance level when multiple, nonindependent significance tests are conducted on the same sample. This issue has not been a concern in manifest variable analyses, although it should be in both Conditions 9 and 10. We will treat this issue briefly in the chapter on latent variables.

A COMBINATION OF THE FIRST AND SECOND TESTS OF CONFIRMATION/DISCONFIRMATION

In the preceding condition (Condition 9) we described how it is possible to confirm/disconfirm predictions furnished by structural (path) models and functional (path) equations. This first test of confirmation/ disconfirmation addresses predictions that estimated values of structural parameters (path coefficients) included in functional equations should be significantly different from zero. The second test of confirmation/ disconfirmation described in the present section addresses predictions that estimated values of structural parameters (path coefficients) not included in functional equations (i.e., omitted parameters) should *not* be significantly different than zero. The strongest case for confirmation/ disconfirmation is made if both tests are conducted, which requires at least some overidentified equations to conduct the second test.

To review how the tests are combined, consider the path equation for z_4 in Figure 2.18, which may be viewed as:

$$z_4 = (p_{41}^* = 0)z_1 + p_{42}z_2 + p_{43}z_3 + u_4 \qquad [2.49]$$

$$= p_{42}z_2 + p_{43}z_3 + u_4 \qquad [2.50]$$

The first test of confirmation/disconfirmation tests the predictions that the sample OLS estimates of p_{42} and p_{43}, or $\hat{p}_{42}$ and $\hat{p}_{43}$, are significant. If both estimates are significant, we have partial confirmation for this structural equation. The term "partial confirmation" is used because the values of p_{42} and p_{43} are estimated conditional on the assumption that $p_{41} = 0$. If $\hat{p}_{42}$ and/or $\hat{p}_{43}$ are nonsignificant (the interpretation of significance is left to the investigator), then this functional equation, and therefore the structural model, are disconfirmed, although we recommend that one still proceed to the second test of confirmation/disconfirmation. The second test concerns the prediction, based on the assumption that $p_{41}^* = 0$, that $\hat{p}_{41}^*$ is not significant. The test requires another OLS analysis to obtain a value of $\hat{p}_{41}^*$. If $\hat{p}_{41}^*$ is not significant, then the prediction has been confirmed and the functional equation is said to be (logically) consistent with, or to have a good fit with, the data, given that $\hat{p}_{42}$ and $\hat{p}_{43}$ are significant. If, however, (a) either $\hat{p}_{42}$ or $\hat{p}_{43}$, or both, is nonsignificant, and/or if (b) $\hat{p}_{41}^*$ is significant, then (c) the functional equation and the model are disconfirmed. Either source of disconfirmation (i.e., the first or second test) implies that the equation and the model are logically inconsistent, or fail to have a good fit, with the data.

To summarize, if all functional equations in a structural model pass the first test of confirmation/disconfirmation, and if all overidentified functional equations pass the second test of confirmation/disconfirmation, then the structural model is said to have a good fit with the data, or to be logically consistent with the data. We can say, therefore, that the structural model is confirmed because it has passed both tests required for confirmation. However, we can not conclude that the structural model that generated the predictions is a "true model." By true we mean that the model and functional equations accurately represent causal processes. On the other hand, if a structural model is disconfirmed by either test, we have a strong, but not necessarily unequivocal, case for concluding that the model is false. These points are discussed in the next chapter, in which we address "causal inference."

3

Causal Inference with
Manifest Variables

> *The insidious thing about the causal point of view
> is that it leads us to say: "Of course, it had to
> happen like that." Whereas we ought to think: It
> may have happened* like that—*and also in many
> other ways.*
>
> — Ludwig Wittgenstein (1980)

We begin this section by restating the third principle for the logical foundation of confirmatory analysis (the principles were presented in Condition 9, Chapter 2). The principle is:

Confirmation of predictions implies corroborative support for the structural model represented by the functional relations and equations. Disconfirmation of predictions implies that one or more components of the structural model (functional relations and equations) is false, in which case it is concluded that the structural model as proposed originally is invalid.

We focus first on confirmation. The corroborative support provided by confirmation implies completion of the following progression: (a) causal hypotheses have been made and formally specified in a structural model and in functional equations; (b) conditions pertaining to the appropriateness of theoretical models (Conditions 1 through 7) and operationalization of variables (Condition 8) have been reasonably satisfied; (c) a set of predictions regarding significance of structural parameters and/or reproduction of a correlation (variance/covariance) matrix have been derived from the structural model and functional equations; and (d) the predictions have been confirmed by empirical tests. This progression suggests that one is in the position to make the judgment, or *causal inference*, that the causal hypotheses on which the structural model and functional equations are based are useful for explaining how and why the endogenous variables in the model occurred and are related to other endogenous as well as exogenous variables. Explanation is possible because structural models and functional equations provide explicit, quantitative statements of theory that, presumably, specify the rules that govern the occurrences of natural events and the structure of observed relationships among naturally occurring events (Heise, 1969). Confirmation of a structural model suggests that these rules are useful and may be used to infer the causal processes that are, and were, operating.

One must be mindful that it is necessary to make a number of untestable assumptions in the process of conducting a confirmatory analysis. By untestable assumptions we mean that reasonable satisfaction of subsets of conditions from Conditions 1 through 8 is based on "faith" and not on empirical tests. For example, with cross-sectional data one cannot test the stability condition (Condition 7), operationalize a cyclical recursive model (Condition 4), or attempt to control bias resulting from an unmeasured variables problem (Condition 5). Consequently, reasons must be offered for assumptions that the model is stable and in an equilibrium-type condition, that causal relations are noncyclical within a temporal bound, and that the unavoidable unmeasured variables problem is not sufficiently serious to preclude confirmatory analysis. Prior research may furnish a basis for assumptions, but an investigator cannot avoid the fact that he or she is relying on faith when he or she assumes that untested conditions are reasonably satisfied.

The issue of reasonable satisfaction is also important in regard to conditions that can be tested empirically. It is usually necessary to rely on reasonable satisfaction, rather than perfect satisfaction, of conditions or subsets of conditions that can be subjected to empirical tests. For example, perfect reliability is seldom attained in manifest variable studies. As discussed in Condition 8, high reliability is generally considered sufficient for reasonable satisfaction of the reliability assumption, although no unequivocal definition exists for "high," and the effects of measurement error in elaborate models is often unpredictable. Other assumptions that are potentially testable, but for which reasonable satisfaction is considered sufficient, include the construct validity of manifest variables, interval measurement scales, and linearity. Although reasonable satisfaction of empirically testable assumptions is considered sufficient for proceeding with confirmatory analysis, the cumulative effects of various, presumably nonserious, violations are essentially unknown.

Untested assumptions, in combination with reasonable rather than perfect satisfaction of tested assumptions, suggest that confirmation of a structural model is not synonymous with proof that the model is true or correct. Confirmation implies only that those assumptions that were tested by empirical analysis provided corroborative support for the structural model. This support may disappear, however, if an *un*tested assumption is shown later to be false, or if what appears to be reasonable satisfaction of an empirically tested assumption is in fact unreasonable. These points lead us to the crucial conclusion that *it is possible to confirm a false structural model*. On the other hand, *it is also possible to disconfirm a true model*. For example, a nonsignificant parameter estimate between variables thought to be causally connected may be due to imprecision in the measurement of the variables rather than to lack of true causal connection (see Cook & Campbell, 1979). Thus, disconfirmation is not necessarily synonymous with disproof of a structural model, although, as discussed shortly, disconfirmation, in comparison to confirmation, has stronger implications for the usefulness of a structural model.

Before contrasting confirmation and disconfirmation, allow us to furnish a simple illustration of how it is possible to confirm a false structural model. Consider Figure 3.1, which presents a false path model and a true path model for a manifest variable design. The difference between the models is that the true model includes an additional, exogenous cause of z_3 that is correlated with z_2, but not with z_1. This suggests that z_a is an unmeasured relevant cause of z_3 in the false model, which implies that Condition 5 (self-containment) is violated in the z_3 equation. However, note the predictions for the two models. Both the false and true models predict that $\dot{p}_{21}$ and $\dot{p}_{32}$ will be significant (first test of confirmation/disconfirmation discussed in Chapter 2, Condition 9). The difference between the models is that $\dot{p}_{32}$ in the false model will be biased in an upward direction due to lack of a control for z_a (assuming relations are linear and positive, and disregarding suppressors). Furthermore, both models predict that $\dot{p}_{31}$* will be nonsignificant (second test of confirmation/disconfirmation discussed in Chapter 2, Condition 10). The consequence of this situation is that the true model furnishes no clear case for disconfirming the false model if one were to employ the false model in a confirmatory analysis. In other words, given that the true model is in fact true, the false model would be confirmed.

Numerous other illustrations could be used to demonstrate how it is possible to confirm false models (see Duncan, 1975). The simple example in Figure 3.1 makes the point that confirmation does not imply truth in a structural model. We should also mention that this point is often characterized in a different manner in the confirmatory literature. The characterization is as follows: (a) a structural model will generate one and only one set of correlations (variances/covariances) among manifest variables, although (b) a particular correlation matrix may be generated by more than one structural model. Thus, two or more structural models may generate the same correlation matrix, and demonstration that a model

FALSE MODEL

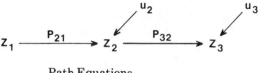

Path Equations

$$z_2 = p_{21}z_1 + u_2$$
$$z_3 = (p_{31}^* = 0)z_1 + p_{32}z_2 + u_3$$

Predictions

$\hat{p}_{21}$ and $\hat{p}_{32}$ are significant.

$\hat{p}_{31}$ is not significant.

TRUE MODEL

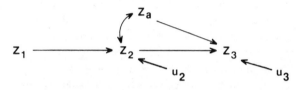

Path Equations

$$z_2 = p_{21} + u_2$$
$$z_3 = (p_3 = 0)z_1 + p_{32}z_2 + p_{3a}z_a + u_3$$

Predictions

$\hat{p}_{21}$, $\hat{p}_{32}$, and $\hat{p}_{3a}$ are significant.

$\hat{p}_{31}^*$ is not significant.

Figure 3.1   Confirmation of a False Model

reproduces a correlation matrix does not imply that it is a true, or a unique, structural model. This characterization may be tied to our example in Figure 3.1 by noting that $\hat{p}_{32}{}^* = 0$ implies that $\hat{r}_{31} = \hat{p}_{21}\hat{p}_{32}$ in both the true and false models (given that z_1 and z_a are unrelated in the true model).

This problem has been a subject of concern in the philosophical literature, as well as to us in advocating confirmatory analysis. We will now draw from the philosophical and other literatures to explore this issue further, our objectives being to point out a logical asymmetry between confirmation and disconfirmation, to discuss the role of causal inference in science, and to suggest approaches to confirmatory analysis that furnish a comparatively stronger base for causal inference.

Returning to the question of confirmation, we have endeavored to point out that confirmation of predictions regarding the significance (first test) and nonsignificance (second test) of estimated structural parameters, where predictions were deduced for causal hypotheses, can not be used to establish the *truth* of the causal hypotheses. To maintain fidelity with the philosophical literature, we shall refer to predictions pertaining to the significance/nonsignificance of estimated structural parameters as "correlational hypotheses." Thus, given confirmation of a correlational hypothesis, to conclude that the causal hypothesis (P) is true because the correlational hypothesis (Q) deduced from it is true (confirmed) would involve committing the fallacy of affirming the consequent. This fallacy occurs in arguments of the form, "P implies Q: Q is true; therefore, P is true." The fallacy lies in the possibility that P logically may be false even though Q is true. The only case in which the truth of P could be inferred from the truth of Q would be if the truth of P were both *necessary and sufficient* for the truth of Q. With empirical phenomena this is not feasible because one can never rule out the logical possibility that other reasons exist for Q to be true than those considered when deducing that Q is implied by P. Try as we do to establish closed systems, we never can be certain that we have done so. On the other hand, it is not a fallacy to conclude that a causal hypothesis (P) is false if the correlational hypothesis (Q) deduced from it is false (i.e., disconfirmed). This is the form of the argument known by logicians as modus tollens, which has the form: "P implies Q: Q is false; therefore, P is false." Note, however, that this logic does not consider the possibility that a correlational hypothesis may be falsified because of specification errors, especially imprecision in the measurement of variables. Thus, even falsification of correlational hypotheses is not unequivocal, which suggests that one should be circumspect about using a single disconfirmation to falsify a causal hypothesis (see Cook & Campbell, 1979; Popper, 1935/1959).

For reasons such as those discussed above, the philosopher Popper (1935/1959) has argued that scientists can never deduce the validity of a general proposition about the world from the truth of a proposition concerning a particular event deduced from the general proposition. On the other hand, Popper argued that one can correctly infer the falsity of a general proposition from the falsity of a proposition concerning a specific event deduced from the general proposition. Thus, as far as deductive logic is concerned, Popper argued that science can only *infer* the falsity of general theoretical propositions from particular events, never their validity. Nevertheless, Popper recognized the inclination of scientists to act as if their general theories are true when empirical consequences deduced from them are confirmed in experience. He euphemistically referred to these situations as those in which theories are "corroborated" by the confirmation of their particular consequences.

We have already discussed the point that the inference that a causal hypothesis is true when a consequence (prediction) deduced from that hypothesis is confirmed in experience would involve the commission of a logical fallacy. The logical possibility always exists that the prediction deduced from the causal hypothesis is confirmed for reasons other than those we considered when formulating the causal hypothesis. This limitation on the possibility for logical inference from empirically confirmed consequences, is, as discussed in the early part of this chapter, a function of the fact that it is not possible to test empirically all conditions required for confirmatory analysis, or to be assured that empirically tested assumptions have been fully satisfied. It follows directly that causal inference based on confirmatory analysis must be tenuous, which is to say, subject to alternative explanations. In other words, the limitation comes down to a limitation associated with all attempts to establish inductive forms of reasoning where one seeks to generalize from particulars in experience. On the other hand, the inference that a causal hypothesis is false when a prediction deduced from that hypothesis is disconfirmed in experience is not an invalid inference as long as one is committed to act as if the deduced consequence is false. It is a question of the correct use of deductive logic, not whether deductive logic leads to necessary truths about the world. Thus, one appears to be in a better position to infer the falsity of causal hypotheses rather than to infer their validity on the basis of experience. This is essentially the position advocated by Popper (1935/1959) and echoed by others (see Cook & Campbell, 1979; Duncan, 1975; Heise, 1975; Namboodiri et al., 1975).

There is something disturbing, however, about a position that suggests that all we can do in science is negate something, never affirm it. This position seems to run counter to our experiences in which scientific theories are offered as explanations of phenomena. It runs counter to the passion with which we and others affirm the truth of a scientific idea or the confidence we have when we use laws of physics to build bridges and to operate space shuttles. To be a scientist involves committing oneself to the affirmation of corroborated theories while at the same time submitting them continuously to empirical tests.

In our view, one must understand Popper's (1935/1959) emphasis on the falsification of theory as the outcome of an analysis of what could rationally be concluded in attempts to validate scientific theories. Popper explicitly ruled out as irrelevant for his analysis psychological (extralogical) concerns such as how theories might be formulated or developed from experience. Presumably, he would also rule out as irrelevant psychological concerns about what people would do once they have subjected a theory to the test. Thus, if people act as if a theory is true when it is merely corroborated, this must be for Popper merely a quirk of human behavior having no rational justification on the basis of the evidence used to validate the theory. But being a matter of extralogical behavior, it is beyond the confines of his analysis. There can be no question that acting as if a theory is true when it has been merely corroborated—which we may regard as a form of inductive behavior—is an important aspect of the scientific enterprise. Thus, if Popper's account of the scientific enterprise seems distorted to us, it is because it is actually limited to only the logical aspect of the enterprise.

It may be disheartening to find that corroboration of a structural model guarantees neither that the model is unassailably correct nor that it yields a unique explanation of relations among variables in the model. But, as we have endeavored to explain, this is the limitation of inductive "inference." What one must keep in mind is that the goal of confirmatory analysis in science is to attempt to explain how and why variables occur and are related. An intuitive approach to causality and causal explanation in psychological research involves proposing functional relations among variables in the form of structural models (theories). If the causal explanations represented by functional relations (equations) are empirically corroborated by data, this does not mean that we will enter into a state of suspended animation. Rather, we will seek to disseminate our inferences regarding causal explanations so that others may test them. We also seek to apply the explanations to solve problems, a process that furnishes additional sources of confirmation/disconfirmation. We continue in these and other endeavors until some other explanation comes along to replace the present one, or until we encounter one, and preferably more than one, instance in which it is clearly disconfirmed. One must strive to obtain explanations for events, even if to do so involves ambiguities and pitfalls.

But what happens if a particular set of observations leads to the corroboration of not just one but of two or more distinct causal theories? Popper (1935/1959) considered this problem, and suggested that theories that are more easily falsifiable are to be preferred to those that are less easily falsifiable. To illustrate this rationale, consider that an easily falsifiable manifest variable model is one in which a reasonably parsimonious structure is used to explain a large number of observed correlations among manifest variables. In other words, the number of parameters that is predicted to equal zero is large in comparison to the number of parameters that is free to vary and to be estimated, which is to say that the model is highly overidentified. Thus, we have a comparatively large number of overidentifying restrictions, any one of which could disconfirm the model. In contrast, if only a few parameters are predicted to equal zero and the rest are left to be estimated, then only a few overidentifying restrictions remain with which to test goodness of fit. Using Popper's suggestion, the former model should be preferred over the latter model because it is more easily falsified (and parsimonious). The larger the number of overidentifying restrictions (i.e., the higher the degree of overidentification), the more likely the model is to be falsified. (Note that we are dealing here only with the second test of confirmation/disconfirmation. This test is considered by many to be the more crucial test of goodness of fit because nonsignificant, estimated structural parameters of minor theoretical relevance can be theory trimmed without major theoretical damage to a model. Nevertheless, a nonsignificant estimate of a parameter of major theoretical significance is seriously damaging to a theoretical model and results in disconfirmation based on the first test of confirmation/disconfirmation.)

A second procedure that builds faith in a corroborated structural model is to subject multiple, highly overidentified structural models to confirmatory analysis. In general, psychology has no dearth of theories regarding the causes of human events. In fact, the problem is often too many competing theories rather than too few theories. Each theory represents an alternative explanation of events, and the recommended procedure is (a) to develop a highly overidentified structural model for each theory, where each model includes causal hypotheses that conflict with those of the other models, (b) to subject each structural model to a confirmatory analysis, and (c) to contrast the results of the confirmatory analyses and ascertain which one of the structural models has the best fit with the data (i.e., provides the most plausible explanation). It is possible, of course, that two or more models will still have essentially equivalent fits with the data. This is a worthwhile finding, however, because the investigator will not now accept blindly one model as corroborated. Furthermore, assuming that some models were disconfirmed, the investigator has a basis for identifying a reduced set of plausible models. The next step is to articulate further each plausible model in the interest of deriving conflicting hypotheses that can be tested in future confirmatory analyses.

In conclusion, no claim can be made that causal inferences lead to unique or unassailably correct causal explanations. It must be recognized that accumulation of scientific knowledge may provide a basis for refuting an inference at some future date. The process of causal inference rests on the premise that we will use the knowledge that is presently available to attempt to explain why psychological phenomena occur. This is the historical premise of science; it is what one does when he or she behaves as a scientist.

4

An Overview of Latent Variable Structural Models

INTRODUCTION

☐ Up to this point we have discussed linear causal modeling with observed or manifest variables. We will now consider the more general case in which some of the variables of a linear causal model are *latent* or unobserved variables. As defined earlier, a latent variable is a hypothetical or theoretical construct, which is to say, an unobserved variable presumed to exist within a structural model but for which direct measurements are not available.

Linear models with latent and manifest variables are not new in psychology. Psychologists have worked with such models for over 60 years in connection with common factor analysis and the classical theory of reliability with its "true" and "error" scores. However, structural equation modeling with latent variables became practical only after statisticians working in the area of factor analysis (Jöreskog, 1970) saw ways to generalize these efforts to encompass linear structural equation modeling (Wiley & Wiley, 1970; Keesling, 1972; Wiley, 1973; Jöreskog, 1973, 1978; Jöreskog & Sörbom, 1979, Jöreskog & Goldberger, 1975). These developments in statistical theory provided the basis for the development and distribution of general-purpose computer programs for structural equation modeling with latent variables such as Jöreskog and Sörbom's (1978) LISREL IV program and McDonald's (1978, 1980) COSAN program. As a result, increasing numbers of psychologists are today discovering the usefulness of structural equation models in their research, while increasing numbers of sociologists, econometricians, and geneticists are using structural equation models with latent variables.

REASONS FOR LATENT VARIABLE MODELS

There are a number of reasons for considering the use of latent variables in modeling causal relationships.

First, since most of our theoretical constructs are abstractions, it is convenient to distinguish between a hypothetical construct as a latent variable and a concrete realization of it in a particular manifest variable.

Second, the concrete realization of a construct is nonunique; the same theoretical construct may be operationalized in any number of ways. Thus, we can think of a domain of manifest observed variables, all of which have in common the same underlying construct. For example, general intelligence may be measured by various tests—for example, the Stanford-Binet, the Wechsler Adult Intelligence Scale (WAIS), Raven's Progressive Matrices, and the Lorge-Thorndike Test. In principle, the number of ways in which a construct may be implemented operationally through manifest variables is unlimited.

Third, our observed variables may involve fallible measurements, which means that in addition to the effects of the hypothesized constructs, the values of our variables may also reflect errors of measurement of an unsystematic nature. Attempts to estimate structural parameters with manifest variable approaches when the variables contain nonnegligible errors of measurement may lead to serious bias in the estimates.

Fourth, measurement of manifest variables may include systematic or nonrandom sources of error, such as variation due to method, context, or person variables. These too, if overlooked or ignored, will lead to serious bias in estimates of structural parameters. Latent variable approaches provide means to deal with both random and nonrandom measurement errors.

Finally, we may not be able to devise direct, univocal measures of the theoretical construct in question because the effects of the theoretical construct may never occur in isolation apart from the effects of other causal variables. For example, we may never be able to devise a measure of general intelligence (conceived of as the capacity to perceive relationships) without its effects being confounded with other variables, such as the various capacities involved in coding the content of the stimulus materials (e.g., verbal, figural, numerical). In general, it is situations such as the above that may be treated with models involving both manifest and latent variables.

DEVELOPING LATENT VARIABLE MODELS

Consider the *latent structural model* shown in Figure 4.1a. This model is essentially the model of the causes and effects of perceived role overload presented earlier in connection with Figure 2.1. However, in this case the variables in the model are represented by *perfectly reliable latent variables*. They are perfectly reliable latent variables because they correspond to hypothetical constructs that have not yet been operationalized by linking them to specific manifest measures. The four hypothetical constructs or latent variables are (1) management's expectations regarding quality of employees' role performance (expected quality), (2) management's expectations regarding quantity of employees' role performance (expected quantity), (3) employees' perceptions of role overload (role overload), and (4) employees' state anxiety. The model states that among employees in an organization, the more their supervisors expect high quality of performance, and the more their supervisors expect high quantity of performance, the more the employees will perceive role overload, which in turn will increase the employees' levels of state anxiety. The unlabeled disturbance terms assigned to perceptions of role overload and to state anxiety, however, indicate that there may be other causes of these variables.

For the sake of illustration, let us assume that the conditions for the appropriateness of a theoretical model (Conditions 1 through 7) are satisfied and that this model is an accurate representation of causal relationships. Also let us assume, again for the sake of illustration, that the correlation between the two latent exogenous variables, expected quality of role performance and expected quantity in role performance, is zero.

So far, we have stated our model only in terms of latent variables. It is not possible to estimate the strengths of causal relationships with latent variables alone because the latent variables are unmeasured. To estimate the strengths of these causal relations, it is necessary to operationalize each of the latent variables in terms of manifest variables that are believed to be caused by a latent variable. In this sense, each latent variable has the role of a common factor, and the manifest variables serve as *manifest indicators* of the common factor.

Figure 4.1b presents possible manifest indicator variables for each of the latent variables. This is referred to as the *measurement model* because it specifies presumed causal relations between latent variables (causes) and the manifest or measured variables (effects) that serve as indicators of the latent variables. For example, four indicators of expected quality of work performance might be role demands regarding (a) reduction in waste (reduction–waste), (b) reduction in number of faulty units produced (reduction–faulty units), (c) increased number of inspections (increased inspections), and (d) increased dependability of product in tests of randomly selected units (increased dependability). The small ϵ (epsilon) associated with each manifest indicator of expected quality is a disturbance term that includes all causes of the manifest variable other than the latent variable, such as measurement error and nonrandom measurement errors.

Multiple indicators are considered necessary for expected quality of work because either (a) expected quality can be manifested in a number of ways, or (b) individual indicators may be measured with error, or both a and b. In contrast, only one manifest indicator variable is associated with

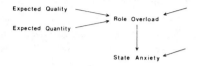

Figure 4.1a   Latent Structural Model

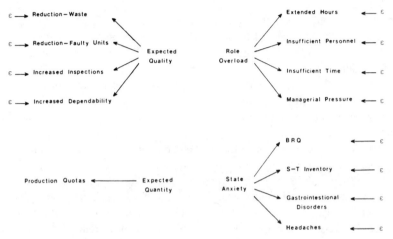

Figure 4.1b   Measurement Model Linking Latent Variables to Manifest Indicators

Figure 4.1   Illustrations of a Structural Model with a Measurement Model for a Latent Variable Analysis

the quantity-of-work latent variable, namely, the degree to which production quotas are satisfied (production quotas). Furthermore, the production-quotas variable has no disturbance term. The use of one manifest indicator variable denotes that the manifest variable is regarded as a *perfect indicator* of the latent variable. This means that the indicator is the primary way that the latent variable is manifested and that the indicator contains neither random nor nonrandom measurement errors. This appeared reasonable inasmuch as production quotas are the key measures of quantity of work, are publicly stated, and the degree to which they are satisfied is measured objectively.

Such is not the case for the role-overload and state-anxiety latent variables, for which multiple manifest measurements are often available, each of which contains error. Thus, multiple indicators are needed, which for role overload might be the extent to which employees perceive (a) the need to work extended hours (extended hours), (b) an insufficient number of employees to accomplish role demands (insufficient personnel), (c) insufficient time to complete tasks (insufficient time), and (d) managerial pressure for productivity (managerial pressure). The four manifest indicators of state anxiety might include two self-report questionnaires for state anxiety, such as (a) the Behavioral Reactions Questionnaire (BRQ; Endler & Magnusson, 1977) and (b) the State-Trait Anxiety Inventory (S—T Inventory; Spielberger, 1977), and two physiological indicators, such as (c) gastrointestinal distress and (d) headaches. Each of the manifest indicators for role overload and state anxiety are also believed to be caused by a disturbance.

When manifest variables are regarded as nonperfect indicators of latent variables, the goodness of fit of the measurement model must be tested. In the present example, this suggests that the goodness of fit of the indicators for quality of work, role overload, and state anxiety must be tested. The test takes the form of a confirmatory factor analysis, and is designed to ascertain if manifest indicator variables are related to latent variables in the manner predicted by the measurement model. The test is discussed later in this section.

Given reasonable satisfaction of the goodness of fit of the measurement model, it is possible to proceed to estimate the strengths of the causal connections among the latent variables and to test the goodness of fit of the latent structural model. Statistical procedures for accomplishing these tasks are also explained later. At this time we note only that the estimation and testing processes involve combining the measurement model with the latent structural model. The combined models for this illustration are shown in Figure 4.2. A model taking the form of Figure 4.2 is often referred to as a "latent variable model" or a "latent variable structural equation model."

LATENT VARIABLE MODELS VERSUS MANIFEST VARIABLE MODELS: THE QUESTION OF RELIABILITY

A major drawback of manifest variable models is that they will yield biased estimates of structural parameters and path coefficients linking latent, hypothetical construct variables when these variables are represented by fallible (not perfectly reliable) manifest indicator variables in a manifest variable analysis. For example, consider first the path model shown in Figure 4.3a. This is the latent structural model presented in Figure 4.1a. The variables in the model are represented by perfectly reliable, standardized latent variables. They are considered standardized because units of measurement are arbitrary, and zero means and unit variances are convenient.

Again, for the sake of illustration, let us assume that this model is an accurate representation of causal relationships. Furthermore, let us assume that in the population of employees to be considered, the (population) path coefficients associated with the latent variables are as they are given

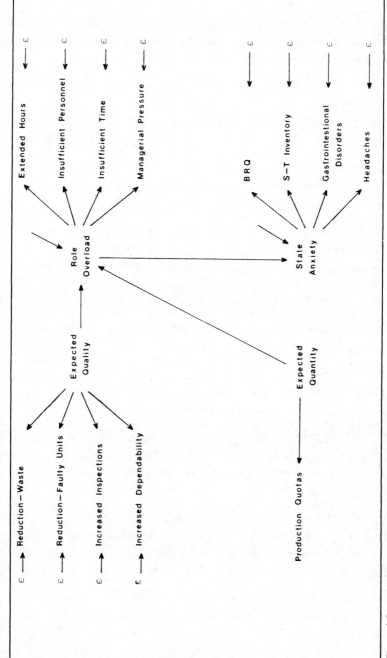

Figure 4.2   An Illustration of a Latent Variable Model

in Figure 4.3a. (Primes denote path coefficients linking latent variables). Note that the magnitudes of these path coefficients suggest that perceptions of role overload are influenced more by role expectations regarding quality of performance ($p'_{31} = .60$) than by role expectations regarding quantity of performance ($p'_{32} = .50$). Again, let us assume that the correlation between the two latent exogenous variables is zero. Finally, we assume that the two exogenous variables do not relate directly to the latent state-anxiety variable.

Suppose that for each latent variable of the model we now choose one manifest variable to serve as an indicator of the latent variable. But suppose, as often happens, that many of the manifest indicators are not perfectly reliable. Then consider Figure 4.3b, which is a latent variable model that includes both the structural and measurement models. That is, we have added four standardized manifest variables to the model, which, with the exception of production quotas, are fallible indicators of the respective latent variables. The three fallible indicators are easily identified because they are viewed as effects of a disturbance designated by ϵ. Disturbance terms are regarded as latent variables and are considered here to be in standardized form. Moreover, these latent disturbances are regarded as consisting exclusively of errors of measurement in this illustration. This means then that the measurements (scores) on each fallible manifest variable are presumed to be a function of both a latent variable and random measurement error.

Given standardized variables, the causal effects of the latent variables on the manifest variables may be represented as path coefficients. In fact, because we assume that the ϵ consist only of random measurement error, the path coefficients associated with the arrows going from the latent variables to their manifest indicators represent the square roots of the reliabilities of the manifest variables. For example, the path coefficient linking the expected-quality latent variable to its manifest indicator, increased dependability, is .81; the corresponding reliability, shown in parentheses, is .65. Note that only production quotas, the manifest indicator for the latent variable of expected quantity of role performance, has a reliability of 1.00. As before, this means that the manifest variable is a perfect indicator of the latent variable. The reliabilities of the remaining three manifest variables are less than 1.00, indicating random error in measurement and the lack of perfect correspondence between latent and manifest variables.

By processes to be explained later in this chapter, it is possible to solve for the correlations among the four manifest variables using the path coefficients shown in Figure 4.3b. These correlations can then be used to solve for the path coefficients linking the manifest variables by the OLS procedures discussed in Chapter 2. The results of the path analysis on the manifest variables are reported in Figure 4.3c.

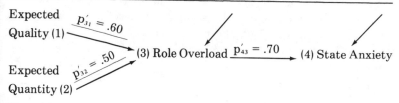

Figure 4.3a   Latent Structural Model with Path Coefficients Linking Latent Variables

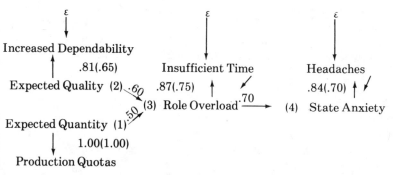

Figure 4.3b   Latent Variable Model with One Manifest Indicator for Each Latent Variable

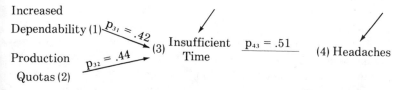

Figure 4.3c   Manifest Variable Model with Biased Estimates of Path Coefficients

Figure 4.3   Illustration of Bias in Estimates of Path Coefficients Resulting from Measurement Error in Manifest Variables

It is now interesting to compare the path coefficients in the manifest variable model (which do not have primes) in Figure 4.3c with the "correct" path coefficients of the latent variable model in Figure 4.3a. The corresponding values for these path coefficients are not the same. This means that if we use a manifest variable approach with fallible indicators of latent variables to estimate the path coefficients among the presumed perfectly reliable latent variables, then the estimates will be biased. In this illustration the estimates are all attenuated. Moreover, the bias is sufficient to lead one to reverse the relative importance of causes on a dependent variable. For example, in Figure 4.3c the path coefficient relating the indicator for expected quality of role performance (i.e., increased dependability) to the indicator for role overload (i.e., insufficient time) has a value of .42 (p_{31} = .42). This value is less than the path coefficient relating the indicator for expected quantity of role performance (production quotas) to the role overload indicator (p_{32} = .44). This is just the reverse of the "correct" situation in Figure 4.3a, where the path coefficients are $p_{31}' = .60$ and $p_{32}' = .50$, respectively.

In sum, measurement error in manifest variables may have serious consequences for confirmatory analysis. If the measurement error is regarded as nontrivial, then corrective procedures are required. Corrective options include the latent variable form of analysis to be described here, as well as other procedures described elsewhere, such as correction for attenuation in path analysis (see Kenny, 1979), and instrumental variables and two-stage least squares (see Goldberger, 1973; James & Singh, 1978).

SUMMARY

Random measurement error is not the only reason for considering latent variable models. In fact, good reasons exist for using a latent variable approach even if manifest variables can be measured with a high degree of reliability. Consider the points made earlier—that many latent variables (hypothetical constructs) are abstractions and can be operationalized by any number of manifest indicator variables. An important aspect of confirmatory analysis with latent variables is a test of the goodness of fit of an a priori measurement model, which is to say, a test of whether multiple manifest indicators are related to latent variables by a structure hypothesized by the investigator. In effect, this is a test of the construct validity of the manifest indicators and, by implication, of the adequacy of the proposed latent variables. Thus, a latent variable analysis makes possible a test of construct validity, another key measurement concern. Of at least equal importance is the fact that (a) given a good fit between a proposed measurement model and the observed data on manifest indicators, then (b) it is possible to estimate the strengths of causal relations among the latent variables. As in manifest variable models, the causal relations among latent variables are estimated within the context of a structural model relating the latent variables. Goodness-of-fit tests based on the logic of Condition 10 are performed if the latent structural model is overidentified.

In summary, latent variable analysis provides the opportunities (a) to work with perfectly reliable causes and effects, (b) to test the goodness of fit of a presumed measurement model, and (c) to test the goodness of fit of a structural model relating latent variables both in terms of estimating causal parameters and in terms of testing overidentifying restrictions.

One does not partake of the benefits of a latent variable approach without paying a heavy price. The lesser part of the price is that one must conquer a complex and often cumbersome terminology. More demanding is a requirement that one have a methodological sophistication that exceeds even that required in the most complex multivariate course generally offered in psychology. However, we believe the price is worthwhile for those desiring the benefits. In the discussion to follow, we have tried to ease the pain by focusing on the logic of the approach and merely overviewing many of the statistical equations. However, we believe that it is important to maintain fidelity with what truthfully is a very complex procedure. It is also noteworthy that the pitfalls of the latent variable procedures are not as well known as those associated with the manifest variable procedures, which is due to the fact that the latent variable approaches were developed much later than the manifest variable approaches. Finally, our attention in this chapter is focused on the operational aspects of latent variable analysis. However, as reviewed at the end of this chapter, the seven conditions pertaining to the appropriateness of theoretical models for confirmatory analysis are every bit as important for latent variable models as they are for manifest variable models.

REPRESENTATION OF STRUCTURAL MODELS WITH LATENT VARIABLES

NOTATION

With the need now to distinguish between manifest and latent variables in our discussion, we need a new notation. The notation we will use, with minor modifications on our part, was suggested by Bentler and Weeks (1980). In Figure 4.4 we show the hypothetical structural model of Figure 4.3a in the new notation. In this notation latent exogenous and latent endogenous variables are represented in structural diagrams by letters enclosed in circles or ellipses. Latent exogenous variables are designated by the Greek letter ξ (xi) with subscripts, while latent endogenous variables are designated by the Greek letter η (eta) with subscripts. Disturbance terms or variables are always treated as latent variables and are identified by the Greek letter ϵ (epsilon) with subscripts but without enclosing circles or ellipses.

As in structural diagrams with manifest variables, causal connections between variables are indicated by arrows, with each arrow pointing from a causal variable to an effect variable. The absence of an arrow between two variables indicates the lack of a direct causal connection between these variables. Associated with each arrow is a structural parameter that indicates the number of units of change in the effect variable resulting from a unit change in the causal variable, holding all other causes of the effect constant. A structural parameter corresponding to a missing arrow is regarded as fixed and equal to zero. The structural parameter associated with an arrow from an exogenous variable to an endogenous variable is designated by the Greek letter γ (gamma) with subscripts, the left-most subscript indicating the number of the endogenous variable and the right-most subscript indicating the number of the exogenous variable. The structural parameter associated with an arrow from one endogenous variable to another endogenous variable is indicated by the Greek letter α (alpha) with subscripts, with the left-most subscript indicating the number of the endogenous variable that is the effect variable and the right-most subscript indicating the number of the endogenous variable that is the causal variable. The structural parameter associated with an arrow from a disturbance variable to an endogenous variable is designated by the Greek letter δ (delta) with subscripts. Two-headed arrows connecting pairs of exogenous variables or disturbance variables indicate nonzero covariance relations between these variables.

In Figure 4.4 ξ_1 and ξ_2 are latent exogenous variables. Both are causes of latent endogenous variable η_1 but not of latent endogenous variable η_2. The two-headed arrow between latent exogenous variables ξ_1 and ξ_2 indicates a presumed nonzero covariance between them. Latent endogenous variable η_1 is in turn a cause of latent endogenous variable η_2. Variables ϵ_1 and ϵ_2 are disturbance variables, each associated with its respective endogenous variable. The disturbance variables are presumed to be uncorrelated.

A model with all latent variables in it, like the model in Figure 4.4, cannot be tested empirically until it is operationalized by linking the latent variables to manifest variables in an appropriate way. The linkage of a latent variable to manifest variables in a model is accomplished by including multiple manifest *indicator* variables that are presumed to be effects of (i.e., caused by) the latent variable. A sufficient number of manifest indicator variables are required so that the structural parameters indicating the effects of the latent variables on the indicator variables will be overidentified. This allows one not only to estimate uniquely these structural parameters but also to test the presumptions about the relations between manifest indicator variables and the latent variables. Such a situation is illustrated in Figure 4.5, which shows four indicator variables $y_1, \ldots, y_4$, each an effect of latent exogenous variable ξ_1 and one of the mutually uncorrelated disturbance variables $\epsilon_1, \ldots, \epsilon_4$. Figure 4.5 also serves to introduce notation for manifest variables in structural models with both manifest and latent variables. Notice that variables $y_1, \ldots, y_4$ are enclosed in boxes. This means they are manifest variables. They are furthermore designated by the letter y, which indicates that they are

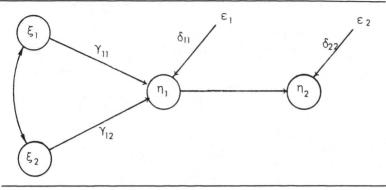

Figure 4.4   Structural Model with Six Latent Variables

ξ_1 and ξ_2 are exogenous variables.

η_1 and η_2 are endogenous variables.

ϵ_1 and ϵ_2 are distrubance variables.

manifest endogenous variables. The Greek letter γ (gamma) is again used to indicate a structural coefficient of a causal relation between an exogenous variable and an endogenous variable. Moreover, the Greek letter δ (delta) is again used to indicate the structural coefficient of the effect of a disturbance variable on an endogenous variable.

Our notation also permits us to have manifest exogenous variables. As shown later, these will be designated by the letter x enclosed in a box. However, manifest variables selected as indicators of a latent exogenous variable are ordinarily endogenous and not exogenous variables. This is because the manifest variables chosen as indicators of a latent exogenous variable are usually effects of not only the latent exogenous variable in question, but of extraneous variables as well, which are subsumed under the respective disturbance variables attached to the manifest indicator variables. Not the least important of these extraneous variables will be errors of measurement. Furthermore, the effects of a latent variable on its manifest indicator variables may be measured in different units of measurement, which would be reflected in different values for the structural parameters relating the latent variable to its respective manifest indicator variables.

However, before we proceed, we must consider how we would treat an ideal situation in which we had more than one presumably "pure," disturbance-free manifest indicator variable of a latent variable. Figure 4.6 illustrates just such a model. Variables $y_1, \ldots, y_4$ are disturbance-free manifest indicators of latent exogenous variable ξ_1. By "disturbance-free" in this case we mean that each indicator variable has only the latent variable ξ_1 as a cause. There are no extraneous causes in addition to the latent variable ξ_1. In this example the indicator variables are perfectly

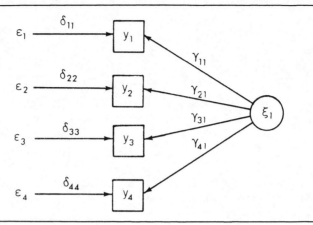

Figure 4.5   **A Structural Model for a Latent Variable with Four Indicator Variables**

correlated with the latent exogenous variable (and with one another). They differ among themselves in having different values for the structural parameters relating them to the latent exogenous variable because, say, they are measured with different units of measurement.

When we have more than one disturbance-free indicator of a latent variable, we should discard all but one of these for use in a model. This will avoid the problem of singularity for the variance/covariance matrix of the manifest variables that arises from having several variables that are simple linear combinations of other variables in the analysis. (A singular or noninvertable sample variance/covariance matrix for the manifest variables would preclude obtaining estimates of the structural parameters of the model). The indicator variable retained and the latent variable it "indicates" can then be treated as simply identical. That is, we can replace the latent variable by the manifest variable in the model. If the latent variable replaced by a "disturbance-free" manifest indicator has a disturbance term, because the latent variable is an endogenous variable as well, then the manifest indicator acquires the disturbance term of the original latent variable. This disturbance is not the disturbance of which the manifest indicator is "disturbance-free." Saying that the manifest indicator is a disturbance-free indicator simply means that, relative to the latent variable as a cause of the indicator, there are no other extraneous causes. This says nothing about the extraneous causes of the latent variable that the indicator may replace.

Thus, given these notational considerations, we might have a model like that in Figure 4.7. In this model we have one latent exogenous variable, ξ_1, linked to four manifest variables, $y_2, \ldots, y_5$, each of which is also linked to one of four disturbance variables $\epsilon_2, \ldots, \epsilon_5$. We also have a single manifest exogenous variable x_2. Variables ξ_1 and x_2 are also causes

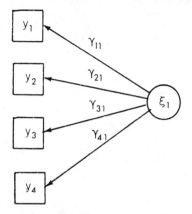

Figure 4.6   A Structural Model for Four Perfectly Reliable Indicators of a Single Latent Variable

of a manifest endogenous variable, y_1, to which is also drawn a disturbance variable ϵ_1 representing a component of y_1 not caused by the exogenous variables. Note that with this example we have introduced a manifest exogenous variable and have denoted it by the subscripted letter x contained within a box. Also we have used the Greek letter γ (gamma) to denote structural parameters relating exogenous variables to endogenous variables, while δ (delta) denotes the structural parameter relating a disturbance variable to an endogenous variable.

A situation in which one has four exogenous manifest variables regarded as causes of a single latent variable, which we illustrate by a model in Figure 4.8, should not be confused with a situation in which one has four manifest indicator variables, each an effect of a common latent variable, such as is illustrated in Figure 4.7. In Figure 4.8 we presume that the manifest variables $x_1, \ldots, x_4$ are perfectly reliable but not strongly correlated, exogenous variables. Each of these manifest exogenous variables is a distinct cause of latent endogenous variable η_1, which also is an effect of a latent disturbance variable ϵ_1. Latent variable η_1 is in turn a common cause of manifest indicator variables $y_2, \ldots, y_5$, each with its respective disturbance variable $\epsilon_2, \ldots, \epsilon_5$. Again γ refers to structural parameters relating exogeneous to endogenous variables, α to structural parameters relating endogenous to endogenous variables, and δ to structural parameters relating disturbance terms to endogenous variables.

Note also that in these models we have numbered variables in the following way: Exogenous variables are grouped together and latent exogeneous variables are numbered first, before manifest exogenous variables are numbered. Similarly, endogenous variables are grouped together and latent endogenous variables are numbered before manifest endogenous

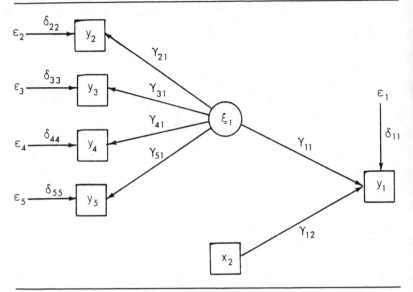

Figure 4.7   A structural model with two exogenous variables and five endogenous variables where ξ_1 is a latent variable with four indicators, $y_2 \ldots , y_5$; x_2 is a manifest exogenous variable; and y_1 is a manifest endogenous variable caused by ξ_1 and x_2.

variables. Disturbance variables receive the number of the corresponding endogenous variable.

STRUCTURAL EQUATIONS

Consider the structural model in Figure 4.9. This model represents an operationalization of the latent construct variables of the model in Figures 4.3a and 4.4. Note that the model contains both latent and manifest exogenous variables as well as latent and manifest endogenous variables. ξ_1 is a latent exogenous variable operationalized by four manifest endogenous indicator variables $y_{11}, \ldots , y_{14}$. x_2 is a manifest exogenous variable. ξ_1 and x_2 are both causes of a latent endogenous variable η_1, as indicated by the arrows from ξ_1 and x_2 to η_1. Four manifest endogenous variables $y_3, \ldots , y_6$, serve as indicators of η_1 as indicated by the arrows from η_1 to these variables. η_1 is also a cause of latent endogenous variable η_2, which in turn serves as a common cause of manifest endogenous indicator variables $y_7, \ldots , y_{10}$. Further note that each endogenous variable in this model has one of the latent disturbance variables $\epsilon_1, \ldots , \epsilon_{14}$ associated with it. Also observe that there are no double-headed arrows between ξ_1 and x_2, indicating that these exogenous variables are uncorrelated, while there are also no double-headed arrows among any of the disturbance variables, indicating that they too are mutually uncorrelated.

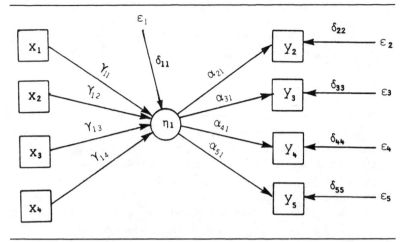

Figure 4.8   A structural model in which four manifest exogenous variables $x_1 \ldots ,$
x_4 are causes of a latent variable η_1, which in turn is a common cause
of manifest endogenous variables $y_2 \ldots , y_5$.

As in the case with models with manifest variables, we may express the
model in Figure 4.9 by a system of simultaneous equations. One equation
is developed for each latent or manifest endogenous variable, which means
we shall have fourteen equations. Each equation includes the latent and/or
manifest variables that have a direct effect on the endogenous variable,
including disturbance variables. This system of equations follows:

$$
\begin{aligned}
\eta_1 &= & & \gamma_{11}\xi_1 &+ \gamma_{12}x_2 &+ & \delta_{11}\epsilon_1 \\
\eta_2 &= \alpha_{21}\eta_1 &+ & & & & \delta_{22}\epsilon_2 \\
y_3 &= \alpha_{31}\eta_1 &+ & & & & \delta_{33}\epsilon_3 \\
y_4 &= \alpha_{41}\eta_1 &+ & & & & \delta_{44}\epsilon_4 \\
y_5 &= \alpha_{51}\eta_1 &+ & & & & \delta_{55}\epsilon_5 \\
y_6 &= \alpha_{61}\eta_1 &+ & & & & \delta_{66}\epsilon_6 \\
y_7 &= & \alpha_{72}\eta_2 &+ & & & \delta_{77}\epsilon_7 \\
y_8 &= & \alpha_{82}\eta_2 &+ & & & \delta_{88}\epsilon_8 \\
y_9 &= & \alpha_{92}\eta_2 &+ & & & \delta_{99}\epsilon_9 \\
y_{10} &= & \alpha_{10,2}\eta_2 &+ & & & \delta_{10,10}\epsilon_{10} \\
y_{11} &= & & \gamma_{11,1}\xi_1 &+ & & \delta_{11,11}\epsilon_{11} \\
y_{12} &= & & \gamma_{12,1}\xi_1 &+ & & \delta_{12,12}\epsilon_{12} \\
y_{13} &= & & \gamma_{13,1}\xi_1 &+ & & \delta_{13,13}\epsilon_{13} \\
y_{14} &= & & \gamma_{14,1}\xi_1 &+ & & \delta_{14,14}\epsilon_{14}
\end{aligned}
$$

$$[4.1]$$

MATRIX EQUATIONS

The model in Figure 4.9 is a relatively simple, linear structural model
with latent variables. But latent variable models can become much more

complex. For instance, a model may involve many latent causal and effect variables, each of which is represented by a number of manifest indicator variables. In other latent variable models, the exogenous variables may be intercorrelated. Disturbance variables may also be mutually intercorrelated. Ordinary algebraic notation thus becomes extremely cumbersome to deal with in structural models with latent variables. And so, latent variable models are usually described with matrix algebraic equations.

There have been a number of notational systems proposed for representing structural equation models by equations in matrix algebra. A very popular system of matrix notation is used in connection with the LISREL computer program of Jöreskog and Sörbom (1978). This notation distinguishes between a structural equation model and a measurement model. Distinguishing between these two models is based on the assumption that all structural equation models are ultimately hypothetical models involving latent variables. But to confirm a structural equation model we must link the hypothetical structural model to observed variables by constructing, for each hypothetical latent variable of the structural model, a number of manifest variables that measure effects of the latent variable. The latent variables of the structural model are then regarded as common factors of the manifest indicator variables. The measurement model thus refers to the structure expressed as a confirmatory factor-analytic model of the relationship between the hypothetical latent variables and their manifest indicator variables. However, a quirk of the LISREL notation is that no manifest indicator variable may be an effect of both a latent exogenous and a latent endogenous variable at the same time. Furthermore, the distinction in the LISREL notation between the structural parameters of the structural equation model and the "factor loadings" of the measurement model introduces unnecessary complications in the algorithm and the computer code needed to implement the estimation of these parameters.

In addition to the LISREL notation, a number of other notations have been proposed, apparently in an attempt to find a general model that contains all structural models—including structural equation models, analysis of covariance structure models, and common factor-analysis models—as special cases. Of note are McDonald's (1978, 1980) Covariance Structure Analysis model (COSAN) and associated program, and Bentler's (1979) model. McArdle (1979, 1980) proposed that all these models and their notations are special cases of each other. He suggested that these models could all be seen as special cases of a very simple but general model in which there is no distinction notationally between a structural model and a measurement model nor a need for the multiple levels of nested orders of factors, as had been proposed by McDonald (1978) or Bentler (1976). Bentler and Weeks (1980) proposed a matrix notation for a general structural equation model that may be seen as a specialization of McArdle's (1979). We shall use the Bentler and Weeks (1980) matrix notation, with minor modifications, in the present discussion.

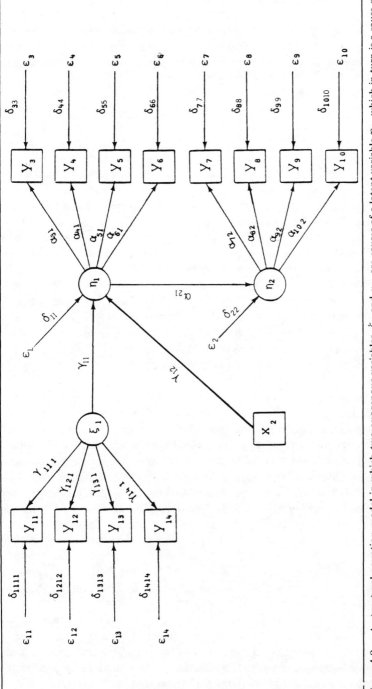

Figure 4.9   A structural equation model in which two exogenous variables, ξ_1 and x_2, are causes of a latent variable η_1, which in turn is a cause of latent endogenous variable η_2. Each of the latent variables in the model is represented by four manifest variables.

According to Bentler and Weeks (1980), there are in structural equation models two basic kinds of variables—independent and dependent variables. In structural diagrams dependent variables are those variables to which arrows point from other variables. Independent variables do not have causal arrows pointing to them. Now, an examination of any structural diagram such as Figure 4.9 will show that both latent and manifest exogenous variables (ξ and x) as well as latent disturbance variables (ϵ) have no causal arrows pointing to them. They are independent variables. On the other hand, latent and manifest endogenous variables (η and y) have arrows pointing to them and are therefore dependent variables. We will now see how this distinction between independent and dependent variables is made in matrix notation for structural equation models with manifest and latent variables.

The "expanded" matrix equation representing the 16-variable model in Figure 4.9 is given in Table 4.1. Dependent variables are represented in a random vector η^* (eta star) that may be partitioned as $\eta^{*'} = [\eta', y']$, where η' is a (transposed) random subvector of latent dependent variables and y' is a (transposed) random subvector of manifest dependent variables. (By "transposed" is meant that the array has been rearranged so that rows become columns and columns become rows. For a single-column vector, a one-dimensional array, transposing this vector means the column becomes a row of elements—which we do here to make it convenient to display the vector in the text). The number of latent dependent variables in η' is indicated by m_1; the number of manifest dependent variables in y' is indicated by m_2. The total number of dependent variables is indicated by m, where $m = m_1 + m_2$. The order of η^* is thus m × 1.

Independent variables are all included in a single random vector ξ^* (xi star). This vector may be partitioned to distinguish between manifest and latent exogenous variables and disturbance variables. Thus we may write $\xi^{*'} = [\xi', x', \epsilon']$, where ξ' stands for a (transposed) subvector of latent exogenous variables, x' stands for a (transposed) subvector of manifest exogenous variables, and ϵ' stands for a (transposed) subvector of latent disturbance variables. The number of latent exogenous variables included in ξ' is n_1; the number of manifest exogenous variables in x is n_2; and the number of disturbance variables in ϵ' is equal to m (the number of dependent variables). The number of independent variables in $\xi^{*'}$ is thus $n_1 + n_2 + m = n$, and so the order of ξ^* is n × 1.

The structural parameters α_{ij} that relate dependent to dependent variables are included in the square m × m matrix A (alpha). Each row of A corresponds to one of the dependent variables and contains the structural parameters of those other dependent variables that are causes of that dependent variable. The structural parameter in the ith row and j^{th} column of A thus represents the amount of change in the ith variable that results from a unit of change in the jth dependent variable. If the element in the ith row and j^{th} column is a zero, this means that the jth dependent variable is not a cause of the ith dependent variable. The elements of the diagonal of $\underline{A}$ are thus ordinarily zero, meaning that a dependent variable does not cause itself. In recursive models the order of the dependent variables can be arranged so that the $\underline{A}$ matrix is lower triangular, that is, only zeros are above the diagonal of $\underline{A}$, implying that a dependent variable only causes other dependent variables beyond it in their relative order. In nonrecursive models such as those involving reciprocal causation, the $\underline{A}$ matrix will have nonzero elements both below and above the diagonal.

The structural parameters that relate independent to dependent variables are contained in the matrix $\underline{\Gamma}^*$ (gamma star). The matrix $\underline{\Gamma}^* = [\underline{\Gamma}:\underline{\Delta}]$ is partitioned into the $m \times (n_1 + n_2)$ matrix $\underline{\Gamma}$ and the $m \times m$ matrix $\underline{\Delta}$ (delta). The rows of $\underline{\Gamma}$ correspond to the different dependent variables. The columns of $\underline{\Gamma}$ correspond to the different exogenous variables. A zero element in the ith row and k^{th} column of $\underline{\Gamma}$ means that the kth exogenous variable is not a cause of the ith variable. In the present example $\underline{\Gamma}$ is a 14×2 submatrix. $\underline{\Delta}$ contains the structural parameters relating the dependent variables to their respective disturbance variables. The rows of $\underline{\Delta}$ thus also correspond to the different dependent variables, while the columns of $\underline{\Delta}$ correspond to the different disturbance variables. Normally, $\underline{\Delta}$ is a diagonal matrix (sometimes even an identity matrix) with zeros everywhere except in the principal diagonal. That $\underline{\Delta}$ is a diagonal matrix reflects the fact that each dependent variable is directly associated with a different disturbance variable. Thus δ_{ii} is the structural parameter relating the ith variable to its corresponding disturbance variable. In the present example $\underline{\Delta}$ is a 14×14 matrix.

We have summarized the notation we will use in Table 4.2. Let us now turn to a more compact form for the general matrix formulation of the linear structural equation model with latent and manifest variables. This form is given in the general case by:

$$\begin{bmatrix} \underline{\eta} \\ \underline{y} \end{bmatrix} = \underline{A} \begin{bmatrix} \underline{\eta} \\ \underline{y} \end{bmatrix} + [\underline{\Gamma}:\underline{\Delta}] \begin{bmatrix} \underline{\xi} \\ \underline{x} \\ \underline{\varepsilon} \end{bmatrix} \qquad [4.2a]$$

or more simply by

$$\underline{\eta}^* = \underline{A}\underline{\eta}^* + \underline{\Gamma}^*\underline{\xi}^* \qquad [4.2b]$$

The dependent variables in $\underline{\eta}^*$ are found on both sides of equations 4.2a and 4.2b. This is not the usual form in which a structural equation is written. Wiley (1973) recommends the following: Bring the expression containing the matrix $\underline{A}$ from the right side over to the left side of the equation and then factor $\underline{\eta}^*$ from the resulting expression to obtain $(\underline{I} -$

TABLE 4.1
An Explicit Rendering of the Matrix Equation for the System of Simultaneous Equations in Equation 4.1

$$
\underset{\underline{\eta}^*}{
\begin{bmatrix}
n_1 \\ n_2 \\ Y_3 \\ Y_4 \\ Y_5 \\ Y_6 \\ Y_7 \\ Y_8 \\ Y_9 \\ Y_{10} \\ Y_{11} \\ Y_{12} \\ Y_{13} \\ Y_{14}
\end{bmatrix}}
=
\underset{\underline{A}}{
\begin{bmatrix}
0 & 0 & 0 & 0 & 0 & 0 & 0 & 0 & 0 & 0 & 0 & 0 & 0 & 0 \\
\alpha_{21} & 0 & 0 & 0 & 0 & 0 & 0 & 0 & 0 & 0 & 0 & 0 & 0 & 0 \\
\alpha_{31} & 0 & 0 & 0 & 0 & 0 & 0 & 0 & 0 & 0 & 0 & 0 & 0 & 0 \\
\alpha_{41} & 0 & 0 & 0 & 0 & 0 & 0 & 0 & 0 & 0 & 0 & 0 & 0 & 0 \\
\alpha_{51} & 0 & 0 & 0 & 0 & 0 & 0 & 0 & 0 & 0 & 0 & 0 & 0 & 0 \\
\alpha_{61} & 0 & 0 & 0 & 0 & 0 & 0 & 0 & 0 & 0 & 0 & 0 & 0 & 0 \\
0 & \alpha_{72} & 0 & 0 & 0 & 0 & 0 & 0 & 0 & 0 & 0 & 0 & 0 & 0 \\
0 & \alpha_{82} & 0 & 0 & 0 & 0 & 0 & 0 & 0 & 0 & 0 & 0 & 0 & 0 \\
0 & \alpha_{92} & 0 & 0 & 0 & 0 & 0 & 0 & 0 & 0 & 0 & 0 & 0 & 0 \\
0 & \alpha_{10\,2} & 0 & 0 & 0 & 0 & 0 & 0 & 0 & 0 & 0 & 0 & 0 & 0 \\
0 & 0 & 0 & 0 & 0 & 0 & 0 & 0 & 0 & 0 & 0 & 0 & 0 & 0 \\
0 & 0 & 0 & 0 & 0 & 0 & 0 & 0 & 0 & 0 & 0 & 0 & 0 & 0 \\
0 & 0 & 0 & 0 & 0 & 0 & 0 & 0 & 0 & 0 & 0 & 0 & 0 & 0 \\
0 & 0 & 0 & 0 & 0 & 0 & 0 & 0 & 0 & 0 & 0 & 0 & 0 & 0
\end{bmatrix}}
\underset{\underline{\eta}^*}{
\begin{bmatrix}
n_1 \\ n_2 \\ Y_3 \\ Y_4 \\ Y_5 \\ Y_6 \\ Y_7 \\ Y_8 \\ Y_9 \\ Y_{10} \\ Y_{11} \\ Y_{12} \\ Y_{13} \\ Y_{14}
\end{bmatrix}}
+
$$

$$
\underset{\underline{\Gamma}^*}{
\begin{bmatrix}
\gamma_{11} & \gamma_{12} & \delta_{11} & 0 & 0 & 0 & 0 & 0 & 0 & 0 & 0 & 0 & 0 & 0 & 0 & 0 \\
0 & 0 & 0 & \delta_{22} & 0 & 0 & 0 & 0 & 0 & 0 & 0 & 0 & 0 & 0 & 0 & 0 \\
0 & 0 & 0 & 0 & \delta_{33} & 0 & 0 & 0 & 0 & 0 & 0 & 0 & 0 & 0 & 0 & 0 \\
0 & 0 & 0 & 0 & 0 & \delta_{44} & 0 & 0 & 0 & 0 & 0 & 0 & 0 & 0 & 0 & 0 \\
0 & 0 & 0 & 0 & 0 & 0 & \delta_{55} & 0 & 0 & 0 & 0 & 0 & 0 & 0 & 0 & 0 \\
0 & 0 & 0 & 0 & 0 & 0 & 0 & \delta_{66} & 0 & 0 & 0 & 0 & 0 & 0 & 0 & 0 \\
0 & 0 & 0 & 0 & 0 & 0 & 0 & 0 & \delta_{77} & 0 & 0 & 0 & 0 & 0 & 0 & 0 \\
0 & 0 & 0 & 0 & 0 & 0 & 0 & 0 & 0 & \delta_{88} & 0 & 0 & 0 & 0 & 0 & 0 \\
0 & 0 & 0 & 0 & 0 & 0 & 0 & 0 & 0 & 0 & \delta_{99} & 0 & 0 & 0 & 0 & 0 \\
0 & 0 & 0 & 0 & 0 & 0 & 0 & 0 & 0 & 0 & 0 & \delta_{10\,10} & 0 & 0 & 0 & 0 \\
\gamma_{111} & 0 & 0 & 0 & 0 & 0 & 0 & 0 & 0 & 0 & 0 & 0 & \delta_{11\,11} & 0 & 0 & 0 \\
\gamma_{121} & 0 & 0 & 0 & 0 & 0 & 0 & 0 & 0 & 0 & 0 & 0 & 0 & \delta_{12\,12} & 0 & 0 \\
\gamma_{131} & 0 & 0 & 0 & 0 & 0 & 0 & 0 & 0 & 0 & 0 & 0 & 0 & 0 & \delta_{13\,13} & 0 \\
\gamma_{141} & 0 & 0 & 0 & 0 & 0 & 0 & 0 & 0 & 0 & 0 & 0 & 0 & 0 & 0 & \delta_{14\,14}
\end{bmatrix}}
\underset{\underline{\xi}^*}{
\begin{bmatrix}
\xi_1 \\ x_2 \\ \varepsilon_1 \\ \varepsilon_2 \\ \varepsilon_3 \\ \varepsilon_4 \\ \varepsilon_5 \\ \varepsilon_6 \\ \varepsilon_7 \\ \varepsilon_8 \\ \varepsilon_9 \\ \varepsilon_{10} \\ \varepsilon_{11} \\ \varepsilon_{12} \\ \varepsilon_{13} \\ \varepsilon_{14}
\end{bmatrix}}
$$

$\underline{A}$) $\eta^* = \underline{\Gamma}^*\underline{\xi}^*$. If we then define $\underline{B} = (\underline{I} - \underline{A})$, we may write the structural equation in the canonical form more like that found in econometic textbooks

$$\underline{B}\eta^* = \underline{\Gamma}^*\underline{\xi}^* \qquad [4.3]$$

Note that the diagonal elements of $\underline{B}$ (beta) must all be unity. The nonzero, off-diagonal elements of $\underline{B}$ will be the negative values of the nonzero, off-diagonal elements of $\underline{A}$. This means that in interpreting the nature of the causal effects, one will have to mentally change the signs of the beta coefficients in the matrix $\underline{B}$. A common mistake is to fail to make these changes.

If we premultiply both sides of equation 4.3 by $\underline{B}^{-1}$ we obtain the "reduced form" of the structural model equation. The reduced-form equation gives dependent variables totally as functions of independent variables. The reduced form for equation 4.3 is:

$$\underline{\eta}^* = \underline{B}^{-1}\underline{\Gamma}^*\underline{\xi}^* \qquad [4.4]$$

The goal of structural equation models is to show how relationships among manifest variables (given by either correlations or covariances) can be explained in terms of the structural equations relating the manifest variables to other (possibly latent) variables of the model. To reach this goal we will need certain "selection" equations that "select" the manifest variables in the subvectors y and x, respectively, from the larger vectors, η^* and ξ^*, of variables (Bentler & Weeks, 1980). Consider the following selection equations:

$$\underline{y} = [\underline{0}:\underline{I}] \begin{bmatrix} \underline{\eta} \\ y \end{bmatrix} \quad \text{and} \quad \underline{x} = [\underline{0}:\underline{I}:\underline{0}] \begin{bmatrix} \underline{\xi} \\ x \\ \epsilon \end{bmatrix} \qquad [4.5a]$$

or

$$\underline{y} = \underline{G}_y\,\eta^* \quad \text{and} \quad \underline{x} = \underline{G}_x\underline{\xi}^* \qquad [4.5b]$$

$\underline{G}_y = [\underline{0}:\underline{I}]$ is a partitioned ($m_2 \times m$) "selection" matrix with $\underline{0}$ an $m_2 \times m_1$ null matrix and $\underline{I}$ an $m_2 \times m_2$ identity matrix. In other words, $\underline{G}_y$ contains zero elements everywhere except for a single element of unity in each row placed in the appropriate column of $\underline{G}_y$ to "select" a corresponding manifest dependent y variable from η^*. Similarly, $\underline{G}_x = [\underline{0}:\underline{I}:\underline{0}]$ is an $n_2 \times n$ selection matrix with the first $\underline{0}$ on the left an $n_2 \times n_1$ null matrix, $\underline{I}$ an $n_2 \times n_2$ identity matrix, and the $\underline{0}$ on the right an $n_2 \times m$ null matrix. In other words, $\underline{G}_x$ contains zero elements everywhere except for a single element of unity in each row placed in the appropriate column of G_x to select a corresponding manifest independent x variable from ξ^*. To illustrate, for the model in Figure 4.9, G_y is a 12 × 14 matrix with 0s for every element except for a single 1 in each row in the column corresponding to a manifest endogenous variable y_i in η^*. Similarly, G_x is a 1 × 16 matrix [0 1 0 0 0 0 0 0 0 0 0 0 0 0 0 0] with unity corresponding to the manifest exogenous variable x_2 in the vector $\xi^{*'} = [\xi_1, x_2, \epsilon']$.

We also need to define a matrix reflecting the variances and covariances among the independent variables of the model. As explained above, all independent variables are included in the random vector ξ^*. Thus, the matrix of variances and covariances among the independent variables is given by the matrix

$$\Phi = E(\xi^* \xi^{*'}) \tag{4.6}$$

where Φ is the Greek letter phi. The model requires that exogenous variables are independent of disturbance variables. This requirement is expressed mathematically by the requirement that $E \ \epsilon \ [\xi' : x'] = 0$, where $E( )$ is the expectation operator. The effect of this requirement appears in the matrix and may be seen in a partitioning of this matrix as

$$\Phi = \begin{bmatrix} \Phi_{\xi\xi} & \Phi_{\xi x} & 0 \\ \Phi_{x\xi} & \Phi_{xx} & 0 \\ 0 & 0 & \Phi_{\epsilon\epsilon} \end{bmatrix} \tag{4.7}$$

where $\Phi_{\xi\xi} = E\ (\xi\xi')$, $\Phi_{\xi x} = E\ (\xi x')$, $\Phi_{xx} = E(xx')$, and $\Phi_{\epsilon\epsilon} = E(\epsilon\epsilon')$. The following terms are assumed to be null matrices in equation 4.7: $\Phi_{\xi\epsilon}$, $\Phi_{x\epsilon'}$ $\Phi_{\epsilon\xi}$, and $\Phi_{\epsilon x}$.

From the reduced-form equation 4.4, the selection equations (equation 4.5) and equation 4.6, we are able to derive the variance/covariance matrix Σ_0. Σ_0 contains the "predicted" variances and covariances among the manifest variables, where by "predicted" is meant that the variances and covariances take on the values they would have if they were generated as functions of the structural parameters of a hypothetical structural equation model. The matrix equations that display Σ_0 as functions of structural parameters and covariances among independent variables are as follows:

$$\Sigma_0 = \begin{bmatrix} \Sigma_{yy} & \Sigma_{yx} \\ \\ \Sigma_{xy} & \Sigma_{xx} \end{bmatrix} \tag{4.8}$$

TABLE 4.2
Symbols Used and Their Meanings in Notation for
Structural Equation Models

Symbol	Meaning
ξ	Latent exogenous variable
η	Latent endogenous variable
ε	Latent disturbance variable
x	Manifest exogenous variable
y	Manifest endogenous variable
α	Structural parameter relating one endogenous variable to another
γ	Structural parameter relating an exogenous variable to an endogenous variable
δ	Structural parameter relating a disturbance variable to an endogenous variable
$\underset{\sim}{\xi}$	Random vector of latent exogenous variables
$\underset{\sim}{x}$	Random vector of manifest exogenous variables
$\underset{\sim}{\varepsilon}$	Random vector of disturbance variables
$\underset{\sim}{\eta}$	Random vector of latent endogenous variables
$\underset{\sim}{y}$	Random vector of manifest endogenous variables
$\underset{\sim}{\xi}*$	Random vector of independent variables $\xi*' = [\underset{\sim}{\xi}, \underset{\sim}{x}', \underset{\sim}{\varepsilon}']$.
$\underset{\sim}{\eta}*$	Random vector of dependent variables $\eta*' = [\underset{\sim}{\eta}', \underset{\sim}{y}']$.
$\underset{\sim}{A}$	Alpha matrix of structural coefficients for endogenous variables.
$\underset{\sim}{B}$	Beta matrix, $\underset{\sim}{B} = \underset{\sim}{I} - \underset{\sim}{A}$.
$\underset{\sim}{\Gamma}$	Gamma matrix of structural coefficients relating exogenous to endogenous variables.
$\underset{\sim}{\Delta}$	Delta matrix of structural coefficients relating disturbance variables to endogenous variables.
$\underset{\sim}{\Gamma}*$	Gamma star matrix, $\Gamma*' = [\underset{\sim}{\Gamma}:\underset{\sim}{\Delta}]$.
$\underset{\sim}{\Phi}$	Phi matrix of covariances among independent variables.
$\underset{\sim}{G}_y$	Selection matrix to select manifest dependent variables from $\eta*$.
$\underset{\sim}{G}_x$	Selection matrix to select manifest independent variables from $\xi*$.

TABLE 4.2 (Continued)

Symbol	Meaning
Σ	Population covariance matrix for manifest variables.
Σ_0	Hypothetical population covariance matrix for manifest variables according to a structural model.
S	Sample covariance matrix for manifest variables.
$\hat{\Sigma}_0$	Estimated hypothetical covariance matrix for manifest variables according to a structural model.

where, according to the model,

$$\Sigma_{yy} = E(yy') = G_y B^{-1} \Gamma^* \Phi \Gamma^{*\prime} B^{-1\prime} G_y' \qquad [4.9a]$$

$$\Sigma_{xy} = E(xy') = G_x \Phi \Gamma^{*\prime} B^{-1\prime} G_y' \qquad [4.9b]$$

$$\Sigma_{xx} = E(xx') = G_x \Phi G_x' \qquad [4.9c]$$

The implications of equation 4.8 and equations 4.9a, 4.9b, and 4.9c are that a predicted or hypothetical variance/covariance matrix Σ_0 for the set of observed variables in random vectors x and y may be derived from the parameter values of a hypothetical structural equation model. Therefore, the degree to which the hypothetical structural equation model reflects reality is given by the degree to which the hypothetical matrix Σ_0 is the same as the empirical variance/covariance matrix Σ for the same variables (in x and y) obtained from measurements of these variables in the world. To make this comparison between the hypothetical matrix Σ_0 and the empirical matrix Σ is the goal of a confirmatory analysis using structural equation models with latent and manifest variables.

SPECIFYING A STRUCTURAL MODEL

One can obtain different models for the same set of manifest and latent variables in ξ^* and η^* by assigning different values to the respective elements of the matrices B, Γ^*, and Φ, known as "parameter matrices," in the structural equation model. In other words, to define a structural equation model with observed and latent variables one must specify the nature of the elements of the parameter matrices of the model. Any particular element of these matrices may be specified (to use terminology popularized by Jöreskog [1973]) in one of three ways:

(1) as a *fixed parameter*, given a value specified prior to the analysis which does not change throughout the estimation process;
(2) as a *free parameter*, whose value is to be estimated from the data conditional on the values of fixed and constrained parameters in the model, or
(3) as a *constrained parameter*, whose value is yoked together with certain other parameters that are all constrained to equal the same value. This value may be free to be estimated conditional on the values of fixed and other sets of constrained parameters.

Specification of a structural model is tied intrinsically to the question of identification. Consequently, we shall discuss identification and then illustrate its application in regard to the model in Figure 4.9.

IDENTIFICATION

It is essential to specify a structural equation model in such a way that the model is identified. Whether a model is identified concerns, in the broadest sense, distinguishing one theory from another theory when operationalizing theory with data (L'Esperance, 1972). With structural equation models, identifying a model involves specifying a priori, according to theory, the fixed values of certain parameters of the model so that (a) no other theoretical model (except one that differs trivially from it in terms of different units of measurement) can have the same *fixed* parameter values, but different free parameter values, and (b) still generate the same hypothetical covariance matrix Σ_0 for the observed variables. In other words, identifying a structural model means fixing the values of an appropriate set of parameters in the model so that the hypothetical covariance matrix Σ_0 associated with this set of fixed parameters will be unique for each distinct complementary set of free parameter values.

Identification also concerns fixing enough parameters of the parameter matrices $\underline{B}, \Gamma^*$, and Φ so that the remaining parameters can then be solved for in terms of the values of the covariances among the manifest variables and the values of the fixed parameters. If an insufficient number and/or inappropriate set of parameters are fixed a priori, the model may not be identified. Then there may be no consistent solutions for the free parameters of the model. In this regard Jöreskog (1979) has indicated the following guidelines for evaluating the identification of one's model: Let s be the number of free and constrained parameters (each distinct constrained parameter being counted only once) in the matrices $\underline{B}, \Gamma^*$, and Φ.

Then a necessary (but not sufficient) condition that all of the free and constrained parameters of the model are identified is that

$$s < (m_2 + n_2)(m_2 + n_2 + 1)/2$$

where the expression on the right is the number of independent elements of the hypothetical variance/covariance matrix Σ_0 for the full set of observed variables, with n_2 x variables and m_2 y variables.

To understand the way identification of a free or constrained parameter may be determined by some elements of the hypothetical covariance matrix Σ_0 and the values of the fixed parameters, let us return to equations 4.9a through 4.9c. These equations imply that the elements of the variance/covariance matrix Σ_0 are functions of the values of the fixed and free parameters in the parameter matrices of the model. If one can find a way to solve uniquely for a given free or constrained parameter from elements of the variance/covariance matrix Σ_0 and the values of the fixed parameters, then the free or constrained parameter is identified. If there is only one way of using elements of Σ_0 to solve for a given free or constrained parameter, then the parameter is just identified. If there is more than one way (using different elements of Σ_0) to solve for the parameter, then the parameter is overidentified. If all free and constrained parameters are just identified, then the model is just identified. If in addition some, but not all, of the free and constrained parameters are overidentified, then the model is partially overidentified. If all free and constrained parameters of the model are overidentified, then the model is overidentified. Finally, applying the term "identified" to a model implies that the model is at least just identified.

To illustrate identification, let us consider the identification of the parameters of the model in Figure 4.9 represented by the system of simultaneous equations in equation 4.1. We assume that in the phi matrix for the model in Figure 4.9 the exogenous variables are mutually uncorrelated with unit variances and that the disturbance variables are also mutually uncorrelated; that is, $\Phi_{\xi\xi}$ and Φ_{xx} are identity matrices, $\Phi_{\xi x} = 0$, and $\Phi_{\epsilon\epsilon}$ is a diagonal matrix. We may then derive the elements of the hypothetical variance/covariance matrix for the observed variables by equations 4.9a through 4.9c. Actually, one does not need in practice to use equations 4.9a through 4.9c per se to find the variances and covariances among the manifest variables according to the model. One can also use processes similar to those discussed in connection with Condition 10 in Chapter 2 to express correlations in terms of path coefficients. These processes involve rules one can apply to the parameters in structural diagrams to determine the variances and covariances in a rather straightforward way (see Costner, 1969; Heise, 1975; Namboodiri et al., 1975). To illustrate these procedures for finding covariances, consider that part of the model in Figure 4.9 that deals with causes of $y_3, \ldots, y_6$, which we have reproduced in Figure 4.10.

This submodel implies that the covariance between y_3 and y_4 is equal to $\alpha_{31}\alpha_{41}\sigma_1^2$, where σ_1^2 is the variance of η_1. The basis for this implication is that y_3 and y_4 have the latent variable η_1 as a common cause. Thus, their covariance, indicated by σ_{34}, should be determined by the extent to which they share common variance attributable to η_1, which is given by multiplying the product of the parameters relating y_3 and y_4 to η_1 times the variance of η_1. However, for simplification we will require that the variances of all latent endogenous variables equal unity. Hence, using the same reasoning, the complete set of covariances among the manifest indicators of η_1 is:

$$\sigma_{34} = \alpha_{31}\alpha_{41} \tag{4.10}$$

$$\sigma_{35} = \alpha_{31}\alpha_{51} \tag{4.11}$$

$$\sigma_{36} = \alpha_{31}\alpha_{61} \tag{4.12}$$

$$\sigma_{45} = \alpha_{41}\alpha_{51} \tag{4.13}$$

$$\sigma_{46} = \alpha_{41}\alpha_{61} \tag{4.14}$$

$$\sigma_{56} = \alpha_{51}\alpha_{61} \tag{4.15}$$

We may also obtain these same results by applying equations 4.9a through 4.9c, where we can take advantage of the fact that the fixed parameters set equal to zero in $\underline{B} = \underline{I} - \underline{A}$, $\underline{\Gamma}^*$, and Φ allow us to simplify expressions for these same covariances as in equations 4.10 through 4.15. In any case, however we obtain them, we have six equations and four unknowns, namely, α_{31}, α_{41}, α_{51}, and α_{61}. This means we may solve this system of six equations in more than one way to obtain estimates of $\alpha_{31}, \ldots, \alpha_{61}$. One solution for these parameters is given by:

$$\alpha_{31} = +(\sigma_{34}\sigma_{35}/\sigma_{45})^{1/2} \tag{4.16}$$

$$\alpha_{41} = +(\sigma_{34}\sigma_{45}/\sigma_{35})^{1/2} \tag{4.17}$$

$$\alpha_{51} = +(\sigma_{35}\sigma_{45}/\sigma_{34})^{1/2} \tag{4.18}$$

$$\alpha_{61} = +(\sigma_{36}\sigma_{46}/\sigma_{34})^{1/2} \tag{4.19}$$

But equations 4.16 through 4.19 do not represent the only possible solutions for the unknown parameters $\alpha_{31}, \ldots, \alpha_{61}$. Parameters α_{31} through α_{61} are overidentified because there is more than one way to solve for each of the four unknown parameters in terms of different

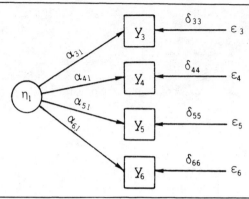

Figure 4.10 A submodel of the model in Figure 4.9 used to illustrate the assessment of the identification of parameters. In this model, $\alpha_{31}, \alpha_{41}, \alpha_{51}$, and α_{61} are overidentified parameters.

elements of Σ_0. For example, we used equations 4.10, 4.11, and 4.13 to obtain the solution for α_{31} in equation 4.16. But we could just as easily have used equations 4.11, 4.12, and 4.15, respectively, to solve for α_{31} as

$$\alpha_{31} = +(\sigma_{35}\sigma_{36}/\sigma_{56})^{1/2} \qquad [4.20]$$

Thus α_{31} is an overidentified parameter, as are the other unknown parameters of this system of equations.

By similar procedures we can solve for parameters $\alpha_{72}, \ldots, \alpha_{10,2}$ in connection with the four indicators of η_2 and for parameters $\gamma_{11,1} \cdots$, $\gamma_{14,1}$ in connection with the four indicators of ξ_1. Because in each of these cases there are four indicators of a common latent variable, the structural parameters relating these indicators to the common latent variable are overidentified.

The free parameter α_{21} relating η_1 to η_2 is also an overidentified parameter. To see this, consider that the covariances between different pairs of manifest indicators of different latent variables may be obtained as the products of structural parameters in causal paths that radiate out from a single latent variable and terminate at each end with one of the manifest indicators (see Figure 4.11). Thus, applying this principle to the causal paths involving the parameter α_{21}, we obtain

$$\sigma_{37} = \alpha_{31}\alpha_{21}\alpha_{72} \qquad [4.21]$$

$$\sigma_{38} = \alpha_{31}\alpha_{21}\alpha_{82} \qquad [4.22]$$

$$\sigma_{39} = \alpha_{31}\alpha_{21}\alpha_{92} \qquad [4.23]$$

$$\sigma_{3,10} = \alpha_{31}\alpha_{21}\alpha_{10,2} \qquad [4.24]$$

Any one of these equations, as well as others involving covariances for pairs of variables from other sets of indicators of η_1 and η_2, respectively, may be used to solve for α_{21}, because the solutions for the other parameters in each of these equations are obtainable using other elements of Σ_0. Parameter a_{21} is therefore very much overidentified. By similar reasoning we can show that γ_{11} and γ_{12} are also overidentified. For example, $\sigma_{x_2 y_3} = \gamma_{12} \alpha_{31}$, $\sigma_{x_2 y_4} = \gamma_{12} \alpha_{41}$, and so on. α_{31} and α_{41} are already determined by other elements of Σ_0.

The structural parameters δ_{33} through $\delta_{14,14}$ associated with the causal paths of disturbance variables ϵ_3 through ϵ_{14} of Figure 4.9 are identified, for they may be determined from the respective diagonal elements of Σ_0 once the other parameters of the model have been determined from the off-diagonal elements of Σ_0. That is, the values estimated for δ_{33} through $\delta_{14,14}$ will reflect the residual variances in variables that cannot be accounted for by the functions indicated in the model.

The structural parameters δ_{11} and δ_{22}, associated with the paths of the disturbance variables ϵ_1 and ϵ_2 for the latent endogenous variables η_1 and η_2, will not be identified unless one makes some specification before analysis that, in effect, specifies the variances of the latent endogenous variables η_1 and η_2. We have already required the variances of latent endogenous variables to equal unity; in other words, we require the following equalities to hold:

$$\sigma_{\eta_1}^2 = \delta_{11}^2 + \gamma_{11}^2 + \gamma_{12}^2 = 1 \qquad [4.25]$$

$$\sigma_{\eta_2}^2 = \delta_{22}^2 + \alpha_{21}^2 = 1 \qquad [4.26]$$

These equalities properly constrain solutions for δ_{11} and δ_{22}. Some computing algorithms for structural equation analysis provide for specifying constraints among parameters such as these (Bentler & Lee, 1982). When they do not, the user must specify arbitrary values for the parameters to fix the metric of their respective latent endogenous variables.

In sum, because all parameters not involving disturbances of the model in Figure 4.9 are overidentified, the model may be said to be overidentified.

It is important to emphasize that the free parameters of the model are just identified or overidentified depending on the assumptions (predictions) made in specifying values for the fixed parameters. It may not be obvious, but the model in Figure 4.9 involves a large number of fixed parameters. For example, the absence of an arrow from ξ_1 to η_2 means that the parameter γ_{21} is equal to, or fixed, at zero. The same is true for the absence of an arrow from x_2 to η_2. Furthermore, every disturbance variable is regarded as a cause of one and only one manifest or latent

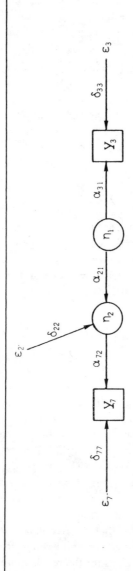

Figure 4.11 Because arrows "radiate" from the common variable η_1, and the latent variables have unit variances, the covariance between the manifest variables y_7 and y_3 is given by the product $\alpha_{72}\,\alpha_{21}\,\alpha_{31}$.

endogenous variable. All arrows pointing from a disturbance to any other variable have parameters fixed at zero (i.e., off-diagonal elements of Δ must be zero). Furthermore, the disturbance variables are presumed to have unit variances and to be mutually uncorrelated, with their covariance matrix $\Phi_{\epsilon\epsilon}$ fixed to be an identity matrix. Two other instances, which do not exhaust all possibilities, are that (a) manifest indicators of latent variables are caused by one and only one latent variable, and (b) the causal relationship between η_1 and η_2 is recursive, implying that $\alpha_{12} = 0$, (i.e., η_2 is not a reciprocal cause of η_1). Finally, the model contains no constrained-equal parameters, although this condition could be implemented if we so desired. For example, we might theorize that α_{31} and α_{41} in equation 4.11 are of equal magnitude. One result of this specification would be that the parameter α_{51} is overidentified (i.e., one would have, in effect, two unknowns in three equations).

IMPLICATIONS OF IDENTIFICATION FOR TESTING GOODNESS OF FIT

As discussed earlier, the degree to which a structural equation model reflects reality is assessed by the degree to which Σ_0, the hypothetical variance/covariance matrix generated according to equations 4.9a through 4.9c, is similar to, or has a good fit with, the matrix Σ, which is the unrestricted, empirical variance/covariance matrix for the same manifest variables. In practice, Σ_0 and Σ are replaced by sample estimates, namely, $\hat{\Sigma}_0$ and S, respectively. Identification has important implications for testing the fit between $\hat{\Sigma}_0$ and S. Consider, first, that there is only one possible solution for the estimate of a just-identified structural parameter. This suggests that estimates for the free and constrained parameters of a just-identified model can always be found in such a way that the resulting $\hat{\Sigma}_0$ matrix exactly equals the matrix S. Just-identified models always have a perfect fit to data. But such good fits are tautological and trivial, and in no way indicate the scientific usefulness of a model. On the other hand, because an overidentified parameter of a model may be estimated in several ways (using different sets of elements of the sample variance/covariance matrix S), different estimated values for the parameter can be obtained. More importantly, the different estimates for an overidentified parameter may be inconsistent (Costner, 1969). In practice, the methods used to estimate an overidentified free or constrained parameter usually take some weighted average of the different solutions for the parameter. As a result, there is some freedom for the sample variance/covariance matrix S to differ from the estimated hypothetical variance/covariance matrix $\hat{\Sigma}_0$. Thus, overidentified models can be falsified when the discrepancy between S and Σ_0 is statistically significant. It follows that an overidentified model is essential for testing the theory on which the identifying conditions are based.

Since structural equation models with latent variables are more complex than those involving only manifest variables, the task of assessing identification is more difficult. Furthermore, because the emphasis is on fixed parameters of the various parameter matrices of the model (essential for the computing algorithms), the identification problem focuses on parameters and not on equations as does the traditional literature on structural equation modeling with manifest variables. One can consult Fisher (1966), Schmidt (1976), Wiley (1973), Werts, Jöreskog, and Linn (1973), or Koopmans and Hood (1953) for general principles of identification. Empirical examples are given by Jöreskog (1979a, 1979b).

ESTIMATION

BASIC PRINCIPLES

In the case of structural models with latent variables, we make the assumption that the distribution of the manifest variables is a function of their variance/covariance matrix. Making this assumption allows us to seek estimates of the free and constrained parameters of the model in the following way: Use as estimates those values for the free and constrained parameters of the matrices B, Γ^*, and Φ that, together with the values of the fixed parameters, make the estimated model variance/covariance matrix $\hat{\Sigma}_0$ for the manifest variables as much like the sample variance/covariance matrix S as possible. We will now show how this principle is implemented in the major methods used to estimate parameters of structural equation models with latent and manifest variables.

A measure of the degree of similarity or fit of the matrix $\hat{\Sigma}_0$ to the matrix S is given by a function of the elements of these matrices known as a loss function. The term "loss function" is derived from the idea that when estimating a parameter one takes a "loss" when the value chosen as an estimate of the parameter differs from the actual value of the parameter. The loss function thus provides a measure of the degree of this loss by measuring some function of the discrepancy between estimate and parameter. A desirable propery of a loss function is that it should take on a large value when the discrepancy between the estimate and the parameter estimated is large and equal zero when there is no discrepancy. In addition, when a number of parameters are to be estimated, the loss function should attempt to combine the individual losses into an overall measure of loss. In the case of structural models with latent variables, we will seek estimates for the free parameters of the structural model so that the estimated variance/covariance matrix $\hat{\Sigma}_0$ derived from these free parameters and the fixed parameters will minimize a loss function defined on $\hat{\Sigma}_0$ and S.

IMPORTANT METHODS

A number of loss functions are available for this purpose. To begin with, one can use least squares (LS) and minimize the function

$$LS = \text{tr}[(S - \hat{\Sigma}_0)'(S - \hat{\Sigma}_0)]$$

This method of estimation minimizes the sum of squared differences between the elements of S and $\hat{\Sigma}_0$. The matrix $(S - \hat{\Sigma}_0)$ represents the element-by-element difference between S and $\hat{\Sigma}_0$. $\hat{\Sigma}_0$ is derived using equations 4.9a through 4.9c with estimated values for the free and constrained elements and a priori values for the fixed elements of the matrices B, Γ^*, and Φ. The sum of squared differences between the elements of the corresponding rows of $(S - \hat{\Sigma}_0)$ is given by the diagonal elements of $(S - \hat{\Sigma}_0)'(S - \hat{\Sigma}_0)$, a square matrix. The sum of the diagonal elements of a square matrix is known as the trace of the matrix and is denoted by "tr[ ]." Thus the sum of the diagonal elements of $(S - \hat{\Sigma}_0)'(S - \hat{\Sigma}_0)$, or the trace of this matrix, gives the sum of squared differences between corresponding elements of S and $\hat{\Sigma}_0$. In other words, the criterion would force us to seek values of the free and constrained elements that would make the sum of squared differences between the elements of the matrices S and $\hat{\Sigma}_0$ as small as possible. Note, however, the term "least squares estimation" in this case does not refer to the ordinary least squares estimation process used with models of manifest variables.

Maximum likelihood estimation begins with a sample from a population whose distributional type is known (e.g., the multivariate normal distribution) and seeks those values for the unknown parameters of the distribution that would make the likelihood of obtaining the sample a maximum. If we used the loss function of maximum likelihood estimation, we would seek to minimize the function

$$ML = \log|\hat{\Sigma}_0| + \text{tr}(S\hat{\Sigma}_0^{-1}) - \log|S| - (m_2 + n_2)$$

which approaches zero as S and $\hat{\Sigma}_0$ become the same. $\log|\hat{\Sigma}_0|$ denotes the logorithm of the determinant of the square matrix $\hat{\Sigma}_0$. The determinant is a number obtained from the elements of the matrix in a way too complex to describe here. Note that if S and $\hat{\Sigma}_0$ are equal, then $\log|\hat{\Sigma}_0|$ and $\log|S|$

will be the same and their difference will be equal to zero. Similarly, if $\underset{\sim}{S}$ and $\underset{\sim}{\dot{\Sigma}}_0$ are the same, $\underset{\sim}{\dot{\Sigma}}_0^{-1}$ will be the matrix inverse of $\underset{\sim}{S}$. Hence, $(\underset{\sim}{S}\underset{\sim}{\dot{\Sigma}}_0^{-1}) = \underset{\sim}{I}$, an identity matrix whose diagonal elements are all unities, the sum of which, given by the trace function, equals $(m_2 + n_2)$, the number of manifest variables. Thus, the difference between $\text{tr}(\underset{\sim}{S}\,\underset{\sim}{\dot{\Sigma}}_0^{-1})$ and $(m_2 + n_2)$ will equal zero in this case. When ML equals zero, it is at an absolute minimum. This absolute minimum is never attained when $\underset{\sim}{S}$ and $\underset{\sim}{\dot{\Sigma}}_0$ are different, but it may be possible to find estimates for the free and constrained elements of $\underset{\sim}{B}, \underset{\sim}{\Gamma}^*$, and $\underset{\sim}{\Phi}$ that make $\underset{\sim}{\dot{\Sigma}}_0$ as much like $\underset{\sim}{S}$ as possible according to this criterion.

Or one can use the loss function of generalized least squares, in which case one would minimize

$$GLS = \text{tr}(I - \underset{\sim}{S}^{-1}\,\underset{\sim}{\dot{\Sigma}}_0)^2$$

As explained previously $\underset{\sim}{S}^{-1}\underset{\sim}{\dot{\Sigma}}_0$ will be an identity matrix (I) when $\underset{\sim}{S}$ and $\underset{\sim}{\dot{\Sigma}}_0$ are identical. Hence the GLS criterion also approaches zero as $\underset{\sim}{S}$ and $\underset{\sim}{\dot{\Sigma}}_0$ become the same.

An advantage of the least squares (LS) method of estimation is that it may be implemented without making any distributional assumptions about the observed variables. On the other hand, the least squares method of estimation does not lend itself to testing the statistical significance of differences indicated by the trace function. In contrast, statistical tests are possible with the maximum likelihood and the generalized least squares methods. To use statistical tests with the maximum likelihood method, the distribution of the manifest variables should follow the multivariate normal distribution. If this assumption is questionable, then the generalized least squares (GLS) procedure may be used. Generalized least squares also makes no distributional assumptions, but still allows for statistical tests. Finally, it is extremely important to note that statistical inference based on maximum likelihood and generalized least squares estimates is possible only with large samples. One reason for requiring large samples is that the chi-square statistics used to test the significance of the maximum likelihood and generalized least squares loss functions are only asymptotically distributed as chi-square. That is to say, the sampling distributions of these chi-square statistics only approximate chi-square distributions in large samples.

The algorithmic procedures for obtaining estimates for the free and constrained elements of a linear structural equation model with latent variables are beyond the scope of this treatment (see Jöreskog, 1973; Bentler & Weeks, 1980). One should know, however, that the procedures are iterative and quite time consuming, even with large, high-speed computers, and may require considerable core memory as well. These procedures estimate all of the unknown (free and constrained) elements of the matrices $\underset{\cdot}{B},\Gamma^*$, and Φ at the same time. This means that lack of fit between data and a model can be spread across all parameter estimates to force an optimal fit. The result is a tendency to obscure which fixed elements are mainly responsible for the lack of fit of the model to data. This is a common problem for all "full-information" estimation techniques; that is, techniques that estimate all free and constrained parameters in a model simultaneously (see Johnston, 1972). On the other hand, if the conditions for confirmatory analysis have been reasonably satisfied, then the estimates furnished by full-information techniques are both consistent and efficient. Unfortunately, applications of latent variable structural modeling in psychology, like those for manifest variables, tend to be extremely weak in regard to attention to the conditions essential for confirmatory analysis, especially in connection with the unmeasured variables problem (Cliff, 1980, Note 1). We will discuss these points later in this chapter.

COMPUTER PROGRAMS

A number of computer programs are available for computing the estimates of the parameters of structural equation models. The program LISREL IV prepared by Jöreskog and Sörbom (1978) is perhaps the most widely available program at this time for structural models with latent variables. However, its use of the notational distinction between the measurement model and the structural equation model is unnecessary and leads to difficulties in treating the case in which a manifest variable is regarded as simultaneously an effect of both latent endogenous and latent exogenous variables. Furthermore, in estimating variances of disturbance variables, LISREL IV frequently produces "Heywood" cases in which the variance estimates are negative. However, a program that implements the structural equation model used in this book would not have Heywood cases when estimating the variances of the disturbance variables, for these could be fixed arbitrarily to unity. The relative contribution of a disturbance variable ϵ_i would then be indicated by the square of the structural parameter δ_{ii}, which is unaffected by the sign of δ_{ii}.

COSAN, a program informally distributed by R. P. McDonald (1978) based on a general model for covariance structure modeling, can be easily used with the notation employed in this book. COSAN has the additional feature of permitting both maximum likelihood and generalized least squares solutions for parameter estimates. Bentler is also developing a program to implement the model of Bentler and Weeks (1980), which should be readily adaptable to the notation of this book. At this writing Jöreskog and Sörbom (1981) have just released version V of the LISREL program. Jöreskog states (personal communication) that LISREL V will be distributed to replace all versions of LISREL IV now in use. Although LISREL V still does not provide for generalized least squares estimation and adheres to the model equation of LISREL IV with attendant problems of Heywood cases in estimation of variances of disturbance terms, the main improvement has been a ten-fold reduction in computing time required to obtain maximum likelihood estimates of the free parameters of a structural equation model. This has been brought about through the use of an improved approach to determining initial values for estimates of the parameters from which to begin the iterative process. The improvement in computing speed should make LISREL V very popular in spite of the minor difficulties we have mentioned.

We continue now with the question of significance tests for the goodness of fit between $\underset{\sim}{\Sigma}$ and $\underset{\sim}{\Sigma}_0$ using $\underset{\sim}{S}$ and $\hat{\underset{\sim}{\Sigma}}_0$.

SIGNIFICANCE TESTING AND GOODNESS-OF-FIT TESTS

TESTING THE SUPPORT FOR A MODEL

Previously, in connection with Conditions 9 and 10 in Chapter 2, we discussed how to evaluate the empirical support for a confirmatory model based on manifest variables. Condition 9, we said, concerns testing whether certain causal parameters are different from zero. It was pointed out that causal relations are indicated by nonzero structural parameters in structural equations. Thus, empirical support for causal relationships is given by statistical tests that reveal that the corresponding estimates of free structural parameters differ significantly from zero. Condition 10, on the other hand, concerned the fit of a model to data. This, we pointed out, can be assessed by taking advantage of the fact that the estimated and fixed structural parameters of a structural equation model determine an estimate of a hypothetical variance/covariance (correlation) matrix for the manifest variables under the assumption that the model is valid. If the estimate of the hypothetical variance/covariance matrix derived from the fixed and estimated free parameters of the structural equations does not differ significantly from the observed (unrestricted) estimate of the variance/covariance matrix for the manifest variables, then we say that the model fits or is consistent with the data.

In the case of structural equation models with latent variables, we can perform tests to determine whether both Conditions 9 and 10 are satisfied. However, how one performs these tests will be constrained by the kinds of statistical tests that are possible with latent variable models. As described briefly above, all of the available algorithms for estimating the free parameters of a structural equation model use full-information methods of estimation. This means all free and constrained parameters of the model are estimated simultaneously. These full-information algorithms usually provide three kinds of statistical tests to test hypotheses about the parameters of a model: (a) confidence interval tests applied to estimates of individual free parameters of the model, (b) tests comparing nested models, and (c) tests of overall goodness of fit of $\hat{\Sigma}_0$ to $\underline{S}$. The first two ways of testing statistical hypotheses lend themselves to methods for assessing whether Condition 9 is satisfied, that is, whether certain free structural parameters are equal to zero or not. The third way provides a basis for assessing whether Condition 10 concerning the goodness of fit of the model to data is satisfied. However, ways b and c are special cases of the same chi-square goodness-of-fit test and will be discussed together, although they concern different substantive questions.

TESTS OF INDIVIDUAL PARAMETERS

The latent variable literature contains little information about the use of confidence intervals to test hypotheses about individual free parameters. Nevertheless, confidence interval tests are possible if parameter estimates are obtained by either full-information maximum likelihood or generalized least squares estimation. The tests are based on estimates of the standard errors of the free parameter estimates derived from the "information matrix," which is generated as a byproduct of the estimation algorithm (see Bentler & Weeks, 1980; Jöreskog, 1973). The standard errors for the free parameter estimates, however, are conditional standard errors; they are conditional on the fixed and constrained parameters of the model. Thus, confidence interval tests of whether free parameters associated with expected causal pathways differ significantly from zero will be meaningful and unbiased only if the specifications regarding fixed and constrained parameters have been determined to have an acceptable goodness of fit to the data. In any case, one has estimates of standard errors and consequently confidence interval tests for just those free parameters of interest when assessing satisfaction of Condition 9.

The application of these confidence interval significance tests should be straightforward. For each free parameter of the model one can construct a confidence interval around the estimate of the parameter using the estimate of the standard error of the parameter. If the confidence interval does not include zero, then one can conclude that the parameter differs significantly from zero, thereby indicating a causal connection between the variables in question.

However, when the researcher seeks to test hypotheses about a number of different parameters of the model with a series of tests (i.e., one test per free parameter), he or she may want to control for the probability of making at least one Type I error of incorrectly rejecting a null hypothesis when it is true, over the series of tests. To do this the researcher will have to have a way to compute this probability. This can be done exactly if one knows that the tests are mutually independent and the level of significance of each test. But in most situations one will have a series of tests of parameters estimated from a single sample, and the tests will not be mutually independent. It follows that the conditional probability of making a Type I error on a test, given one has already made a Type I error on a previous test, will not be given by the nominal level of significance used for the test. A number of general procedures are available for dealing with this situation, many of which revolve around the Bonferroni method of defining more stringent levels of significance for individual tests of significance. These procedures, which are reviewed in Larzelere and Mulaik (1977) and Stavig (1981), have the major drawback of being less powerful than procedures that involve a series of tests known to be statistically independent. Nevertheless, power may not be a major concern with the large samples required for goodness-of-fit testing with latent variable methods. The alternative to using confidence intervals for testing hypotheses about individual parameters is based on the overall goodness-of-fit tests. We will first describe the goodness-of-fit test and then return to the alternative procedure for testing individual parameters. (Before departing from this point, we should mention that the logic described above for controlling for Type I errors in latent variable models applies also to manifest variable models).

GOODNESS-OF-FIT TESTS

After one has obtained maximum likelihood estimates of the free and constrained parameters, he or she can then generate the estimated model variance/covariance matrix $\hat{\Sigma}_0$ and compare this for goodness of fit with the sample variance/covariance matrix S estimated in the usual way under no restrictions. To do this one can compute the statistic

$$F = N \left[\log|\hat{\Sigma}_0| - \log|S| + \text{tr}(S\hat{\Sigma}_0^{-1}) - (m_2 + n_2)\right]/2$$

which, when the sample size N is very large, is approximately distributed as chi-square with $(m_2 + n_2)(m_2 + n_2 + 1)/2 - s$ degrees of freedom. s is the number of independent free and distinct constrained parameters of the model. If the sample value of this statistic exceeds the critical value of chi-square with the respective degrees of freedom at the specified level of significance, the model is rejected for lack of fit to the data. However, one must keep in mind that this test actually concerns a test of the appropriateness of the values chosen for the parameters fixed to specify the model. That is to say, the statistical hypothesis tested by the overall goodness-of-fit test is that the fixed parameters' values are what they have been fixed to. The test does not test hypotheses about the free parameters of the model; these have been estimated in such a way as to make the fit of the model to the data as close as possible, conditional on the values of the fixed parameters. And so, any lack of fit will be a result of the fixed parameter values and not of the free parameters. Thus, if the test yields a significant goodness-of-fit statistic, one then must consider that Condition 10 is not satisfied, that one's specification of the model in terms of fixed and constrained parameters is possibly not correct. On the other hand, if the overall goodness-of-fit test statistic is not significant, it means that Condition 10 is satisfied, that is, the specification of the model is consistent with the data.

TESTS OF INDIVIDUAL PARAMETERS USING THE F STATISTIC

One can use the above chi-square goodness-of-fit statistic F to test hypotheses about individual (and even groups of) parameters in a model. Thus, this statistic can also be used to assess whether Condition 9 concerning hypotheses about the free parameters of the structural model has been satisfied. To apply the chi-square goodness-of-fit statistic F for this purpose, one must make a comparison between two models: one with the parameter in question fixed to the hypothesized value; the other a model that is identical to the first model except that the parameter (or parameters) in question is (are) free to be estimated. The model with the value of the parameter(s) fixed by hypothesis will ordinarily yield a larger chi-square statistic than the one with the same parameter(s) allowed to be free. The difference between these two chi-squares is also a chi-square statistic, known as the difference chi-square, with degrees of freedom equal to the difference in degrees of freedom between the original chi-squares. If the difference chi-square is significant, one rejects the null hypothesis about the fixed parameter(s). This approach is illustrated below.

A PRIORI SEQUENCES OF TESTS

Bentler and Bonnet (1980) have recently reviewed the problem of conducting a series of independent statistical tests about individual parameters of a structural equation model with latent variables. The purpose of such a series of tests is not to explore data, but to test a number of a priori hypotheses in connection with the parameters of a particular model included within a nested sequence of models. According to Roy (1958), one can construct a series of independent statistical tests of individual parameters by specifying an a priori sequence of nested models whose goodness of fit to the data is to be tested, beginning first with a test of the goodness of fit of an initial overidentified model. Each subsequent model must differ from the previous model only in having additional fixed parameters over and beyond those of the previous model. Each model, therefore, is a specialization of the previous model in having the previous models' same fixed parameters as well as additional ones. Once the a priori sequence of models has been specified, then a sequence of statistical tests is performed as follows:

For such a sequence of models, let F_i and F_{i+1} be the chi-square values with degrees of freedom d_i and d_{i+1}, respectively, for the goodness-of-fit tests of models i and i+1, respectively. Then the test of the effect of not fixing the additional parameters in the $(i + 1)^{st}$ model is given by the difference chi-square value $F_d = F_{i+1} - F_i$, which has $d = (d_{i+1} - d_i)$ degrees of freedom. This sequence of tests continues until one rejects the null hypothesis. To go on beyond this point with tests of subsequent models would be logically inconsistent, because subsequent models would contain parameter values that were rejected in some previous test. With such a series of tests one could test the specification of a model (Condition 10) and then examine the causal connections between variables (Condition 9). (See also the discussion in Mulaik [1972, pp. 411-417] or Larzelere and Mulaik [1977] for the description of analogous tests in multivariate step-down regression).

It must be pointed out that to achieve a series of independent statistical tests with an a priori, nested sequence of models, one pays the price of being constrained to testing hypotheses about parameters in the order in which they are fixed in specifying the nested sequence of models. Furthermore, because the sequence of statistical tests ends when a null hypothesis (about the fixed values of one or more parameters) has been rejected, it is essential to arrange the testing of hypotheses about parameters in the order of their relative importance.

Thus, in defining a sequence of models so one can test hypotheses about different parameters of a structural equation model, one will first test hypotheses about those parameters that, when fixed, specify a measurement model relating the manifest variables of the model to different (usually latent) hypothetical construct variables. Next, if the previous hypotheses are accepted, one will test hypotheses about those parameters that, when fixed—in addition to the previously fixed values—specify an overidentified causal structure among the hypothetical construct variables of the model. Then, if the values of previously fixed parameters are consistent with the data, one will go on to test whether further fixing to zero the values of the structural parameters linking hypothetical construct variables to one another is consistent with the data. If so, one will reject the causal structure among the hypothetical construct variables and then test whether additionally fixing to zero the structural parameters relating the manifest indicator variables to the hypothetical construct variables is consistent with the data. This last test is a test of whether any structure exists at all among the manifest indicator variables. We will now illustrate a nested sequence of models in which such a series of tests may be performed.

A NESTED SEQUENCE OF MODELS

To illustrate how, in connection with the model in Figure 4.9, one may construct a priori a nested sequence of models, each subsequent model more restricted than the previous, consider the structural diagrams in Figures 4.12 through 4.16. Figure 4.12 is a diagram of a just-identified model for the thirteen manifest variables of the model in Figure 4.9. According to this model, twelve of the thirteen manifest variables are dependent on nine exogenous latent common factor variables plus twelve disturbance variables. Three of the latent variables, ξ_1, η_1, and η_2, correspond to the same-labeled latent variables of the model in Figure 4.9. The remaining six latent variables, ξ_3 through ξ_8 (represented in Figure 4.12 by slightly smaller circles than those associated with ξ_1, η_1, and η_2) are included only to illustrate a just-identified model that contains as a specialization the more restricted, overidentified model in Figure 4.9. The thirteenth manifest variable (x_2) in Figure 4.12 is a perfectly reliable exogenous variable. Under the assumption that all latent variables are specified to have unit variances, the number of free parameters to estimate in this model is 91: (a) 12 structural coefficients relating disturbances to manifest variables, (b) 45 independent covariances among the 9 latent exogenous variables and the single manifest exogenous variable x_2, (c) the variance of x_2, and (d) 33 structural coefficients relating the 9 latent exogenous variables to the 12 manifest endogenous variables. Since the number of free parameters to be estimated (each corresponding to one of the single or double-headed arrows in the diagram) equals the number of variances and covariances in the population covariance matrix for the thirteen manifest variables, the model is just identified. The model's covariance matrix Σ_0 will fit the population covariance matrix Σ perfectly.

Figure 4.13 is a more restricted, overidentified model representing the model to use to test hypotheses about the specified parameters of the measurement model portion of the model in Figure 4.9. In this model a causal structure is specified relating the manifest variables y_3 through y_{14} to the latent variables ξ_1, η_1, and η_2 of the model in Figure 4.9. But, in contrast to the latent structural model in Figure 4.9, no causal structure is specified in Figure 4.13 among the variables ξ_1, x_2, η_1, and η_2. The model simply allows these variables to be correlated, but in an unspecified way, and it indicates this by the double-headed arrows between these variables in Figure 4.13. The reason the model of Figure 4.13 is a restriction of the just-identified model in Figure 4.12 is because six of the nine latent exogenous (common factor) variables of the just-identified model have been effectively deleted from the model. This has been accomplished by specifying that the structural coefficients linking the six latent exogenous variables with the twelve manifest variables in Figure 4.12 are zero and that the covariances of the six latent variables with the other manifest and latent exogenous variables are zero also. In other words, numerous parameters of the model in Figure 4.12 have been restricted or fixed to equal zero.

A test of the specification of the fixed parameters of the model in Figure 4.13 is then given by a comparison of the goodness-of-fit statistic obtained for the model in Figure 4.13 to the goodness-of-fit statistic obtained for the just-identified model in Figure 4.12 (which is equal to zero).

Figure 4.14 is a structural equation model developed from the measurement model in Figure 4.13 by specifying a causal structure among the variables ξ_1, x_2, η_1, and η_2. In fact, it is the model described previously in connection with Figure 4.9. In this case latent exogenous variable ξ_1 and manifest exogenous variable x_2 are seen to be direct causes of only η_1, while η_1 is a direct cause of η_2. Exogenous variables ξ_1 and x_2 are also presumed to be unrelated. The latent structural model in Figure 4.14 is more restricted than the model in Figure 4.13. If in Figure 4.14 we allowed ξ_1 and x_2 to covary, and included causal arrows from ξ_1 to η_2 and from x_2 to η_2, then the resulting model would be no more restricted than the measurement model in Figure 4.13 and would fit the data as well as the model in Figure 4.13. In other words, we would then have just as many free parameters to estimate in the model of Figure 4.14 as we do in the model of Figure 4.13. By fixing certain parameters equal to zero in the model of Figure 4.14 ($\sigma_{\xi_1 x_2} = 0$, $\gamma_{21} = 0$, $\gamma_{22} = 0$), we have overidentified the structural parameters associated with causal relationships among the variables ξ_1, x_2, η_1 and η_2. Thus the difference in the goodness of fit between the model in Figure 4.14 and the model in Figure 4.13 is the basis for a test of the parameters fixed to specify an overidentified causal

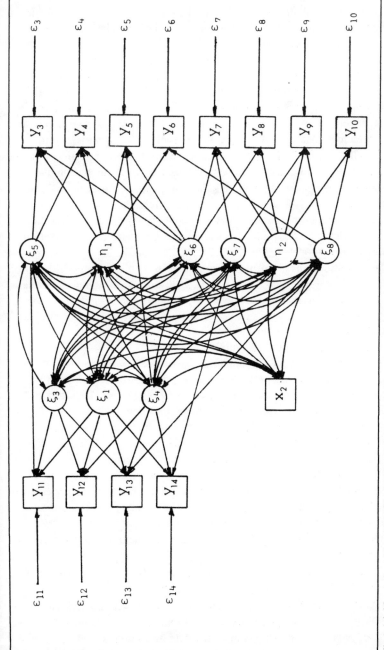

Figure 4.12 A Just-Identified Model Within Which the Model in Figure 4.9 Is Nested

structure among the exogenous and latent endogenous variables of the model in Figure 4.9.

The structural diagram in Figure 4.15 is of an even more restricted model in which the causal paths between the variables of the previous model in Figure 4.14 have been deleted. In other words, the structural coefficients associated with causal connections among the latent variables and the manifest exogenous variable x_2 in Figure 4.14 have all been fixed to zero. A comparison of the goodness of fit of this model with the goodness of fit of the model in Figure 4.14 would be the basis for determining whether the causal structure between the exogenous and latent endogenous variables of the model in Figure 4.14 exists or not.

Finally, the model in Figure 4.16 is the most restricted model of all in this sequence. No structure is hypothesized to exist among the manifest variables. This model we will call the "null model," because it hypothesizes that the variables are all mutually uncorrelated.

Now, a sequence of statistical tests may be performed as follows: First, compare the just-identified model of Figure 4.12 with the more restricted measurement model in Figure 4.13. The test of the difference between these two models is given by the chi-square test of the goodness of fit of the model in Figure 4.13 to the data. If one *accepts* the null hypothesis (that the model in Figure 4.13 fits the data), one can then go on to perform subsequent tests; otherwise, one must stop, since any subsequent model would have fixed parameters whose values were already rejected in testing the first overidentified model.

Given acceptance of the model in Figure 4.13, one can then compare the model in Figure 4.14 with the model in Figure 4.13. The model in Figure 4.14, being the more restricted, *becomes the null hypothesis.* The chi-square statistic to use is the *difference* between the chi-square for the goodness of fit of the model in Figure 4.14 and the chi-square for the goodness of fit of the model in Figure 4.13. As noted earlier, the degrees of freedom for the chi-square statistic comparing these two models is the difference in the degrees of freedom between the two goodness-of fit chi-square statistics. If one rejects the null hypothesis, that is, rejects the values of the parameters fixed to specify an overidentified structure among the latent variables and γ_{22}, one must stop further statistical testing and accept the model in Figure 4.13. Acceptance of the model in 4.14 suggests confirmation of the hypothesis regarding fixed values in the structural part of the model. That is, ξ_1 and x_2 are unrelated ($\sigma_{\xi_1 x_2} = 0$), and, further, neither are direct causes of η_2 ($\gamma_{21} = 0$, $\gamma_{22} = 0$).

On the other hand, if one accepts the null hypothesis (meaning the model in Figure 4.14 has acceptable fit), one can then go on and test the difference between the model in Figure 4.15 and the model in Figure 4.14, which is equivalent to a test of whether the structural coefficients, γ_{11}, γ_{12}, and α_{21}, representing causal connections among the manifest exog-

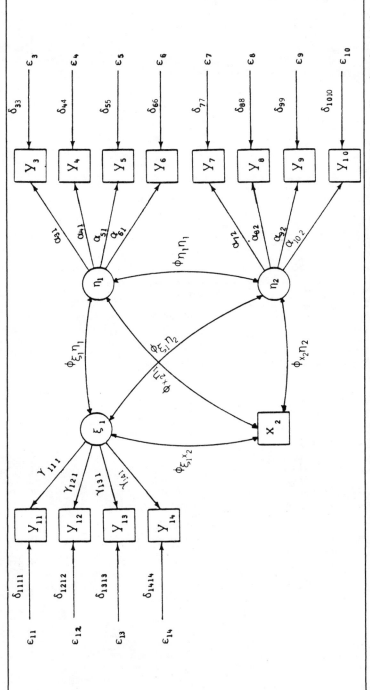

Figure 4.13 Each cluster of four manifest variables is determined by a common latent variable. The latent variables are allowed to be correlated among themselves and with the manifest exogenous variable x_2. Both single- and double-headed arrows correspond to free parameters of the model. This is the measurement model for the model in Figure 4.9.

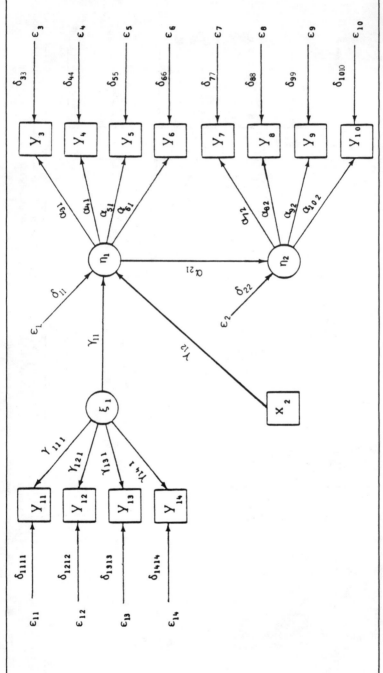

Figure 4.14 A structural model in which two exogenous variables ξ_1 and x_2 are causes of a latent variable η_1, which in turn is a cause of latent endogenous variable η_2. Each of the latent variables of the model is represented by four manifest indicator variables.

enous and the latent variables of the model in Figure 4.14, differ significantly from zero. As before, the chi-square statistic to use for this test is the difference chi-square equal to the difference between the goodness-of-fit chi-square statistics obtained for the models in Figures 4.14 and 4.15, respectively. The difference chi-square has degrees of freedom equal to the difference between the degrees of freedom of the two goodness-of-fit chi-squares. Again, if the difference chi-square test of the difference between these models is significant, one must stop and perform no further significance testing. In that case one accepts the structural model in Figure 4.14.

If the difference chi-square test comparing the models in Figures 4.14 and 4.15 is not significant, then one can make one final test. This is a test of the pathways from the latent variables to the observed variables. Do their structural parameters all simultaneously equal zero? If they do, then there should be no structure among the observed variables. Thus one would test the difference between the model in Figure 4.15 and the model in Figure 4.16. (Actually there is the possibility for intermediate models between the four independent clusters model in Figure 4.15 and the no-structure-among-variables model in Figure 4.16: One might have a model in which just the third common factor is eliminated, leaving variables $y_{11}, \ldots, y_{14}$ mutually uncorrelated as well as uncorrelated with the other manifest variables. A more restricted model would eliminate the second and third factors, leaving the last nine variables mutually uncorrelated as well as uncorrelated with the first three variables, which are assumed to have a single common factor). As before, one performs a chi-square test based on the difference between the goodness-of-fit chi-squares of the models in Figures 4.15 and 4.16, respectively. If one rejects the null hypothesis (i.e., the no-structure model in Figure 4.16 is incorrect), one accepts the previous model of Figure 4.15.

THE NORMED FIT INDEX

There is one serious drawback to the use of the chi-square goodness-of-fit statistic. Just at that point at which the sample size becomes large enough so that the goodness-of-fit statistic becomes distributed with reasonable approximation to the chi-square distribution, it also has sufficient power to detect even minute departures of the data from the model. One will find that, with real-world data, the fit of the model will be rejected almost every time, even when an examination of the residual matrix $(S - \hat{\Sigma}_0)$ reveals most elements of this matrix are small in magnitude. On the other hand, Bentler and Bonnett (1980) point out that if one uses this statistic with *small* samples, he or she will almost always accept the fit of a model to the data for almost any model. Consequently, one would hope to find a way of assessing how well the model captures most

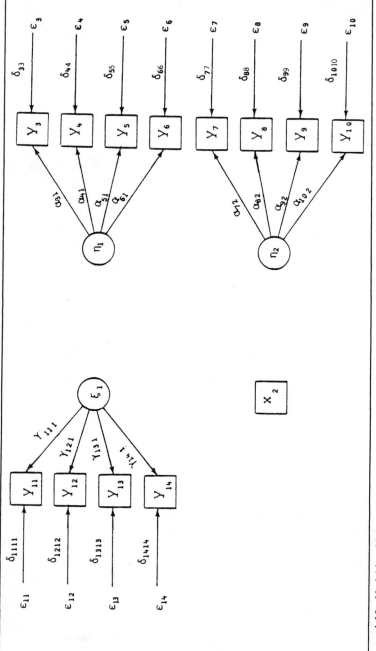

Figure 4.15 Model in which γ_{11}, γ_{12}, and α_{21} have been fixed to equal zero to test the structural model part of Figure 4.14.

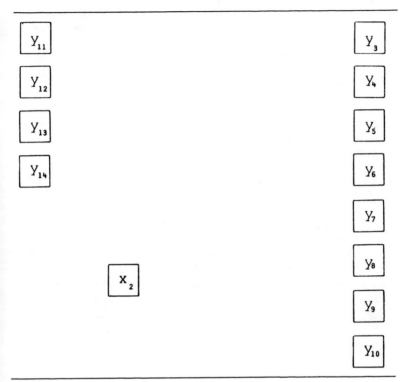

Figure 4.16 "Null" model for set of thirteen variables in which all variables are hypothesized to be mutually uncorrelated. In such a model all paths between variables have been deleted.

of the information in the sample covariance matrix that is independent of sample size.

Bentler and Bonnet (1980) proposed an index they call the *normed fit index*. This index gives the *relative decrease in lack of fit* between two *nested* models, one less restricted than the other. The decrease in lack of fit in going from the more restricted to the less restricted model is compared to a norm. This norm is defined on a nested sequence of increasingly less restricted models that begins with a most restricted "null" model, is followed by the original two nested models, and ends with a just-identified model. The norm for comparison is the decrease in lack of fit in going from the "most restricted" model at one end of the sequence to a just-identified model (which necessarily has no lack of fit) at the other end of the sequence. The most restricted model at the most restricted end of the sequence would fix all free parameters not fixed in the other models in the nested sequence. In many (but not all) instances the most restricted model is the "null" model that predicts no relations among any of the manifest variables. In other words, under this most restricted "null" model, the variance/covariance matrix of the observed variables would be hypothesized to be a diagonal matrix, with all off-diagonal elements equal to zero.

For example, consider the nested sequence of models in going from the model in Figure 4.16 down to the model in Figure 4.12. The model in Figure 4.16 is the "null" model of this sequence. Figure 4.12 displays the just-identified model. The difference in lack of fit between the null model in Figure 4.16 and the just-identified model in Figure 4.12 represents the maximum possible difference in lack of fit between any two models in this sequence of nested models. And so, we can use this maximum possible difference in lack of fit as a norm against which the difference in lack of fit between any two models within the sequence can be compared.

In testing the fit of the null model, the goodness-of-fit statistic is denoted F_0 and is based on a comparison of the differences between the zero covariances of the null model and the actually observed covariances in the sample covariance matrix $\underline{S}$. Now, designate the most restricted "null" model M_0. From the pair of models in question let M_1 denote the *least* restricted model, that is, the model that has the fewest fixed parameters (and yet is still overidentified). Let M_k denote a more restricted submodel of M_1, in that M_k has not only the same fixed parameters of M_1, but other fixed parameters as well, meaning it has fewer free parameters to estimate. Then the normed fit index is given by

$$\delta_{kl} = (F_k - F_l)/F_0 \qquad [4.27]$$

where F is any fit function (LS, ML, GLS) evaluated for the respective models. (The index works with any method of estimation using a fit function that is to be minimized conditional on the fixed parameter values and which takes the value of zero when fit is perfect. Even the LS fit function can be used since probabilistic inference will not be involved in the use of the normed fit index).

Now, a special case of the index given in equation 4.27 would be a comparison of the lack of fit of a given model M_k to the lack of fit of the null model M_0, which is given by

$$\delta_{0k} = (F_0 - F_k)/F_0 \qquad [4.28]$$

If this index is close to unity, then the model M_k has captured most of the information about relationships between the observed variables as given in the sample variance/covariance matrix. This index may be used even if the goodness-of-fit test for M_k using the chi-square statistic is significant, meaning a statistical lack of fit. In other words, the normed fit index provides a nonstatistical assessment of the adequacy of a model's fit to data, which may be used to determine whether, on practical grounds, a model may be of value in describing a particular set of data.

However, a drawback of the normed fit index is that the index takes no account of the reduction in degrees of freedom in going from the null model to the model whose fit is being assessed. For example, a just-identified model with zero degrees of freedom would have a normed fit index of unity. And a barely overidentified model with just a few degrees of freedom relative to the degrees of freedom of the null model would typically have a normed fit index of near unity. One must ask how efficient is the increase in fit in going from the null model with many degrees of freedom to another model with just a few degrees of freedom in terms of the degrees of freedom lost in estimating more parameters? Khattab and Hocevar (1982) recommend the efficiency index

$$\epsilon = (F_0 - F_k)/[F_0(d_0 - d_k)] \tag{4.29}$$

which represents the per parameter (or degree of freedom) average increase in fit, where d_0 is the degrees of freedom of the null model, d_k is the degrees of freedom of the model M_k whose fit to the data is to be assessed, and F_0 and F_k are defined as before.

However, the efficiency index in equation 4.29 is not useful for making comparisons between models in general. One would like to consider how well a model fits data in terms of the parsimony of the model. The parsimony of a model is indicated by the ratio of the number of degrees of freedom in the model to the number of degrees of freedom available in the data as indicated by the degrees of freedom of the null model for those data. When this ratio is unity, all information in the data available for testing the null model is also available for testing the alternative model in question. No information is wasted on estimating parameters. For example, consider two models, M_1 and M_2. Let M_1 be a model applied to 10 variables, while M_2 is applied to 30 variables. The number of degrees of freedom d_{01} in the *null* model for the 10-variable case is $(10 \times 11)/2 - 10 = 45$. The number of degrees of freedom d_{02} for the *null* model of the case with 30 variables is $(30 \times 31)/2 - 30 = 435$. Suppose the degrees of freedom d_1 of the 10-variable model M_1 is 35. Suppose the degrees of freedom d_2 of the model M_2 is 425. Both models differ from their respective null models by 10 degrees of freedom. Yet M_2 would have a parsimony of $425/435 = .977$, while the parsimony of M_1 would be $25/35 = .71$. If M_1 and M_2 both had the same value for the normed fit index, they would both have the same efficiency index as well, but, because M_2 is more parsimonious, its use of the data is superior. Thus, we recommend multiplying the normed fit index by the parsimony of the model to obtain the parsimonious fit index:

$$\pi = (d_k/d_0) [F_0 - F_k)/F_0] \tag{4.30}$$

This index corrects for the high normed fit index values obtained by models that waste data in estimating parameters to get good fits to the data. Note that a just-identified model with zero degrees of freedom would obtain a zero parsimonious fit index value even when its normed fit index value is unity.

We will now illustrate the use of the normed fit indices, as well as estimation, significance testing, and nested models, in an example of a structural model with latent variables.

Example

What follows is a series of analyses based on an artificially generated sample variance/covariance matrix. This matrix was designed to simulate data obtained from a sample of 800 observations on 13 manifest variables having the structural relationships of the model in Figures 4.9 and 4.14. This sample variance/covariance matrix is shown in Table 4.3.

Our first task will be to evaluate the "measurement model" part of the model in Figure 4.9 and Figure 4.14. In this phase of our analysis we will attempt to answer questions such as the following: Have we selected variables that behave as indicators of latent variables in the manner that the manifest variables of the model in Figure 4.9 and Figure 4.14 do? In other words, are manifest variables $y_3, \ldots, y_6$ all related to a single, common latent variable or factor? Can we say the same thing about variables $y_7, \ldots, y_{10}$ or variables $y_{11}, \ldots, y_{14}$? Is variable x_2 uncorrelated with variables $y_{11}, \ldots, y_{14}$? These questions can be answered by testing the model shown in Figure 4.13. To do this we will now seek maximum likelihood estimates of the parameters of the model in Figure 4.13.[6]

The maximum likelihood estimates along with the estimated standard errors of the free parameters of the model in Figure 4.13 are shown in the structural diagram in Figure 4.17. The chi-square test for goodness of fit with 61 degrees of freedom yields a value of 57.4074. The probability of getting a chi-square statistic this large or larger with 61 degrees of freedom is .6069. Hence the goodness-of-fit statistic is not significant at the .05 level, and we can accept the model as consistent with the data.

Having accepted a model in which the variables are divided into homogeneous clusters in the expected manner, we now can focus on the structure among the latent variables of that model. We will assume that, according to theory, the latent variables of the model in Figure 4.17 have a structure like that of Figure 4.9 or Figure 4.14. In specifying this model we will have to fix the values of the two structural parameters relating the disturbance variables ϵ_1 and ϵ_2 to their corresponding latent endogenous variables η_1 and η_2 just so the metric of these endogenous variables will be

TABLE 4.3

Sample Covariances Among 13 Manifest Variables of the Model
in Figure 4.14 for a Sample of 800 Observations

	y3	y4	y5	y6	y7	y8	y9	y10	y11	y12	y13	y14	x2
y3	.99												
y4	.56	1.10											
y5	.60	.63	1.07										
y6	.66	.69	.74	1.14									
y7	.43	.49	.50	.51	1.08								
y8	.37	.42	.42	.46	.64	.94							
y9	.47	.52	.55	.57	.78	.69	1.22						
y10	.35	.40	.41	.45	.61	.53	.65	.93					
y11	.29	.38	.39	.44	.25	.26	.29	.22	.97				
y12	.25	.30	.31	.38	.22	.20	.26	.19	.51	1.00			
y13	.24	.34	.32	.36	.18	.21	.26	.21	.49	.44	.94		
y14	.25	.36	.34	.39	.24	.23	.28	.20	.54	.44	.48	.91	
x2	.43	.47	.50	.51	.35	.33	.40	.29	.03	−.01	−.04	−.00	.96

determined. In Figure 4.18 we show the structural diagram of this model again, but this time with maximum likelihood estimates and estimated standard errors of the values of the structural parameters of this model. The chi-square statistic for this model has 64 degrees of freedom and a value of 57.6570. The probability of getting a chi-square with 64 degrees of freedom this large or larger is .6988. Again, the chi-square statistic is not significant at the .05 level, and so we continue to accept the model. The difference chi-square for the comparison of the models in Figures 4.13 and 4.14 is 57.6570 − 57.4074 = .2496 with 64 − 61 = 3 degrees of freedom. This is not significant. Hence the specification of the causal structure among the exogenous and latent endogenous variables is consistent with the data.

Because the chi-square goodness-of-fit statistic is not significant, we may now test hypotheses about various free parameters of the model in Figure 4.18. One way we could do this at this point is to perform confidence interval tests of whether the various free parameters of this model are equal to zero or not. For example, we may wish to test the hypothesis that the structural parameter α_{21} relating the first latent endogenous variable to the second latent endogenous variable is equal to zero. The maximum likelihood estimate of α_{21} is equal to .729 and has a standard error of .054. An approximate 95 percent confidence interval estimate of α_{21} is thus $[.729 - 2(.054) < \alpha_{21} < .729 + 2(.054)]$ or

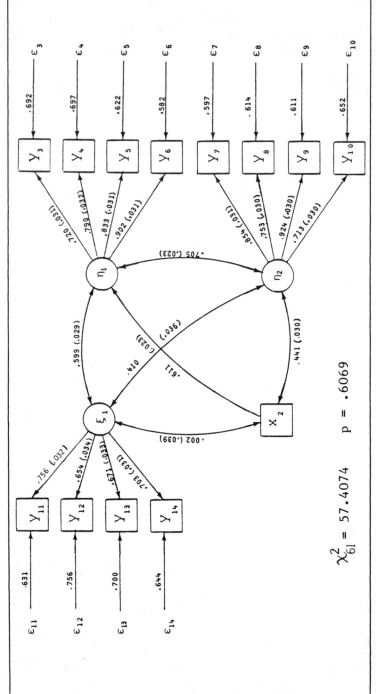

$$\chi^2_{61} = 57.4074 \qquad p = .6069$$

Figure 4.17 Model in Figure 4.13 shown with maximum likelihood estimates of structural parameters and covariances among variables indicated in the diagram. Numbers in parentheses are standard errors of the corresponding parameter estimates.

$[.611 < \alpha_{21} < .837]$. Since the interval does not include zero, we reject the hypothesis that α_{21} is equal to zero (see Jöreskog & Sörbom, 1979). In Figure 4.18 the standard errors of each of the free structural parameters of the model are indicated in parentheses next to the corresponding maximum likelihood estimates of these parameters. A test of this form could be performed for each free parameter in turn. However, the tests in such a sequence of tests will not be independent and will have an unknown bias after the first test.

Instead of performing at this point a series of confidence interval tests of the free parameters, we may also proceed with the remainder of the a priori sequence of tests described earlier. The remaining tests will test hypotheses about select free parameters of the model in Figure 4.14 and 4.18 using difference chi-square statistics. To begin with, consider the model in Figure 4.15. This is a model nested within the previous model in Figure 4.14 in which the structural parameters pertaining to the relationships between the two exogenous and the two latent endogenous variables (i.e., $\gamma_{11}, \gamma_{12}, \alpha_{21}$) have all been fixed to zero. All other fixed parameters are the same. For the model in Figure 4.15, the chi-square goodness-of-fit statistic with 67 degrees of freedom is equal to 1120.5375, which is significant at the .05 level. The difference chi-square between this model (Figure 4.15) and the previous model (Figure 4.14 or 4.18) is 1061.8805 – 1120.5375 = 57.675, with 3 = 67 – 64 degrees of freedom, which is significant at the .05 level. This means that fixing to zero the three additional parameters pertaining to causal relationships among the two exogenous and the two latent endogenous variables produces a definite lack of fit of the model to the data. Hence there must be nonzero relationships between these variables as specified by the causal connections hypothesized between them.

Because the chi-square statistic for goodness of fit of the model in Figure 4.15 is significant, we cannot proceed with any further statistical tests for the fit of further restricted models nested within the previous models. They would all be rejected. We thus end up accepting the structural equation model repeated in Figures 4.9, 4.14, and 4.18 as adequately fitting the thirteen variables.

However, we may further wish to apply the normed fit index to the model in Figure 4.18. To obtain this value we first must obtain the value of the chi-square goodness-of-fit statistic for a "null" model that proposes that the covariances between different variables of the set of thirteen manifest variables are all zero. In other words, the hypothetical model variance/covariance matrix $\hat{\Sigma}_0$ is presumed to be a diagonal matrix with zeros in its off-diagonal positions. This would correspond to the model illustrated in the structural diagram in Figure 4.16. In this case the value of the chi-square goodness-of-fit statistic with 78 degrees of freedom is computed to be 5029.1802, which is significant at the .05 level. But the

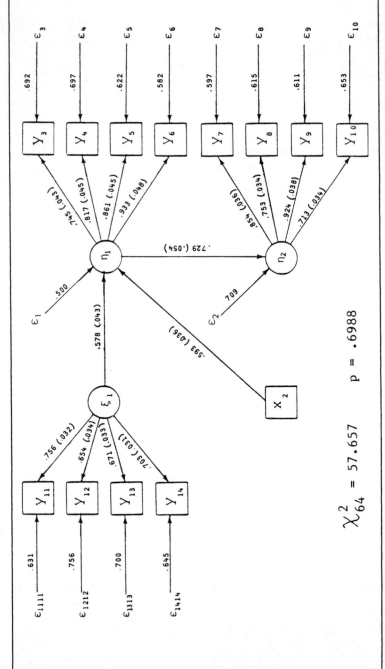

$$\chi^2_{64} = 57.657 \qquad p = .6988$$

Figure 4.18 Structural equation model of Figure 4.14 shown with maximum likelihood estimates of free parameters of the model.

normed fit index for the model in Figure 4.18 is (5029.1802 – 57.675)/5029.1802 = .9885, with an associated reduction in degrees of freedom in going from the null model to the structural equation model of (78 – 64) = 14.

The efficiency index for the model in Figure 4.18 is .9885/14 = .0706. The parsimonious fit index is (64/78) × .9885 = .811. These results mean we have gained considerable improvement in fit at the expense of very little loss in degrees of freedom in going from the null model to the structural equation model to account for the relationships among the thirteen manifest variables. This provides considerable support for the model in Figures 4.9, 4.14, and 4.18.

APPLICATIONS

A number of latent variable models are available in addition to the recursive model we used to illustrate latent variable designs. References to a large number of studies are furnished in the Annual Review chapter on "Multivariate Analysis with Latent Variables: Causal Modeling," by Bentler (1980). One can also find overviews of a number of important designs in Jöreskog (1978) and more complete illustrations in Jöreskog and Sörbom (1979). Of special interest are models that can be used to test assumptions associated with selected conditions for confirmatory analysis, using latent variable designs. For example, an overview of latent variable models for testing reciprocal causation (Condition 4) was presented recently by Maruyama and McGarvey (1980). (Unfortunately, these authors made the unwarranted assumption that disturbances for reciprocally related, latent endogenous variables were unrelated.) Tests for moderators, which help to specify boundaries for theory (Condition 6), have been addressed by Werts, Rock, Linn, and Jöreskog (1976), Werts, Rock, and Grandy (1979), and Werts, Rock, and Linn (1979). The question of stability of structural models (Condition 7) has been investigated in growth and longitudinal studies (Jöreskog, 1979; Jöreskog & Sörbom, 1979; Werts, Jöreskog & Linn, 1972). Finally, questions concerning the operationalization of variables and constructs (Condition 8), such as method variance and other forms of nonrandom measurement error, have received considerable attention in the latent variable literature (see Alwin & Jackson, 1980; Kalleberg & Kleugel, 1975; Mulaik, 1975; Mellenbergh, Kelderman, Stijlen & Zondag, 1979; Werts, Rock, Linn, & Jöreskog, 1976; Werts, Breland, Grandy, & Rock, 1980).

THE CONDITIONS FOR CAUSAL MODELING
WITH LATENT VARIABLE MODELS

By now it should be clear that to do confirmatory analysis with latent variable structural models, one still has to satisfy the ten conditions for confirmatory analysis described earlier (Chapter 2) for models with manifest variables. So far, our discussion of latent variable models has focused on methodological procedures for determining whether structural parameters associated with hypothesized causal connections between variables are indeed not equal to zero (Condition 9) and whether the specifications of fixed parameters in the identification of the model are consistent with the data (Condition 10). We also furnished references regarding models and tests for causal direction (Condition 4), moderators (Condition 6), stability and stationarity (Condition 7), and construct validity (Condition 8). This might suggest that researchers using latent variable models have addressed conditions for confirmatory analysis in a meaningful and thorough manner. However, such has not always been the case. It is our impression that many of the conditions have been violated, often seriously, in published confirmatory analysis using latent variables. We shall review below our more serious concerns.

Violations of Conditions 1, 2, and 5. We have observed numerous studies with violations of the self-containment condition (Condition 5), where obvious relevant causal variables have been omitted from latent variable structural models. These omissions of relevant causes have seemed *not* to be due to a dearth of knowledge or theory available to investigators in the field, but due to a superficial regard for theory and available knowledge (violations of Conditions 1 and 2) accompanying the rush to implement a new methodology. In fact, violations of Conditions 1 and 2 may be the root of most misuses of confirmatory methods with latent variables, and for us this is evidenced by the many studies in the literature in which little or no effort has been made to provide theoretical justification for the model to be analyzed. It is time that theoretical concerns receive at least equal emphasis as methodological concerns in latent variable analysis.

Misinterpretations of Disturbance Variables (Disturbance Terms). Another common mistake is to short-circuit the distinction between disturbance variables and residual variables. Disturbance variables are not "residual variables," that is, variables representing variation in the endogenous variables after effects due to preceding causal variables in functional equations have been partialed out in the *estimation* process. In this case residual variables are always uncorrelated with causal variables in structural equations because of the mathematics of partialing. As with manifest variable models, the correct way to view disturbance variables is to regard them as causal effects on the endogenous variables due to such things as omitted causal variables, random shocks, and misspecifications of equations.

The extraneous causal influences acting on an endogenous variable may or may not be correlated with the causal variables included explicitly in the functional equation for an endogenous variable. If in a functional equation the disturbance variable is correlated with the causal variables (for example, the disturbance includes relevant causes), then the functional equation and the system of functional equations will not be self-contained (i.e., a violation of Condition 5), and it will be impossible to determine in a consistent way the effects of the causal variables on the endogenous variables. Thus, we must have good reasons to assume that the disturbance variables are uncorrelated with the causal variables in functional equations. In other words, we must know of no plausible unmeasured extraneous variable that acts upon an endogenous variable and at the same time correlates with the causal variables of the endogenous variable. If this is the case, then in the estimation process residual variables can be tentatively identified with disturbance variables.

In a related vein, another frequent mistake with latent variable models is to presume without prior justification that the disturbance variables contain only error of measurement. Often the variances of the disturbance terms are interpreted as "error variances" and used to estimate the reliability of certain manifest variables. But as we have already indicated, the disturbances may contain *true* variance that is associated with omitted causal variables not included in the study. Another misinterpretation is to assume that the disturbance variables are like unique factors in common factor analysis, which are always mutually uncorrelated. But it is quite possible to have correlated disturbance variables because omitted, relevant causal variables represented in different disturbances can be correlated. Most estimation algorithms allow one to estimate these correlations, but such estimation is meaningful only in certain types of designs, such as nonrecursive and time-series models.

In summary, disturbance variables are often misunderstood and misinterpreted in latent variable models. To a great extent this appears to be again attributable to the lack of attention to Conditions 1, 2, and 5.

Exploratory Rather than Confirmatory Analysis. A serious misuse of the methodology of confirmatory analysis with latent variables is to "play" with fixing and freeing the elements of the parameter matrices. That is, a researcher may conduct numerous analyses with different fixed and free parameters until a model is found that best fits the data. It is also not unknown for some researchers to change assumptions regarding causal direction for the same purpose. This is nothing but exploratory analysis and does not represent a confirmatory analysis. Stated simply, a confirmatory analysis tests only a priori models that have a strong theoretical base. This does not preclude, however, testing several a priori models on the same sample.

Failure to Overidentify Parameters. Another shortcoming of many confirmatory analyses using both manifest and latent variables is to fail to overidentify the structural parameters of the measurement portion of a model, that is, the connections between latent variables and their manifest indicators. As mentioned earlier in this chapter, overidentification is essential if one is to specify a model in ways in which it can be potentially falsified. As it most often happens, failure to overidentify parameters occurs when a researcher selects only a few manifest indicators to represent each latent variable. Unfortunately, unequivocal guidelines are not available at the present time concerning the number of manifest indicators per latent variable required for overidentification to test all important hypotheses. However, as a heuristic, we suggest that each latent variable in a model be represented by at least four manifest indicator variables. In this case the structural parameters of the "measurement" submodels relating each set of manifest indicators to their respective latent variables will be overidentified, and it should be possible to test the measurement aspects of the model.

These are our most serious concerns with respect to the use of latent variables in confirmatory analysis. They are by no means exhaustive of all the concerns in this area. In fact, many of the issues we raised in regard to manifest variable models, such as the need for equilibrium-type conditions and specification of causal intervals in time-series analysis, apply equally to latent variable models. We will not attempt to document all of these issues again for latent variable models. Rather, we suggest that the users of the latent variable approach have been at least as cavalier as users of the manifest variable approach in regard to theoretical justifications for using confirmatory analysis. We recommend strongly that theoretical issues be given greater attention in latent variable designs.

CAUSAL INFERENCE WITH LATENT VARIABLES

There are dangers and difficulties for causal inference in using the latent variable concept because it implies explanation in terms of unseen, not directly measurable, processes and/or entities. The danger is that when a model with latent variables appears consistent with data, one may fail to entertain the possibility of alternative models for the same data. Latent variables can never be regarded as representing unique explanations of any phenomenon. This is especially to be remembered in latent variable models because the number of latent variables, including latent disturbances, will always exceed the number of manifest variables. As a consequence, the latent variables can never be uniquely determined from the manifest variables; what is manifest and seen cannot uniquely define what is latent and unseen. This result is now well known for the latent variable model of exploratory common factor analysis (see Mulaik & McDonald, 1978; McDonald & Mulaik, 1979 for reviews of this problem in factor analysis). But the result also generalizes from common factor models to structural equation models with latent variables.

There are two important aspects to the problem of indeterminacy for latent variables: (1) Scores on latent variables are not uniquely defined. (2) The identity of latent variables is not uniquely determined from the manifest variables dependent on them.

When a structural equation model with latent variables fits a set of data, one may naturally want to have a way to obtain measurements on the latent variables. Borrowing the factor score concept from factor analysis, some have tried to obtain these measurements by regressing the latent variables onto the manifest variables, using information about the covariances among the manifest variables and between the manifest variables and the latent variables, as the basis for the regression estimates. However, the regression estimates of the latent variables are not equivalent to the latent variables, differing from them by an indeterminate amount whose variance is equal to the error of estimate in estimating the latent variable from the manifest variables. It is the unpredictable part of the latent variable that is indeterminate. There is no unique solution for this part. Hence, one can construct more than one solution for the latent variable by combining the predictable part—obtained from the regression of the latent variable onto the manifest variables—with a variable independent of the predictable part, chosen arbitrarily to stand for the unpredictable part. When the squared multiple correlation for predicting a latent variable is less than .70, then quite possibly two alternatively constructed solutions for the same latent variable can be correlated not just zero, but negatively with one another. The use of constructed or estimated "factor scores" to stand for a latent variable is not recommended when the multiple correlation for predicting a latent variable is less than .80. When the multiple correlation is less than .80, such scores may show moderate to strong correlations with other variables while possibly the real latent variable in question has only zero to moderate correlations with these other variables.

More problematic is the indeterminacy in the identity of latent variables in structural equation models. To be sure, a researcher performs a confirmatory analysis with an interpretation already given to the latent variables of the analysis. If the model is disconfirmed because the latent variables do not relate to their respective manifest indicators as expected by hypothesis, then one may question either the choice of indicators, or more seriously, the interpretations attached to the latent variables of the model that led one to believe that the manifest variables would be linked together through the latent variables.

But what can one conclude if the model is corroborated by showing acceptable fit between latent and manifest variables? Is the model corroborated because the manifest variables have as causes the latent variables presumed at the outset to be causes of them? Or is the model corroborated because the manifest variables have some other variables as causes? In particular, could there be other variables having the *same* pattern of relationships with the manifest variables as one's hypothetical latent variables, but distinct from them? The mathematics of indeterminacy for latent variables allows for this. But there is no way to resolve such questions other than to try to make explicit all possible alternative interpretations for the results and then to perform further studies to differentiate between the interpretations. But the indeterminacy of latent variables is not a fatal flaw of latent variable models. It is a reflection of the indeterminacy in all inductive attempts to use empirical observations to confirm theories by examining whether consequences deduced from the theories do indeed occur as expected. We emphasized this point earlier in Chapter 3.

We recognize that there are those who are uncomfortable with unseen causes, latent variables, and hypothetical constructs. In fact, inspired by the nineteenth-century writings of the empiricist philosophers Mach and Pearson, the followers of the positivist movement in the philosophy of science sought between 1920 and 1950 to exlude from science all reference to unseen causes, believing that incorrigible knowledge could only be derived from sensory experience and hence from those things that were observed. Since the 1950s the philosophy of science has taken a more pragmatic and less dogmatic and absolutistic position with respect to knowledge. The result is that the use of "unseen causes" is accepted now with greater tolerance, as long as the unseen causes allow one to unify broader domains of experience than before and are interpreted in terms of categories that in principle may eventually be observable or predict novel, observable results. It is interesting to note that Mach resisted atomic theory in physics because atoms were often given an independent reality over and beyond the observable phenomena to which they were theoretically tied, while Pearson opposed the Mendelian theory of the segregation of unit characters in the germ cells for nearly twenty years after Mendel's work was discovered in 1900, partly because Mendel's theory was too theoretical and not merely descriptive. In a way, these scientists' reluctance to take seriously what were at the time hypothetical constructs led them to resist what were to become the next major developments in their respective fields. Thus to "see" things differently, and this includes in some cases "seeing" in things what is not directly visible in them, may be essential first steps to achieving better understanding of the relationships between things in our world.

Notes

1. Theories of stress often differentiate between (a) qualitative overload, which refers to demands that exceed physical and/or personnel resources, and (b) quantitative overload, which refers to demands that exceed available time limits but not physical/personnel resources (see Katz & Kahn, 1978). Both sources of overload are addressed in the illustration.

2. The conditional function has the form of the linear regression function (Lord & Novick, 1968). Other functions, such as maximum likelihood functions, may be employed to represent functional relations (see Jöreskog & Sörbom, 1979).

3. Methodology has also been developed for nominal and ordinal scales of measurement (see Carter, 1971; Boyle, 1970; Heise, 1972; Lyons, 1977; Spaeth, 1975).

4. The latter assumption satisfies the "rank condition" required for identification, which is beyond the mathematical scope of this treatment. It implies that estimates of structural parameters will not be subject to at least severe bias resulting from multicollinearity (see Billings & Wroten, 1978; Johnston, 1972).

5. Points 1 through 3 are analogous to conventional contrasts between standardized and unstandardized regression weights, which are not elaborated here. Decomposition of correlations is treated in Condition 10.

6. In actuality the sample variance/covariance matrix in Table 4.3 was created in the following way: First, 800 observations on the 15 mutually uncorrelated independent variables of the model in Figures 4.9 and 4.14 were generated using a computer random-number generator that produces numbers that are approximately normally distributed with means of zero and standard deviations of unity. The sample variance/covariance matrix for these 15 artificially generated variables was then calculated and used as a sample estimate Φ of the matrix of covariances among the independent variables of the model in Figure 4.14. Then after fixing the zero and other fixed elements of the matrices Λ, Γ, and Δ to specify the model in Figure 4.14, arbitrary values were then chosen for the remaining "free" parameters of these matrices and the resulting sample variance/covariance matrix was derived using equations 4.9a-4.9c. Thus the matrix in Table 4.3 simulates a sample variance/covariance matrix taken from a population distributed according to the multivariate normal distribution consistent with the model in Figure 4.14.

7. The estimates of the free parameters of the models discussed in this section were obtained using the program LISREL IV (Jöreskog & Sörbom, 1978).

References

Alwin, D. F., & Jackson, D. J. Measurement models for response errors in surveys: Issues and applications. In K. F. Schuessler (Ed.), *Sociological methodology, 1980.* San Francisco: Jossey-Bass, 1979.

Bandura, A. The self-system in reciprocal determinism. *American Psychologist,* 1978, 33, 344-358.

Bentler, P. M. Multistructure statistical model applied to factor analysis. *Multivariate Behavioral Research,* 1976, 11, 3-25.

Bentler, P. M. Linear simultaneous equation systems with multiple levels and types of latent variables. In K. G. Jöreskog & H. Wold (Eds.), *Systems under indirect observation,* 1979.

Bentler, P. M. Multivariate analysis with latent variables: Causal modeling. *Annual Review of Psychology,* 1980, 31, 419-456.

Bentler, P. M., & Bonett, D. G. Significance tests and goodness of fit in the analysis of covariance structures. *Psychological Bulletin,* 1980, 88, 588-606.

Bentler, P. M., & Lee, S. Y. *Structural models with polynomial constraints.* Paper presented at the Annual Meeting of the American Educational Research Association, New York, March 23, 1982.

Bentler, P. M., & Weeks, D. G. Linear structural equations with latent variables. *Psychometrika,* 1980, 45, 289-308.

Billings, R. S. & Wroten, S. P. Use of path analysis in industrial/organizational psychology: Criticisms and suggestions. *Journal of Applied Psychology,* 1978, 63, 677-688.

Blalock, H. M. Causal inferences, closed populations, and measures of association. *American Political Science Review,* 1967, 61, 130-136.

Blalock, H. M. Theory building and causal inferences. In H. M. Blalock & A. B. Blalock (Eds.), *Methodology in social research.* New York: McGraw-Hill, 1968.

Blalock, H. M. *Theory construction.* Englewood Cliff, NJ: Prentice-Hall, 1969.

Blalock, H. M. (Ed.), *Causal models in the social sciences.* Chicago: Aldine-Atherton, 1971.

Blalock, H. M., Wells, C. S., & Carter, L. F. Statistical estimation with random measurement error. In E. F. Borgatta & G. W. Bohrnstedt (Eds.), *Sociological methodology.* San Francisco: Jossey-Bass, 1970.

Bohrnstedt, G. W., & Carter, T. M. Robustness in regression analysis. In H. L. Costner (Ed.), *Sociological methodology.* San Francisco: Jossey-Bass, 1971.

Borgatta, E. F., & Jackson, D. J. (Eds.). *Aggregate data: Analysis and interpretation.* Beverly Hills, CA: Sage, 1980.

Bowers, K. S. Situationism in psychology: An analysis and a critique. *Psychological Review,* 1973, 80, 307-336.

Boyle, R. P. Path analysis and ordinal data. *American Journal of Sociology*, 1970, 75, 461-480.

Bradley, J. *Mach's philosophy of science*. London: Athlone Press, University of London, 1971.

Bunge, M. *Causality*. Cambridge, MA: Harvard University Press, 1959.

Byerly, H. C. *A primer of logic*. New York: Harper & Row, 1973.

Campbell, D. T., & Fiske, D. W. Covergent and discriminatory validation by the multitrait-multimethod matrix. *Psychological Bulletin*, 1959, 56, 81-105.

Capaldi, N. *Human knowledge*. New York: Pegasus, 1969.

Carroll, J. B. The nature of data, or how to choose a correlation coefficient. *Psychometrika*, 1961, 26, 347-372.

Cliff, N. *Some cautions concerning the application of causal modeling methods*. Paper presented at a National Institute for Justice Workshop on Research Methodology and Criminal Justice Program Evaluation, Baltimore, March, 1980.

Cohen, J., & Cohen, P. *Applied multiple regression/correlation analysis for the behavioral sciences*. New York: John Wiley, 1975.

Cook, T. D., & Campbell, D. T. The design and conduct of quasi-experiments and true experiments in field settings. In M. D. Dunnette (Ed.), *Handbook of industrial and organizational psychology*. Chicago: Rand McNally, 1976.

Cook, T. D., & Campbell, D. T. *Quasi-experimentation: Design and analysis issues for field settings*. Chicago: Rand McNally, 1979.

Costner, H. L. Theory, deduction, and rules of correspondence. *American Journal of Sociology*, 1969, 75, 245-263.

Cronbach, L. J., & Meehl, P. E. Construct validity in psychological tests. *Psychological Bulletin*, 1955, 62, 281-302.

Dansereau, F., Jr., Graen, G., & Haga, W. J. A vertical dyad linkage approach to leadership within formal organizations: A longitudinal investigation of the role making process. *Organizational Behavior and Human Performance*, 1975, 13, 46-78.

Darlington, R. B. Multiple regression in psychological research and practice. *Psychological Bulletin*, 1968, 69, 161-182.

Darlington, R. B., & Rom, J. F. Assessing the importance of independent variables in nonlinear causal laws. *American Educational Research Journal*, 1972, 9, 449-462.

Deegan, J., Jr. Specification error in causal models. *Social Science Research*, 1974, 3, 235-259.

Dilman, I. *Induction and deduction: A study in Wittgenstein*. Oxford: Basil Blackwell, 1973.

Dubin, R. Theory building in applied areas. In M. D. Dunnette (Ed.), *Handbook of industrial and organizational psychology*. Chicago: Rand McNally, 1976.

Duncan, O. D. Partials, partitions, and paths. In E. F. Borgatta & G. W. Bohrnstedt (Eds.), *Sociological methodology, 1970*. San Francisco: Jossey-Bass, 1970.

Duncan, O. D. *Introduction to structural equation models*. New York: Academic, 1975.

Ekehammer, B. Interactionism in personality from a historical perspective. *Psychological Bulletin*, 1974, 81, 1026-1048.

Endler, N. S., & Magnusson, D. Toward an interactional psychology of personality. *Psychological Bulletin*, 1976, 83, 956-974.

Endler, N. S., & Magnusson, D. The interaction model of anxiety: An empirical test in an examination situation. *Canadian Journal of Behavioral Science*, 1977, 9, 101-107.

Feigl, H. De principiis non disputandum . . . ? In Black, M. (Ed.), *Philosophical analysis.* Englewood Cliffs, NJ: Prentice-Hall, 1963.

Firebaugh, G. A rule for inferring individual-level relationships from aggregate data. *American Sociological Review,* 1978, 43, 557-572.

Fisher, F. M. *The identification problem in econometrics.* New York: McGraw-Hill, 1966.

Georgescu-Roegen, N. *The entropy law and the economic process.* Cambridge, MA: Harvard University Press, 1971.

Goldberger, A. S. Efficient estimation in overidentified models: An interpretive analysis. In A. S. Goldberger & O. D. Duncan (Eds.), *Structural equation models in the social sciences.* New York: Seminar Press, 1973.

Goldberger, A. S., & Duncan, O. D. *Structural equation models in the social sciences.* New York: Seminar Press, 1973.

Gordon, R. Issues in multiple regression. *American Journal of Sociology,* 1968, 73, 592-616.

Griffin, L. J. Causal modeling of psychological success in work organizations. *Academy of Management Journal,* 1977, 20, 6-33.

Hannan, M. T. Problems of aggregation. In H. M. Blalock (Ed.), *Causal models in the social sciences.* Chicago: Aldine, 1971.

Heise, D. R. Problems in path analysis and causal inference. In E. F. Borgatta (Ed.), *Sociological methodology,* 1969. San Francisco: Jossey-Bass, 1969.

Heise, D. R. Employing nominal variables, induced variables, and block variables in path analysis. *Sociological Methods & Research,* 1972, 1, 147-173.

Heise, D. R. *Causal analysis.* New York: John Wiley, 1975.

Hemphill, C. G., & Oppenheim, P. Logic of explanation. *Philosophy of Science,* 1948, 15, 135-175.

Hume, D. [*An enquiry concerning human understanding*] (E. Steinberg, Ed.). Indianapolis: Hacket, 1977. (Originally published, 1748.)

James, L. R. The unmeasured variables problem in path analysis. *Journal of Applied Psychology,* 1980, 65, 415-421.

James, L. R. A test for asymmetric relationships between two reciprocally related variables. *Multivariate Behavioral Research,* 1981, 16, 63-82.

James, L. R., & Jones, A. P. Organizational structure: A review of structural dimensions and their conceptual relationships with attitudes and behavior. *Organizational Behavior and Human Performance,* 1976, 16, 74-113.

James, L. R., & Jones, A. P. Perceived job characteristics and job satisfaction: An examination of reciprocal causation. *Personnel Psychology,* 1980, 33, 97-135.

James, L. R., & Sells, S. B. Psychological climate: Theoretical perspectives and empirical research. In D. Magnusson (Ed.), *Toward a psychology of situations: An interactional perspective.* Hillsdale, NJ: Lawrence Erlbaum, 1981.

James, L. R., & Singh, K. An introduction to the logic, assumptions, and basic analytic procedures of two-stage least squares. *Psychological Bulletin,* 1978, 85, 1104-1122.

Jeffreys, H. *Theory of Probability* (2nd ed.). Oxford: Clarendon, 1948.

Johnston, J. J. *Econometric methods* (2nd ed.). New York: McGraw-Hill, 1972.

Jöreskog, K. G. A general method for the analysis of covariance structures. *Biometrika,* 1970, 57, 239-251.

Jöreskog, K. G. A general method for estimating a linear structural equation system. In A. S. Goldberger & O. D. Duncan (Eds.), *Structural equation models in the social sciences.* New York: Seminar Press, 1973.

Jöreskog, K. G. Structural analysis of covariance and correlation matrices. *Psychometrikia*, 1978, 43, 443-477.

Jöreskog, K. G. Statistical estimation of structural models in longitudinal developmental investigation. In J. R. Nesselroade & P. B. Baltes (Eds.), *Longitudinal research in the study of behavior and development*. New York: Academic, 1979. (a)

Jöreskog, K. G. Statistical models and methods for analysis of longitudinal data. In K. G. Jöreskog and D. Sörbom, *Advances in factor analysis and structural equation models*. Cambridge, MA: Abt Books, 1979. (b)

Jöreskog, K. G., & Goldberger, A. S. Estimation of a model with multiple indicators and multiple causes of a single latent variable. *Journal of the American Statistical Association*, 1975, 70, 631-639.

Jöreskog, K. G., & Sörbom, D. *LISREL IV users guide*. Chicago: National Educational Resources, 1978.

Jöreskog, K. G., & Sörbom, D. *Advances in factor analysis and structural equation models*. Cambridge, MA: Abt Books, 1979.

Jöreskog, K. G. & Sörbom, D. *LISREL V: Analysis of linear structural relationships by maximum likelihood and least squares methods*. Research Report 81-8, Department of Statistics, University of Uppsala, Uppsala, Sweden, 1981.

Kalleberg, A. L., & Kluegel, J. R. Analysis of the multitrait-multimethod matrix: Some limitations and an alternative. *Journal of Applied Psychology*, 1975, 60, 1-9.

Katz, D., & Kahn, R. L. *The social psychology of organizations* (2nd ed.). New York: John Wiley, 1978.

Keesling, J. W. *Maximum likelihood approaches to causal flow analysis*. Ph.D. thesis, University of Chicago, Chicago, Illinois, 1972.

Kenny, D. A. *Correlation and causality*. New York: John Wiley, 1979.

Kenny, D. A. Cross-lagged panel correlation: A test for spuriousness. *Psychological Bulletin*, 1975, 82, 887-903.

Khattab, A., & Hocevar, D. *Significance testing in confirmatory factor analytic models*. Paper presented at the Annual Meeting of the American Educational Research Association, New York City, New York, March 22, 1982.

Koopmans, T. C., & Hood, W. C. The estimation of simultaneous linear economic relationships. In W. C. Hood & T. C. Koopmans (Eds.), *Studies in econometric methods*. New York: John Wiley, 1953.

Kritzer, H. M. Political protest and political violence: A nonrecursive causal model. *Social Forces*, 1977, 5, 630-640.

Larzelere, R. E., & Mulaik, S. A. Single-sample tests for many correlations. *Psychological Bulletin*, 1977, 84, 557-569.

L'Esperance, L. "Interdependence vs. recursiveness: A review of the debate and notions of causality in economics." In Brunner, Karl (Ed.), *Problems and issues in current econometric practice*. Columbis, OH: College of Administrative Science, Ohio State University, 1972.

Lord, F. M., & Novick, M. R. *Statistical theories of mental test scores*. Reading, MA: Addison-Wesley, 1968.

Lyons, M. Techniques for using ordinal measures in regression and path analysis. In K. F. Schuessler (Ed.), *Sociological methodology, 1977*. Jossey-Bass: San Francisco, 1977.

Mahoney, M. J. Reflections on the cognitive-learning trend in psychotherapy. *American Psychologist*, 1977, 32, 5-13.

Maruyama, G., & McGarvey, B. Evaluating causal models: An application of maximum-likelihood analysis of structural equations. *Psychological Bulletin*, 1980, 87, 502-512.

McArdle, J. J. The development of general multivariate software. In J. Hirschbuhl (Ed.), *Proceedings of the Association for the Development of Computer Based Instructional Systems*. Akron, OH: University of Akron Press, 1979.

McArdle, J. J. Causal modeling applied to psychonomic systems simulation. *Behavioral Research Methods and Instrumentation*, 1980, 12, 193-209.

McDonald, R. P. A simple comprehensive model for the analysis of covariance structures. *British Journal of Mathematical and Statistical Psychology*, 1978, 31, 59-72.

McDonald, R. P. A simple comprehensive model for the analysis of covariance structures: Some remarks on applications. *British Journal of Mathematical and Statistical Psychology*, 1980, 33, 161-183.

McDonald, R. P., & Mulaik, S. A. Determinacy of common factors: A nontechnical review. *Psychological Bulletin*, 1979, 86, 297-306.

Mellenbergh, G. J., Kelderman, H., Stijlen, J. G., & Zondag, E. Linear models for the analysis and construction of instruments in a facet design. *Psychological Bulletin*, 1979, 86, 766-776.

Merton, R. K. *Social theory and social structure*. Glencoe, IL: Free Press, 1968.

Miller, A. D. Logic of causal analysis: From experimental to nonexperimental designs. In H. M. Blalock (Ed.), *Causal models in the social sciences*. Chicago: Aldine-Atherton, 1971.

Mischel, W. On the future of personality measurement. *American Psychologist*, 1977, 32, 246-254.

Mulaik, S. A. *The foundations of factor analysis*. New York: McGraw-Hill, 1972.

Mulaik, S. A. Confirmatory factor analysis. In D. J. Amick and H. J. Walberg (Eds.), *Introductory multivariate analysis for educational, psychological, and social research*. Berkeley, CA: McCutchan, 1975.

Mulaik, S. A., & McDonald, R. P. The effect of additional variables on factor indeterminacy. *Psychometrika*, 1978, 43, 177-192.

Namboodiri, N. K., Carter, L. R., & Blalock, H. M. *Applied multivariate analysis and experimental designs*. New York: McGraw-Hill, 1975.

Ostrom, C. W. *Time series analysis: Regression techniques*. Beverly Hills, CA: Sage, 1978.

Pearson, K. *The grammar of science*. London: Adam & Charles Black, 1911. (Originally published, 1892.)

Pervin, L. Performance and satisfaction as a function of individual-environment fit. *Psychological Bulletin*, 1968, 69, 56-68.

Pindyck, R. S., & Rubinfeld, D. L. *Econometric models and economic forecasts*. New York: McGraw-Hill, 1976.

Popper, K. R. *The logic of scientific discovery* [*Die, Logik der Forschung*]. New York: Basic Books, 1959. (Originally published, 1935.)

Roberts, K. H., Hulin, C. L., & Rousseau, D. M. *Developing an interdisciplinary science of organizations*. San Francisco: Jossey-Bass, 1978.

Roy, J. Step-down procedure in multivariate analysis. *Annals of Mathematical Statistics*, 1958, 29, 1177-1187.

Rozelle, R. M., & Campbell, D. T. More plausible rival hypotheses in the cross-lagged panel correlation techniques. *Psychological Bulletin*, 1969, 71, 74-80.

Schlick, M. Causality in everyday life and in recent science. In H. Feigl & W. Sellars (Eds.), *Readings in philosophical analysis*. New York: Appleton-Century-Crofts, 1949.

Schmidt, P. *Econometrics*. New York: Marcel Dekker, 1976.

Schoenberg, R. Strategies for meaningful comparison. In H. L. Costner (Ed.), *Sociological Methodology, 1972*. San Francisco: Jossey-Bass, 1972.

Simon, H. A. On the definition of the causal relation. *Journal of Philosophy,* 1952, 49, 517-528.

Simon, H. A. Causal ordering and identifiability. In W. C. Hood and T. C. Koopmans (Eds.), *Studies in econometric methods*. New York: John Wiley, 1953.

Simon, H. A. *Models of discovery*. Dordrecht, Holland: R. Reidel, 1977.

Simon, H. A., & Rescher, N. Cause and counterfactual. *Philosphy of Science,* 1966, 33, 323-340.

Singh, B. K. Path analysis in social science research. In B. K. Singh (Ed.), "Recent trends in social analysis." *Indian Journal of Extension Education: Special Volume on Methodology,* 1975.

Spaeth, J. L. Path analysis. In D. J. Amick & H. J. Walberg (Eds.), *Introductory multivariate analysis for educational, psychological, and social research*. Berkeley, CA: McCutchan, 1975.

Specht, D. A., & Warren, R. D. Comparing causal models. In D. R. Heise (Ed.), *Sociological methodology, 1976*. San Francisco: Jossey-Bass, 1976.

Spielberger, C. D. State-trait anxiety and interactional psychology. In D. Magnusson & N. S. Endler (Eds.), *Personality at the crossroads: Current issues in interactional psychology*. Hillsdale, NJ: Lawrence Erlbaum, 1977.

Stavig, G. R. Multiple comparison tests for path analysis and multiple regression. *Journal of Experimental Education,* 1981, 50, 39-41.

Stolzenberg, R. M. The measurement and decomposition of causal effects in nonlinear and nonadditive models. In K. F. Schuessler (Ed.), *Sociological methodology, 1980*. San Francisco: Jossey-Bass, 1979.

Strotz, R. H., & Wold, H. O. Recursive versus nonrecursive systems. An attempt at synthesis. In H. M. Blalock, Jr. (Ed.), *Causal models in the social sciences*. Chicago: Aldine-Atherton, 1971.

Theil, H. *Principles of econometrics*. New York: John Wiley, 1971.

Travers, R.M.W. Letter to the editor. *Educational Researcher,* 1981, 10, 32.

Tukey, J. W. Causation, regression, and path analysis. In O. Kempthorne, T. A. Bancroft, J. W. Gowen, & J. L. Lush (Eds.), *Statistics and mathematics in biology*. New York: Hofner, 1964.

Werts, C. E., Breland, H. M., Grandy, J., & Rock, D. R. Using longitudinal data to estimate reliability in the presence of correlated measurement errors. *Educational and Psychological Measurement,* 1980, 40, 19-29.

Werts, C. E., Jöreskog, K. G., & Linn, R. L. A multitrait-multimethod model for studying growth. *Educational and Psychological Measurement,* 1972, 32, 655-678.

Werts, C. E., Jöreskog, K. G., & Linn, R. L. Identification and estimation in path analysis with unmeasured variables. *American Journal of Sociology,* 1973, 78, 1469-1484.

Werts, C. E., & Linn, R. L. Path analysis: Psychological examples. *Psychological Bulletin,* 1970, 74, 193-212.

Werts, C. E., & Linn, R. L. Considerations when making inferences within the analysis of covariance model. *Educational and Psychological Measurement,* 1971, 31, 407-416.

Werts, C. E., & Linn, R. L. Corrections for attenuation. *Educational and Psychological Measurement,* 1972, 32, 117-127.

Werts, C. E., Linn, R. L., & Jöreskog, K. G. Estimating the parameters of path models involving unmeasured variables. In H. M. Blalock (Ed.), *Causal models in the social sciences.* Chicago: Aldine-Atherton, 1971.

Werts, C. E., Rock, D. A., & Grandy, J. Confirmatory factor analysis applications: Missing data problems and comparison of path models between populations. *Multivariate Behavioral Research,* 1979, 14, 199-213.

Werts, C. E., Rock, D. A., & Linn, R. L. Estimation and testing of partial covariances, correlations, and regression weights using maximum likelihood factor analysis. *Educational and Psychological Measurement,* 1979, 39, 29-37.

Werts, C. E., Rock, D. A., Linn, R. L., & Jöreskog, K. G. Comparison of correlations, variances, covariances, and regression weights with or without measurement error. *Psychological Bulletin,* 1976, 83, 1007-1013.

Wiley, D. E. The identification problem for structural equation models with unmeasured variables. In A. S. Goldberger & O. D. Duncan (Eds.), *Structural equation models in the social sciences.* New York: Seminar Press, 1973.

Wiley, D. E., & Wiley, J. A. The estimation of measurement error in panel data. In H. M. Blalock (Ed.), *Causal models in the social sciences.* Chicago: Aldine-Atherton, 1971.

Wittgenstein, L. [*Culture and value*] (G. H. Von Wright, Ed., Peter Winch, trans.). Chicago: University of Chicago Press, 1980.

Wright, S. The method of path coefficients. *Annals of Mathematical Statistics,* 1934, 5, 161-215.

Wright, S. Path coefficients and path regressions: Alternative or complementary concepts? *Biometrics,* 1960, 16, 189-202.

Young, J. W. The function of theory in a dilemma of path analysis. *Journal of Applied Psychology,* 1977, 62, 108-110.

Zajonc, R. B. Feeling and thinking: Preferences need no inferences. *American Psychologist,* 1980, 35, 151-175.

Zedeck, S. Problems with the use of "moderator" variables. *Psychological Bulletin,* 1971, 76, 295-310.

About the Authors

LAWRENCE R. JAMES is Professor in the School of Psychology at the Georgia Institute of Technology. His research interests include cognition and perception as they relate to behavior and organizations, leadership, and quantitative techniques.

STANLEY A. MULAIK is Professor in the School of Psychology at the Georgia Institute of Technology. He has published work on multivariate statistical analysis, including work on factor-analytic models and on linear causal modeling with latent variables.

JEANNE M. BRETT is Associate Professor of Organization Behavior at the Kellogg Graduate School of Management at Northwestern University. Her primary research interests are the impact of work on the family and conflict management in industrial relations.